100

The Hormel

Legacy:

100 Years

of Quality

GEO. A. HORMEL & COMPANY

Library of Congress Catalog Number: 90-93553

Printed in the United States of America

Writing, editing and production
Dr. Doniver A. Lund, St. Peter, Minnesota
V. Allan Krejci, Geo. A. Hormel & Company
Yeager Pine & Mundale, Minneapolis, Minnesota

Proofreading
Meri G. Harris and Sharon M. Barnes, Geo. A. Hormel & Company

Design
Nancekivell Design Office, Minneapolis, Minnesota

Typography
Peregrine Publications, St. Paul, Minnesota

Printing
Diversified Graphics, Inc., Minneapolis, Minnesota

ACKNOWLEDGEMENTS

Several people and organizations deserve recognition for their part in making this book a reality. They include Dr. Doniver Lund, professor of history, Gustavus Adolphus College, St. Peter, Minnesota, principal researcher and coauthor; V. Allan Krejci, Hormel director of public relations, who provided writing, editing and project coordination as well as his extensive knowledge of company events, policies and philosophies; Meri G. Harris, administrative assistant, and Sharon M. Barnes, secretary, public relations, for their tireless involvement, specifically for close and painstaking proofreading of chapter drafts and printer's proofs, and Gene A. Lifka and Mark N. Reed, Hormel Audio Visual Services Department, for research and printing of historical photographs.

Geo. A. Hormel & Company employees, retirees and family members contributed more than 1,200 possible title suggestions for this Centennial history book.

The winning title appearing on this cover, *The Hormel Legacy*, was submitted by Ben and Joyce Eblen. Ben, a company retiree since 1971, spent 20 years at the Austin, Minnesota, plant. The subtitle, *100 Years of Quality*, was entered by Helen Moss, a retiree with 18 years of service in the Buffalo, New York, meat products district sales office.

William R. "Randy" Mylius, a grocery products sales representative for the New Orleans, Louisiana, district, was awarded third place in the "Name That Book" contest for his title suggestion.

Special acknowledgements are also due the Minneapolis-based account team of Yeager Pine & Mundale for their invaluable research, writing and project organizational efforts; Nancekivell Design Office, providers of book design from concept to completion; Peregrine Publications, book typographers, and Diversified Graphics, Inc., custom printers.

In 1991, Hormel celebrates an event that comes but once in a lifetime – its Centennial year.

This commemorative event provides an opportune time to pause and reflect upon the rich and dynamic heritage that shaped Geo. A. Hormel & Company. This book was created to honor the first 100 years, to learn from them, to be inspired by them – and to preserve this unique story for the next century.

In *The Hormel Legacy*, you will read about the people, the key decisions and the major events that propelled Geo. A. Hormel & Company from a fledgling entrepreneurial enterprise in an abandoned creamery to its present-day status as America's largest independent meat and food processor. Over the years, the company has experienced times of great achievement as well as great hardship – times colored and shaped by human energy, commitment and trust.

The people in this story are many. Hormel employees and retirees, numbering in the thousands, contributed hard work, loyalty, creativity and leadership. Hormel stockholders, producers, suppliers and communities became valued business partners. Customers and consumers the world over provided the gift of confidence by purchasing Hormel products. All are the reason this company – and this book – are realities. Unfortunately, space does not permit individual recognition of employees and nonemployees alike who made valuable contributions to this century of success and achievement.

Throughout this story, you will see a company with a culture built on strong, solidly based values. While much has changed in the food industry and world in 100 years, these values – integrity, an uninterrupted quest for quality and innovation, a respect for each other and a commitment to community – define Hormel today. This book offers a rare opportunity to underscore these values – as well as ensure their place in the company's future.

Most histories take a long look back. This book, in addition to being retrospective, is forward looking and filled with lessons to help guide Hormel in its next 100 years. Join us in celebrating both 100 years and the chapters yet unwritten.

CHAPTER ONE

Immigrants and Travelers 1860-1891

"I used to wonder what it would be like to spend a day in the sun with nothing to do but fish."

George A. Hormel

1860

George A. Hormel in 1880.

The Civil War splits the nation.

PRE-1860

1830 John George Hormel, father of George A. Hormel, born January 24 in Schwalbach, Germany.

1833 The Hormel family immigrates to the United States and settles in a German-American community in Buffalo, New York.

1836 Susanna Wilhelmina Decker, mother of George A. Hormel, born November 15 in Neuwied, Germany.

1856 John Hormel and Susanna Decker marry December 28 in Buffalo, New York.

More than a century ago, George A. Hormel prepared himself for a life of innovation and hard work. His career took him from the unpaved streets of Toledo, Ohio, where he landed his first job as a paperboy, to the gritty packinghouses of Chicago, Illinois, where he worked 14-hour days for $10 a month. Hormel's ultimate success would amaze friends and competitors alike.

The Hormel home in Toledo, Ohio.

Susanna Decker Hormel (1890), John G. Hormel. (1896)

1860-1875

1860 Abraham Lincoln is elected the 16th president of the United States.
▪ John and Susanna's third child, George A. Hormel, born December 4 in Buffalo, New York.

1861 Civil War erupts with the Confederate attack on Fort Sumter, South Carolina.

1865 Lincoln is assassinated at Ford's Theater, Washington, D.C.
▪ The Civil War ends.
▪ The Hormel family moves to Toledo, Ohio, and starts a tannery business with Ferdinand Heyer.

1868 George A. Hormel lands his first job as a paperboy for the *Toledo Democrat.*

1873 The Panic of 1873 brings financial hardship to millions, including the Hormel family. George Hormel, age 13, quits school and works to help support his family.

President Abraham Lincoln.

1875 George moves to Chicago, Illinois, to work in Uncle Jacob Decker's meatpacking house at $10 a month, plus room and board.

1876-1891

1879 George leaves the meatpacking business for Kansas City, Missouri, and takes a job as a traveling wool and hide buyer for Major J. N. Dubois.

1880 George becomes a hide buyer for Oberne, Hosick & Company, covering northern Iowa and southern Minnesota.

1887 George moves to Austin, Minnesota, where he and Albrecht Friedrich become partners in Friedrich & Hormel, a meat market and packinghouse.

1891 The partnership dissolves and Geo. A. Hormel & Company is established in Austin, Minnesota.

1891

Friedrich & Hormel, Butchers and Packers, FINE SUGAR CURED Hams, Shoulders, Bacon, Lard, and Dried Beef. ALSO DEALERS IN Hides, Wool, Tallow, Pelts and Furs. Hormel, Minnesota.

The first ad for Friedrich & Hormel appeared in The Austin Register *in 1890.*

Reaching its Centennial year in 1991, Geo. A. Hormel & Company attained widespread industry recognition for a corporationwide transformation that dramatically and successfully changed its business focus.

One hundred years following its small beginning in the late 19th century, the company was no longer known as a production-driven pork processor but as an innovative marketer of value-enhanced, consumer-branded products. Hormel foods were being served in the homes of American families throughout the United States as well as in Europe, England, Japan, the Philippines and numerous other major foreign markets.

More than 8,300 employees, including subsidiaries, helped bring the diversified family of Hormel products into the marketplace in Centennial year 1991. And stockholders, confident and pleased with the company's financial strength and continued growth, numbered 9,100 on the New York Stock Exchange. Fiscal 1990 sales had risen to more than $2.6 billion. Equally significant, the *Fortune* 500 directory, while based on 1989 sales data, ranked Geo. A. Hormel & Company 190th among the nation's 500 largest industrial companies.

The Hormel ancestral home in Schwalbach, Germany.

In 1991, Geo. A. Hormel & Company had sales offices in most major metropolitan areas of the United States; processing plants located in 11 cities; distribution centers in four states, and nine wholly owned subsidiaries, including an international enterprise that continued to broaden its presence and strengthen its position as a major company operation.

Equally impressive, while other well-known and often larger century-old meatpackers had disappeared from the scene by 1991, Geo. A. Hormel & Company completed its first 100 years as the largest independent meat and food processor in America.

A FATHER AND ROLE MODEL – Young George A. Hormel had the right "incubator" to nurture his entrepreneurial grit and persistence. George's father, John, was born in Schwalbach, Germany, in 1830. Just three years later, the Hormel family pulled up stakes, immigrated to the United States and settled in the growing German community of Buffalo, New York.

Twenty years later, another German family whose history would intertwine with John Hormel also settled in Buffalo. They were the Deckers of Neuwied, Germany, whose experience in the meatpacking business spanned centuries. Ludwig Decker, determined to duplicate his success at home, had chosen to leave a prosperous business in Neuwied. With Ludwig came his attractive teenage daughter, Susanna.

A FORTUITOUS MEETING – Susanna Decker and John Hormel were part of the fast-growing, industrious and pious German-American community in Buffalo. The city had grown from nearly 9,000 in 1830 to more than 80,000 in 1860. The German community was tight knit and sociable and it was inevitable that these first-generation Americans would meet.

It was not inevitable that the pair would fall in love, but John Hormel and Susanna Decker did, and they were married in 1856. John, 26, had worked on a riverboat plying the Mississippi and he had dreams of settling new territories and starting a business of his own. Susanna was a responsible and mature 20-year-old who had been employed as a servant in the Buffalo home of President Millard Fillmore.

John and Susanna Hormel immediately started a family and their third child is the reason for this publication. George A. Hormel was born in December 1860, the same year Lincoln was elected president and the Pony Express began regular service between St. Joseph, Missouri, and Sacramento, California. In his own way, John and Susanna's son, George, would be a leader . . . and a racehorse.

John and Susanna Hormel in 1890.

THE TOLEDO KID – In 1865, with the Civil War over and his yen for a business of his own undiminished, John Hormel moved his family to the booming port city of Toledo, Ohio, on the banks of the Maumee River at Lake Erie. It was there that John started a partnership with his friend, Ferdinand Heyer. A skilled tanner, Heyer was supposed to raise his share of the capital for their joint enterprise. However, when Heyer was unable to garner the cash, the ever-optimistic John went ahead and formed the partnership despite Susanna's objections. John Hormel's way of dealing fairly with people would serve young George well in the years ahead, although later it also almost destroyed the prosperous company George ultimately built.

TOUGH ON THE OUTSIDE, CARING WITHIN – Life for George Hormel, growing up in Toledo in the 1860s and 1870s, was simple and hard. Most streets in town were unpaved and mudholes flourished after a rain. Parks were rare, fire and police protection were scarce and inefficient. In the backyard of every house, if they could afford them, families kept pigs, chickens, cows and horses. The privy was out back, too, freezing cold in winter and stinking hot in summer. The privy was also perilously close to the well where the family pumped its drinking and cooking water.

In the mid-1860s, John Hormel started a tannery business in Toledo, Ohio, with his friend Ferdinand Heyer.

The births of John and Susanna Hormel's children are recorded in the family's German Bible.

If city living was rough, George's family life was warm and caring. Still, there were few frills and much work. Nearly everything was done by hand. When he was seven, George was given the job of polishing the family's shoes. Here he showed an entrepreneur's knack for focusing on essentials. George thought only the front of the shoes mattered, so he focused polish and brush there and let the devil take the hindmost. When his mother inspected the shoes, she declared, "George, forna ist huey und hinter ist fuey!" (The front is fine, but the back is phooey.) His mother was not stern but she expected good work. Under Susanna's guidance, George Hormel learned that the job could not be fudged. It was an important lesson. In his unpublished autobiography, *The Open Road*, Hormel later wrote, "I learned that it was quicker and easier to do the chore properly the first time. Learned the hard way, this lesson has proved a gold mine to me." In a phrase, Hormel learned how to do it right the first time, a concept that many American companies today have been forced to relearn.

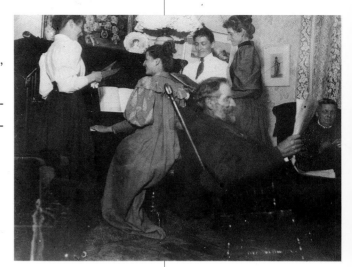

George's sisters entertain the family at the piano.

STOUT VALUES ESPOUSED BY DAD – For his part, John Hormel encouraged his children with his faith, his sense of humor and his love of music. After dinner, Hormel often read from the Bible and pointed out a simple scriptural lesson for the children. Then he'd ask, "How about some music?" and the children would grab their instruments – a Jew's harp, a violin, a guitar – and gather round the piano to play and sing.

Philosophically, John Hormel believed that life was a challenge; it was not full of crushing obligations, it was full of creative opportunities, and he passed these ideas on to his oldest son, George. Hormel lived a deeply religious life which was grounded in faith in the American dream. He believed that only Christian teaching could produce democracy and only Christian living made democracy possible. The streets were not paved with gold, they were filled with mud. But through hard work and perseverance, Hormel believed a man could become rich or, like Lincoln, president.

Hard work was the order of the day. At age eight, George Hormel landed his first job as a paperboy for the *Toledo Democrat*. Papers were distributed first-come, first-served, but the older, stronger boys often made themselves first by force. Here the meek did not inherit the job. George had to fight for his share of the morning news. During this time, George also worked in his father's tannery. He learned to grade and pull

At age eight, George A. Hormel took his first job as a paperboy for the Toledo Democrat.

The five Hormel brothers in 1896: (from left) Ben, Herman, George, John and William (Henry).

By the late 1870s, Chicago, Illinois, was firmly established as "Hog Butcher to the Nation."

wool and to tan hides. When he was 13, the Panic of 1873 closed his father's tannery and put an abrupt end to George's education. He had finished six years of grammar school and would have gone on through the eighth grade. But with the family strapped for cash, George Hormel had to abandon school and go to work like thousands of other young boys. He worked as a lather in construction, as a stevedore and as a jack-of-all-trades in a meat market where he earned $10 a month, plus board. He landed a better job as a woodworker in the railroad shops at $.60 a day. Within a short time, he improved his pay and showed a sense of responsibility by memorizing all the necessary measurements needed for the job. George Hormel's building and woodworking experience would help him years later.

In 1875, the shape of George Hormel's life slowly began to come into focus. His beloved Uncle Jay, Susanna's brother, Jacob Decker, had become the owner of a Chicago, Illinois, packinghouse retail outlet that sold surplus meat products. When George's father queried him about working for Uncle Jay, George piped up immediately, "Yes," and his accommodating Uncle Jay said, "Come along."

George was filled with anticipation and dread because he had never lived anywhere but with his family. "I was so excited I could hardly sleep or eat," Hormel wrote. "Chicago! The 'Gem of the Prairies,' the city destroyed by fire only to rise from its ashes. Who hadn't heard of it; who didn't want to go there?" It was, as the poet Carl Sandburg said, "Hog Butcher to the Nation," precisely the right place for a young man with two generations of meatpacking in his bloodline.

WHAT A WONDERFUL TOWN – For the next year and a half, George worked for Uncle Jay in the Decker packinghouse market. Hogs were butchered and dressed elsewhere, then sold to the retail packinghouses which processed the meat. The packinghouses sold the ham, bacon, pork loins, ribs and tenderloins to retail markets, and the longer lasting cured meat to lumber camps, shipping companies and railroads.

George worked as a cashier when first arriving at his uncle's market in Chicago. Soon afterwards, Uncle Jay hired a woman for that job, quite an innovation in 1875. As a result, George began delivering meat. Because Jacob Decker sold a substantial volume of meat products to lumber camps in Wisconsin and Michigan, George often drove his two-wheeled delivery cart, loaded with corned beef and salt pork, to the noisy, tough Chicago

wharves for waterbound transit. In his spare time, George worked at the
chopping block where he learned how to cut hog carcasses into their principal parts, trim ham and bacon bellies and prepare them for sale.

Even at a youthful 15, Hormel worked 14 hours or more each day for
$10 per month, plus room and board. Chicago life was not gay or pretty,
nor did he see much of it. Hormel woke at 5:30 a.m., drank coffee,
downed bread and butter, meat and potatoes and arrived at work one
hour later. He toiled straight through to lunch when he replenished himself with beans and pork, bread and butter, pie and cold coffee. Sometimes George was home at 6:00 p.m., but often he worked later. In that
case, when he finally did get home, he ate a quick supper and fell straight
into bed. During the winter, he lived in perpetual darkness. Up before
dawn, George worked in a dark and gloomy room, then came home to
dark quarters after dusk.

Despite the grind, George Hormel learned some invaluable lessons. He
had learned from his mother that cleanliness was next to godliness. From
his uncle, he discovered that cleanliness in the packinghouse meant
profits. "Clean food," Jacob Decker would say, "doesn't spoil in a hurry.
Dirty food spoils while you're looking at it." Spoiled food, of course, was
a waste of money. At the same time, Hormel learned how other packinghouses worked. "Packers' methods were wasteful and their handling of
animals inhumane," Hormel observed. "Dirt, grease, blood and offal
covered floors, walls and equipment. Unskilled, ignorant, seasonal
workers were sweated and oppressed; they were as dirty as the premises.
In these packinghouses, the processed meat, ready for the market, was
usually black with flies."

TOMORROW'S VISIONS AND TODAY'S FALLOUT – In 1876, George Hormel
was not the only one appalled by the wasteful and inhumane conditions
in the meat markets of Chicago. So were Edward A. Cudahy, Philip D.
Armour and Gustavus F. Swift. These men, who were business vision-
aries, would become pioneers in the industry. Swift's ideas would revolu-
tionize the meat processing business and the eating habits of the world.
Later, so would George Hormel's. But, at 16 and far from home, he found
the heavy lifting required at the docks each day wore him down. At his
doctor's suggestion, George returned home for a rest. While he was gone,
Uncle Jay, also weary of the grind, sold his business and moved to Texas.

*The five Hormel sisters in
1896: (from left, top row)
Susanna, Elizabeth,
Emma, (bottom row)
Nellie and Charlotte.*

If anything, business toward the end of the nineteenth century was mercurial. The ascent and descent of business fortunes must have been dizzying and frightening. For example, in the three years between 1873-76, Jacob chose to exit the business. George's father, John, now with a large family to feed, lost his tannery and barely assembled enough cash to purchase a rendering plant. But Jacob Decker did not leave the volatile meat-packing business for long. After living in Texas briefly, he returned to the Windy City and started up a new packinghouse market.

When George learned that his uncle had returned to Chicago, he jumped at the chance to work for him again. Having received the health-restoring food of his mother, George took the blessings of his father with him back to Chicago. It was 1876, the nation was 100 years young, General George Custer would soon make his last stand at the Battle of the Little Big Horn against the Sioux and Mark Twain would publish *Tom Sawyer.*

TEENAGE SALESMAN – Working for Uncle Jay's new firm, George Hormel traveled to Indianapolis, Indiana, where he bought pork tenderloins and packed them in galvanized containers and placed them in barrels filled with salt and crushed ice. These barrels were eventually shipped to Europe. George enjoyed his first responsible job and he took to it, quickly figuring out how to bargain with the meat sellers. He realized that on warm days the packers were more anxious to sell their products than on cold days. Hormel bought accordingly, paying less for the meat when the weather was warm. His Uncle Jay, Hormel wrote, " . . . was well pleased with the results of my operation."

George, however, eventually became less than well pleased. Although he liked this job, he felt the pay, $7.50 a week, plus room and board, was too low. George believed he should be paid at least $10 but his uncle did not agree.

Inspired by the American dream to seek his fortune, and believing he would not find it in Chicago, Hormel paid $5 for a train ticket to Kansas City, Missouri. There he hoped to find a better job. He was 19 years old, 6'2" tall, strong and hard and experienced as a tanner-wool puller, a railroad shop helper and a meatpacker. For living expenses, the risk-taker George had less than $5 in his pocket.

At age 19, George A. Hormel moved to Kansas City, Missouri, to seek his fortune.

THE OPEN ROAD – This young man, in search of opportunity, expected the streets of Kansas City to be filled with businesses offering jobs. Instead, Hormel found the city filled with other young Turks like himself. Luckily, he landed a good job, not as a drone in the hide cellars as he expected, but as a seasonal buyer for Major J. N. Dubois, owner of a hide and wool house. Dressed in a frumpy wool Sunday suit and carrying his oilskin bag, Hormel soon found himself riding a train to Pleasant Hill, Missouri, to explore his new territory. There were other buyers on that train – slick, dashing types wearing stylish clothes and toting leather luggage. Against these sophisticated, experienced men, Hormel measured himself. How could he compete?

At first, he couldn't compete. He bought nothing. Business was at a standstill in Pleasant Hill and also at his next stop, Rich Hill. The dealers were not buying wool because they believed the market price was high. Hormel disagreed with the dealers' perspective. The wool prices were fair. Hormel found an unconventional solution. He was willing to buy direct from the breeders and one enterprising dealer offered him a proposition. "You help sack and weigh the wool we buy and pay me a half-cent a pound," he said. "I'll drive you around to the sheep breeders and you can buy all you want." Previously, no one purchased wool this way. Hormel hesitated only long enough to weigh his decision carefully. For two days the young salesman and the dealer combed the countryside buying wool. When the wool reached Kansas City, Major Dubois sent Hormel a telegram: "Congratulations. Wool arriving in fine condition. Keep it up." The risk he had taken worked; from that point on, Hormel purchased all his wool this way.

When George Hormel returned to Kansas City, his boss welcomed him home and offered him a steady job at $75 a month, plus expenses. Hormel, no doubt, went out and bought the necessary trappings for the job – the sharp new suit, the jaunty hard hat and the expensive leather luggage. Then he went back on the road. This time when he returned from his buying trip, he found the company closed. Major Dubois had bolted with $100,000 obtained from fraudulent bills of lading. Hormel was once again out of a job but at least he was an experienced buyer of hides and wool. And he could dress the part.

Hormel searched for more work in Kansas City; he wrote a letter to his father asking for work in Toledo; he took the train to St. Louis. No luck there. Work seemed as scarce as snow in July. Hormel returned to Chicago seeking work at Oberne, Hosick & Company, one of the world's largest dealers in hides, wool, tallow and furs. They needed no wool

George first demonstrated his entrepreneurial spirit as a wool buyer for Major J. N. Dubois.

buyers but Hormel landed a job in the hide cellar as a common laborer, the newest man in the pack. To this lucky fellow fell the task of hefting the heaviest hides. After a month of tossing hides around, Hormel knew he had to quit. The job was exhausting and he was determined to find more challenging, higher paying work.

Luck has a way with entrepreneurs. Luck finds them in the right place at the right time. In Kansas City, for example, Major Dubois had, at first, turned Hormel down for a job. Then, at the last moment, he whistled him back from halfway down the street. In Chicago, at Oberne, Hosick & Company, luck visited once again. On the day Hormel decided to quit the hide cellar, Oberne himself offered him a job as a company buyer.

Hormel was glad for the opportunity. His new headquarters were in Des Moines, Iowa, where the district manager, George Crandale, assigned him to cover most of Iowa and southern Minnesota. Upon arrival, Hormel immediately fell in love with both states — the prosperous farms, the fertile soil, the healthy livestock and the extensive grain crops. "I had no time for play," he wrote, "but Minnesota's cool blue skies and meadows flecked with brilliant flowers were like water to a thirsty man. The dark-shadowed lakes were full of walleye pike, bass and perch. I used to wonder what it would be like to spend a day in the sun with nothing to do but fish."

Map of Austin, Minnesota, in 1874.

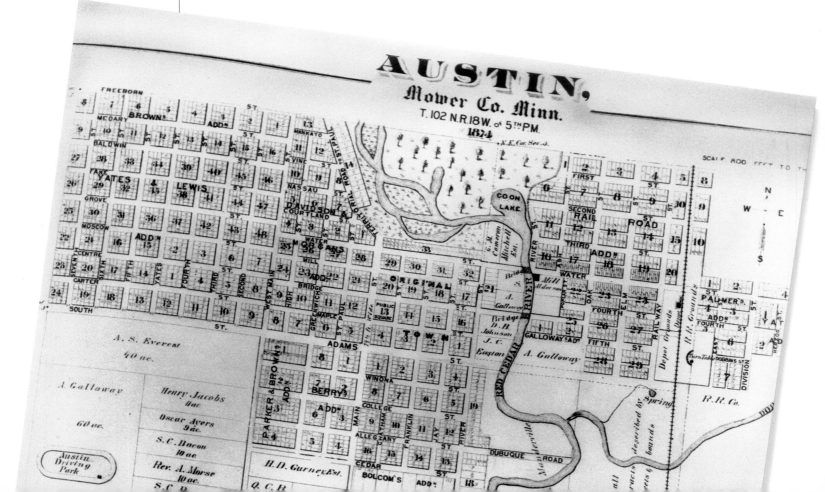

That day would come. George Hormel's talent for intelligent buying had given him a good job and luck had landed him in the right spot. Austin, Minnesota, the northernmost stop on his route, had a burgeoning population of 3,000. Here he often spent weekends with a growing circle of friends. Later, this town would be the site of his company.

Hormel quickly discovered that life on the road was different from toil in the hide cellars and tanneries of Chicago and Toledo. First, the life of a buyer was not physically exhausting. At each stop he would make the rounds, buying hides from two types of customers: butchers who, in those days, slaughtered their livestock and cut it up for sale, and farmers who did their own slaughtering and were happy to sell the hides to him. Second, the life of a buyer gave Hormel newly found spare time. At the end of the day, he returned to his hotel and ate dinner. He had evenings free. Gone were the days when he fell exhausted into a cold bed after putting in a 14-hour day as a laborer.

In the 1880s, what did a young man do with his free time? He roller skated and ice skated. He shot billiards. Although it had been strictly forbidden in his proper Christian home, he played cards. Hormel became an avid poker player and, according to his autobiography, acquired some skill at bluffing and betting. He soon found himself winning and losing sizable stakes. However, his fascination with the game — win or lose — kept him in the red, not the black. Years later, before it became a popular notion, Hormel realized the addictive nature of his gambling. "The itch to gamble," he wrote, "became as insidious as a tippler's urge to drink. I not only lost what I earned but began to draw advances against my future earnings." After many years, despite all his hard work and high earnings, Hormel had saved nothing.

Henry James, the great American novelist, urged a young writer to be one of those people upon whom nothing is lost. Although not a writer, Hormel was one of those people upon whom little was lost. From his struggles with poker, he learned that taking risks could be useful in certain circumstances. The risk he had taken buying wool for Dubois was such an example. Hormel also learned ". . . what life on the road with no anchors would do to me. It was novel and I was young," he wrote, "but when I began to examine critically my older colleagues, I could see what this life had done to them. Most of them had become accustomed to a life which unfitted them for any other."

Austin, Minnesota, was a prosperous town of 3,000 when George A. Hormel settled there.

An avid poker player, George A. Hormel struggled with an "itch to gamble" in his younger years.

Hormel could also see that the leather business fluctuated because it was tied to the whims of fashion. A new low-cut men's boot meant the industry needed less leather and that meant less buying. Hogs, on the other hand, were a steadily growing commodity. They fattened quickly on refuse grain and the leavings of cattle and skimmed milk. They were an incidental source of profit at almost every farm. The population of America was growing and pork would feed this expanding nation.

Hormel believed that someone with his background in hides, wool, tallow and the processing of meat could surely make a go of it. But with his capital gambled away, Hormel could not start an enterprise. Frustrated, he scoured the countryside buying hides from butchers and farmers. Soon luck would deal him another good hand and Hormel would have the foresight to use it to his advantage.

In the spring of 1887, at age 27, George Hormel went home to Toledo to visit his parents, brothers and sisters. When his father questioned him about his future, George must have squirmed when admitting he had not yet made a decision. John Hormel suggested he turn to God for help and to him for financial assistance. During George's next regular trip to Austin, Hormel discovered that the butcher shop of his best customer, Anton Friedrich, had burned down. Friedrich was rebuilding but was not going to operate the new shop himself. He was going to rent it for $60 a

In 1891, George A. Hormel (upper left) with fellow members of Austin's Tennis Club.

month to his son, Albrecht. He suggested George join his son in a partnership. All George needed was $500 to stock the market and ready it
for business.

Visions of earnings lost in poker games must have filled George
Hormel's head. But he didn't let his bad habits stop him; nor did he go
straight to his father. Why not? His younger brother, William, wrote,
"George might have easily gotten this sum from our father but his spirit
of self-reliance and independence led him to do otherwise." Perhaps
shame about his card playing kept him from asking for help. Perhaps it
was his sense of pride. He wanted to show his father he could start this
new enterprise on his own. Whatever the reason, Hormel went to his boss,
George Crandale, and said, "I'd like to borrow $500."

"What for?" Crandale asked.

"I'm going into partnership with Albrecht Friedrich. We're going to run
a meat market and a pork packinghouse."

"But you're overdrawn for $104 already," Crandale said.

"I know. Here's $4. That leaves $100. Lend me $400 more. If I haven't
paid you in six months, I'll come back and work it out."

Crandale shook his head. "You're a good traveling man, George, but a
good businessman? That's something else, and cards and business, they
just don't mix."

"I'm through with cards and all that," said Hormel. "This is my chance
to make more of myself and you can help me."

After thinking it over, Crandale said, "You know, I really believe you
mean it, George. I hate to lose you but I won't stand in your way."

NOT JUST ANOTHER BUTCHER – In August 1887, Hormel wrote his mother
a long, excited letter about his prospects. "I am sure of success at Austin,"
he wrote, "more so than I was in any enterprise. Now don't think I'm going to be just another butcher – that isn't what I am going into. It is the
pork packing business I am about to enter into and, of course, we must
have a packinghouse market to retail the trimmings and offal. I can find
plenty of business to keep the flies from me. So don't say I'm a butcher –
but a pork packer. We must hold our head up in the world. Now laugh!"

George Hormel had the packinghouse business in his blood and it
showed. From his Uncle Jay, he learned about handling, trimming and
curing meat and all the clever and thrifty techniques that make for high-

George's frequent letters kept his parents informed about his life in Austin. He wrote this letter to his mother in August 1887.

George Hormel's first business venture in 1887.

quality products. In his travels, Hormel had seen tremendous waste and inefficiency. Yet those shops were profitable. "If they can run a market profitably that way," he wrote, "imagine how much better I can do running things right."

In October 1887, the Austin firm of Friedrich & Hormel opened for business. There was no ribbon-cutting ceremony and no grand opening celebration. The town's two weekly newspapers ignored the event entirely. Even so, the new business thrived. Albrecht worked the retail market and George handled the production of sausage, ham, bacon and tenderloins. Soon he was making more products than Albrecht could sell. In his resourceful fashion, Hormel sold these extras to retailers in surrounding communities.

In less than two years, the business began to expand and garner news coverage. On July 9, 1889, the *Mower County Democrat* carried this observation: "Friedrich & Hormel is building an extension to its meat market. The business is immense and still increasing." Trade was good, so, in keeping with Hormel's prediction to his mother, the market must have been very "nice and complete."

A SAUSAGE OF HIGH STANDING – In September of the same year, the company purchased a steam engine, boiler and other machinery for the packinghouse and, in the following year, 1890, a reporter for the *Democrat* wrote: "Today a Philadelphia company laid down a large-sized meat chopper at Friedrich & Hormel's meat emporium. The sausage they sold at distant markets last year has given them such a standing in the world that it became necessary to enlarge their manufacturing facilities."

Despite the market's immediate and abundant success, the partners were at loggerheads almost from the start. Like his father, Albrecht Friedrich saw the store as a first-class retail meat market, selling nothing but the best meat. Like his ancestors, Hormel saw the meat market merely as an outlet for a large-scale packinghouse rivaling Swift, Cudahy and Armour. Hormel wanted to turn their little slaughterhouse into a first-class packing plant.

In September 1891, the proprietors of the Austin Packinghouse and Market mutually dissolved their partnership. Friedrich assumed control of the meat market and Hormel took over the packinghouse. "It is Hormel's intention," wrote the reporter for the *Austin Register*, "to carry out the plans heretofore mentioned in these columns by making his packinghouse one of the leading industries in southern Minnesota. Hormel's branch of the business has a wide reputation and it has always been an easy matter to dispose of all the stock they could produce. Mr. Hormel possesses tireless, persistent enterprise and vim, which is bound to bring success." Were both Hormel and the reporter clairvoyant? Considering the size and reputation of Geo. A. Hormel *&* Company today, one has to say, yes.

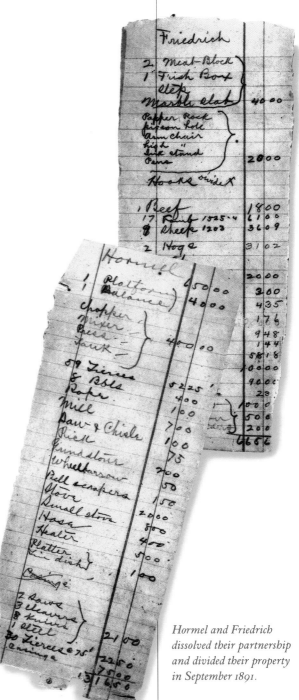

Hormel and Friedrich dissolved their partnership and divided their property in September 1891.

European immigrants pouring into the United States at the turn of the century were loyal consumers of "Hormel's Wonderful Sausage."

Pepperoni, a native Italian food, has been a longtime American favorite and a well-known Hormel specialty.

"I think it was the sausage," George A. Hormel once replied to a question about his company's survival of the Panic of 1893, just two years after its founding. Many people today recognize the crucial role sausage played in the success of the fledgling company. But few understand the vital role sausage has played in the history of the Western world.

When George A. Hormel formed his company in 1891, the art of sausage making was centuries old. The Babylonians enjoyed sausage as early as 1500 B.C., and references to the succulent food are found in the ancient Greek classics of Homer and Aristophanes.

It wasn't until medieval times, however, when more progressive methods of raising livestock emerged, that sausage making put a crimp in the harsh cycle of "feast or famine" dominating the lives of most Europeans. The supply of meat was now more abundant and sausage making made it possible to prevent spoilage and build a supply of food to carry people through lean times. However, the preservation of fresh meat for later use required flavoring of rare spices found only in the East. Caravans to

Asia soon materialized and world travel and trade were born.

The spice trade built great cities and created vast empires, started wars and inspired bold adventurers to take to the seas in search of new routes to the Orient. Marco Polo, Magellan, Vasco da Gama and Christopher Columbus secured their places in history while seeking routes to the East where spice fortunes lay.

In the centuries that followed, sausage making was refined as the regions of Europe adapted their techniques to the demands of custom and climate. Eventually, distinctive sausages came to be identified with particular regions of Italy, Germany and Scandinavia.

Sausage was hung in this Austin plant drying room in 1949.

Until the late 1800s in America, sausage was considered a European specialty and was imported to satisfy the demands of a small market. That changed with the wave of European immigrants that poured into the United States in the 1880s and 1890s, bringing their traditions and tastes with them. George A. Hormel, the son of German immigrants, recognized this new market. He made sausage for the Hormel Provision Market in the company's early years, drawing customers from all over the Midwest.

In 1915, the company created the Dry Sausage Division and expanded its product base from a few items in limited quantities to a larger line capable of meeting the needs of the East Coast market. Guided by Walter I. Bergman, who came from a family of sausage makers, Hormel maintained a commitment to quality and authenticity that gave it a reputation as one of the finest producers of dry sausage in the country. The dry sausage line, which had nearly 25 offerings by 1930, stood at more than 150 products in 1990, all developed with painstaking attention to the discriminating tastes of consumers.

Throughout the years, production of dry sausage has evolved from art to science. No one, according to Antonio E. Alonso, director of the company's Deli Division, can dispute the company's leadership in the marketplace. "Hormel is the largest manufacturer of dry sausage in the country," he says, "and

Today, the Deli Division of Geo. A. Hormel & Company produces a wide variety of dry sausage.

we've been the leader as far back as 1904 when the company name was a leading brand in the neighborhood delis of New York. **Di Lusso** genoa, **Homeland** hard salami and our entire line of pepperoni are consumer favorites."

Genoa salami had its origin in the northern Italian seaport city of Genoa, the birthplace of Columbus. A better name could not have been chosen for the company's most famous dry sausage

product, **Di Lusso** genoa. Properly translated from the Italian word for "deluxe," **Di Lusso** genoa is characteristically a mild, unsmoked and lightly garlic-flavored salami. It is seasoned with spices imported from the Orient to produce a smooth, pleasing flavor. **Di Lusso** genoa is made from specially selected lean meats, hand sewn into a natural casing and roped with 10 hitch cords — traditional wrapping for the finest genoa. The product is unsmoked but

it must be delicately aged for months to ensure an appetizing, beautiful bloom and perfect dryness. It is vacuum-packaged for longer shelf life and overwrapped in a parchment wrapper printed in the Italian colors of red, green and royal purple. "**Di Lusso** genoa requires more skill in preparation than any other sausage and the quality requirements are the highest in the industry," says Alonso.

Hormel has been producing hard salami for

nearly a century. However, in 1978, German-style **Homeland** hard salami, blended with selected, imported spices and "a master's touch of garlic," was introduced. It has become another consumer favorite, says Alonso. "The product's success is a result of the company's exhaustive marketing efforts to provide customers with the authentic, Old World taste admired for generations."

Hormel pepperoni, another Italian-style sausage and one of the most popular sausages in the country, is produced in Austin, Minnesota; Knoxville, Iowa, and Algona, Iowa, sometimes referred to as "the pepperoni capital of the world." This medium-chopped sausage is seasoned with red pepper and fine spices, giving it a hot sensation with a sweet aftertaste.

Thanks to the phenomenal growth of the American pizza market, beginning in the mid-1970s, pepperoni is the number one pizza topping and is now consumed for a wide variety of uses. **Hormel** pepperoni has become the number one pepperoni in the country, sold through retail supermarkets, delis and food-service outlets.

If George A. Hormel were alive today and he was asked to cite a key factor in his company's success, no doubt he would still say, "I think it was the sausage."

Hormel deli products are promoted in this successful advertising campaign.

Homeland hard salami combines imported spices, garlic and a smoky flavor for a top-grade salami that is a consumer favorite.

CHAPTER TWO

The Gritty

Entrepreneur

1891-1927

"I kept constantly before me the challenge: 'Originate, don't imitate!'
and made it one of the key commandments of the organization."
George A. Hormel

1891

George A. Hormel in 1940.

Austin, Minnesota, was small but thriving when George A. Hormel took a partner for life and started his own business venture. Even in 1891, the ambitious young entrepreneur planned for growth well beyond his little retail butcher shop on Mill Street. Just outside of town, he was building a complete meat processing plant where only the best quality would carry the name – Hormel.

1891-1900

1892 George A. Hormel marries Lillian Belle Gleason, February 24.
- George and Lillian's only child, Jay Catherwood Hormel, is born in Austin, Minnesota.
- Geo. A. Hormel & Company erects its first building, a two-story brick structure.
- The company processes 610 hogs.
- Annual sales reach $220,000.

1894 George Hormel's brother, Henry, moves to Austin as minister of the Central Presbyterian Church.

1895 George Hormel's parents move to Austin from Toledo.
- Canadian bacon is developed by Geo. A. Hormel & Company.

1896 Fire destroys much of the Hormel plant. The company rebuilds and expands.
- John Hormel, George's father, dies.

1898 Hormel hires its first full-time salesman.

1899 George Hormel hangs up his cleaver and apron and takes on a full-time management role.

1901-1910

1901 Minneapolis branch opens on Central Avenue.
- Geo. A. Hormel & Company incorporates in Minnesota.
- President William McKinley assassinated; succeeded by Theodore Roosevelt.

1902 Main Street is paved in Austin.
- Company processes 32,646 hogs and sales hit $711,000.

On November 25, 1891, George A. Hormel announced the opening of his new business in the Austin Transcript.

George A. Hormel (far right) and his employees in 1898.

1903 Refrigeration is added to the Hormel plant.
- "Dairy Brand" name is first used.
- Sales reach $860,000.

1904-18 Hormel opens seven distribution centers in Midwest and South.

1906 Federal meat inspection begins. Geo A. Hormel & Company receives high marks for cleanliness and sanitation.

1909 George Hormel buys his first automobile, a White Steamer.

1910 Susanna Hormel, George's mother, dies.

In the early years, Hormel marketed its products under the Dairy Brand label.

1911-1920

1911 First Hormel national advertising appears in *Ladies' Home Journal*.

1912 Annual sales reach $5 million.

1914 Jay C. Hormel leaves college to work for the company.

1917 The United States enters World War I. Jay C. Hormel is first enlisted man from Minnesota, 88th Division, Camp Dodge, Iowa.

1918 World War I ends.

Geo. A. Hormel & Company had developed a substantial export business by the outbreak of World War I.

1919 Company processes 533,200 hogs.
- Sales reach $29.7 million.

1921-1927

1921 Cy Thomson's embezzlement of $1,187,000 is discovered by Jay C. Hormel.

1922 Jay C. Hormel marries Germaine Dubois of La Vernelle, France, in West Kirby, England.

1924 The company processes more than one million hogs for the first time.

1925 The company institutes an insurance plan for employees.

1926 Hormel introduces "Hormel Flavor-Sealed Ham," the first canned ham.
- Austin National Bank fails. It is saved by George A. Hormel and nine Austin businessmen.

1927 Mr. and Mrs. George A. Hormel move to Bel Air, California, leaving their Austin home to the YWCA.
- Canned whole chicken and spiced ham are added to Flavor-Sealed line.

President Theodore Roosevelt.

1927

Jay C. Hormel at 15 months in 1894.

Ladies' Home Journal carried the company's first national advertisement in February 1911.

I n 1891, James Naismith hung a bushel basket on a pole, aimed a ball at it and called the game basketball. Americans needed a little innocent diversion in 1891. The industrial revolution was in full swing, making millionaires out of a few individuals while it kept the majority hoping their turn would come some day. Congress had passed the Sherman Antitrust Act designed to protect smaller businesses from the domination of giant monopolies. Immigrants streamed to America in vast numbers, adding to an ever-growing workforce, and the cities of America continued to burgeon.

IN THE HEART OF THE COUNTRY – Austin, in 1891, was definitely in the country. It was a small, thriving community with nearly 4,000 inhabitants. Located in Mower County, Austin, the county seat, is 10 miles from the Iowa border, approximately 180 miles from South Dakota, 100 miles from Wisconsin and 100 miles from the Twin Cities of Minneapolis/St. Paul. Austin was close to – if not in the center of – the best hog-growing country in the world.

George A. Hormel had been visiting Austin as a last stop on his hide and wool buyer's route for seven years. Afterward, for four years, he had been in partnership with Albrecht Friedrich. During that time, Hormel developed some close friendships in Austin, including Samuel Doak Catherwood and Russell E. Shepherd, attorneys who would ultimately become lifelong associates. "To them," Hormel wrote, "I owe perhaps the greatest gift one man can give another – faith in himself." Hormel liked Austin and enjoyed participating in its community life. He was a member of the Volunteer Fire Department, the Central Presbyterian Church and a charter member of the "Bachelors," a group that organized sleigh rides, bicycle tours, baseball games, dances and oyster suppers (though how they got oysters in Minnesota is anyone's guess).

Hormel must have seen something special in Austin. Although he had fallen in love with the area and had made good friends, Austin and Minnesota should not have been the city and state of first choice for a prospective meatpacker. In the 1880s, Iowa's population was larger than Minnesota's with 1.9 million people compared to 1.3 million. And, more importantly, Iowa produced far more swine – six million compared to only 381,000 in Minnesota.

Before settling in Austin, George A. Hormel traveled northern Iowa and southern Minnesota as a hide and wool buyer.

Although Iowa was the place to locate a pork packing business, Hormel chose southern Minnesota. Did he, like many farsighted entrepreneurs before and after him, foresee the eventual growth and financial importance of Minnesota? (Today, Iowa's population has not risen above three million while Minnesota's surpassed four million in 1980.) Was he taking a gamble? Was it pure luck that led him to Austin? Or was it a combination of all three factors – a lucky, farsighted gamble?

DOWN ON BOURBON AVENUE AND OUT AT THE CREAMERY – Whatever his exact reasons or intuitions, Hormel's decision to base his new company in Austin quickly turned out to be the correct one. Austin and Mower County were growing fast. The area was filled with hardworking Norwegian and German immigrants, mostly farmers owning large parcels of land with deep black soil, and businessmen – grocers, bankers, blacksmiths, doctors and dentists, lawyers and insurance agents.

In late fall 1891, the newest addition to the town's business community was the Hormel Provision Market, a retail shop that sold his meat products. Against his friends' advice, Hormel located his shop on Mill Street, also known as Bourbon Avenue, because it was lined with saloons. His friends warned Hormel that no self-respecting woman would go to his store if she had to step around a staggering drunk. Hormel believed, however, that people would go out of their way for his products and he took the risk.

While Hormel was setting up shop at his Mill Street location, he was also busy building a packing plant on a parcel of land purchased one-half mile northeast of town. With the help of his first employee, George Peterson, a Swedish immigrant, Hormel began converting an abandoned creamery on that site into a slaughterhouse. Here, Hormel's experience working as a carpenter in Toledo's railroad yards came in handy. It served him well in the following years when he and Peterson added new buildings to accommodate the fast-growing enterprise.

Between October and late November 1891, Peterson and Hormel built a runway between the hog pens and the hog-sticking pen; installed a scale; put in a 25-pound sausage stuffer and a power-operated sausage chopper; purchased a two-horsepower steam engine; constructed a brick smokehouse for ham and bacon and a smaller one for sausage, and built a beef slaughterhouse.

The Hormel Provision Market was a retail meat market in Austin that sold Hormel products for more than 30 years. (1891)

In Austin, George A. Hormel (right) met Samuel Doak Catherwood, a young attorney, and the two became lifelong friends. (1887)

The company's first power source was a two-horsepower steam engine.

When Hormel's father visited and heard the engine and the chopper operating in tandem, he was proud. "The little place sounded like industry," John Hormel said, "and gave everyone a confident, busy air." Whatever doubts John may have entertained about his eldest son, they evaporated. After a visit, Hormel's brother, Henry, wrote, "I do not think that father was ever more encouraged. . . . He was convinced of George's business ability and of his unbounded capacity for self-sacrifice for a great cause. It was a comfort to him when he saw the eldest of his five sons so well started in a promising business."

A BUSINESSMAN'S ACUMEN — Hormel's father was comforted by what he saw and also perhaps relieved. Given the pace and thrust of the business world in the 1890s, his eldest son had taken time settling down as the proprietor of his own establishment. No doubt John could still remember the conversation he had with his son in 1887 when George, in debt from gambling, still couldn't decide what he planned to do with his life.

As to his son's business sense, John might have had a few anxious moments. Certainly his son's former boss, George Crandale, had his doubts. But in the four years working in partnership with Friedrich, George Hormel had shown not only his ambitious nature but also his innate business savvy and his willingness to take calculated risks.

Hormel, for example, disliked the common practice in the 1880s, when he was still a partner with Friedrich, of extending credit to customers without stipulating a prompt payment date. Accounts drifted until the customer got around to paying. Floating his hard-earned income — which he could use to make improvements or buy stock — irked Hormel. He wanted to institute a policy of prompt payments within the first 10 days of each month. However, Hormel's partner disagreed, arguing that the fledgling enterprise would lose its customers.

Friedrich was right. In the short run, as Hormel later noted in his autobiography, ". . . we did lose trade, but I collected every bill and, because we sold only quality meat, our wealthier customers, who had left in a huff, soon came back. Our working-class customers came back, too, when they found out how much easier it was paying a one month's bill rather than a two or three months' bill."

Like a good idea whose time has come, Hormel's policy of prompt payment quickly spread throughout Austin. Stationery and advertisements soon carried the statement, "Bills are due the first of the month and must be paid."

Hormel's inborn business sense showed in another way. While working with Friedrich, he was determined to find out which animals were most profitable to sell – pork, beef, veal or mutton – and which to stock. Hormel kept a ledger sheet on each type of animal. On one side he listed the cost and the weight of the animal; on the other, the amount received for each piece sold. In no time, he discovered that veal, beef and mutton were less profitable than pork, whose carcasses could be sold almost completely. "This led us," Hormel wrote, "to specialize in pork. When a customer was in doubt, we always recommended 'a nice cut of pork.'" Hormel now knew what meat was most profitable and he pushed that product. With many products in the future, he would first create the line and then urge the eager public to buy it.

THE UNGRAND OPENING – Sometime between November 1891 and January 1892, without any fanfare, advertisements or stories in the papers, Geo. A. Hormel & Company Pork Packers and Provision Dealers opened for business. Hormel and Peterson were so busy preparing and building that they failed to notice the exact date of the opening. Years later they couldn't even pin it down. Hormel, writing to his son, Jay, in 1941, said, "On Thanksgiving 1891, I walked to the plant which was not anywhere near completed." Questioned at about the same time, Peterson said he thought they slaughtered and dressed the first hog in early November. Ben Hormel, George's brother, established the opening date as Nov. 28, 1891. On that date, Ben, age 14, visited Austin and noted that the plant was in operation. Both he and Peterson agreed that George Hormel himself would be an unreliable witness to the plant's completion and opening date, for Hormel never considered the plant completed.

Although the exact date of the plant's opening is unknown, Hormel captured the sense of accomplishment he must have felt at that time. "Finally the little plant was ready," George wrote. "The icehouse was packed with every ounce of river ice we could squeeze into it. Every tub and kettle, trolley and tool was in its place. The plant was only a few small brick and frame buildings to anyone else. But to me and George Peterson, to my family and the girl I was shortly to marry, those little buildings meant everything. They were our hostages to fortune."

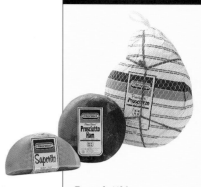

PROSCIUTTI

Prosciutti hams are a traditional Italian favorite and a longstanding specialty product at Geo. A. Hormel & Company.

Selected from among the finest hams available, each prosciutto ham requires several months of dry curing and aging to achieve perfection. Each is carefully hand-rubbed with salt and curing ingredients and massaged to provide an even, sweet and mellow flavor, texture and color.

Prosciutti hams are traditionally sliced paper thin and wrapped around melon. They can be eaten at any meal occasion as a main course or appetizer. They are very popular as a sandwich meat, as an ingredient in pasta dishes or as a topping for veal and sole.

The Hormel family of prosciutti hams includes the traditional bone-in **Primissimo** ham; the skin-on, boneless **Saporito** prosciutto, and the skinless, boneless **Parma Brand** prosciutto ham, the company's best-selling variety.

Lillian Belle Gleason married George A. Hormel in 1892 and put an end to his Bachelor's Club membership. (1905)

AND BABY MAKES THREE – In 1892, George Hormel, a charter member of the Austin "Bachelors," married Lillian Belle Gleason, a 24-year-old teacher at Austin's Franklin School and an organist at the Central Presbyterian Church. Her parents, natives of Massachusetts and Connecticut, had settled in nearby Blooming Prairie. Lillian brought to their marriage "a love of music and books," Hormel wrote, "rare sympathy and good sense, an understanding of human nature and the great patience necessary to surmount the problems and uncertainties of our first years together." Lillian also brought to the marriage her ability to manage the household on the $35 allowance George gave her monthly. At the Hormel Provision Market, she, like everyone else, paid for the cuts of meat. In her spare time, Lillian also helped manage the business. She kept the packinghouse books, calculated the payrolls, wrote ads for the Austin papers, billed customers, addressed circulars and prepared price lists. But, in the fall of 1892, Lillian's spare time disappeared. She gave birth to the couple's only child, Jay Catherwood Hormel, named Jay for his great-uncle, Jacob Decker, and Catherwood for George's best friend, Samuel Doak Catherwood.

In a series of important events in the life of George Hormel, another was the packinghouse now in operation. In addition, construction of a large two-story brick building behind the creamery was underway. To finance the building, Hormel borrowed $1,000 from his father and the rest from the bank.

The first addition to the Hormel plant was a two-story brick building behind the creamery. (1894)

A SLOW BUT STEADY START – The decision to build this structure in
1892 was daring, almost foolhardy, yet it would prove propitious. It put
Hormel deeply in debt, but he was ready for business. At the retail
outlet, Hormel dressed his meatcutters in starched white jackets and caps;
he made sure the shop was neat and clean and stocked with choice meat.
Disregarding the inebriated obstacles on Bourbon Avenue, customers beat
a path to George Hormel's door and soon made the Provision Market the
largest retail meat store in Austin. Toward the end of that first full year in
business, George's brother, Herman, arrived in town, joining Ben, and
took charge of the market, overseeing its growth for the next 30 years.

Business at the packinghouse was also moving into high gear by 1892
standards. By the end of that year, the packinghouse had slaughtered 610
hogs. (Today, the company can process 900 hogs in one hour.) To increase hog capacity, pay his bills and build more facilities, Hormel needed
more money and he chose a variety of means to raise the cash. Hormel
scoured the area for hides and sold them to his old friend, Crandale.
He purchased and shipped poultry and eggs to a Twin Cities-based produce house and, for the Thanksgiving season, dressed turkeys. Despite
these efforts, he invariably found himself short of cash at month's end.

"We were to find that the business often represented a taskmaster so
demanding," he wrote, "that we would ask ourselves how can we be compensated for what this monster has cost us? Many times I would have
gladly served in a less exacting capacity and let someone else feed the
business's rapacious maw with money, energy and ideas. But always
money — it lived on gold!" And just around the corner lay the financial
Panic of 1893.

THREATS FROM WALL STREET AND CHICAGO – Starting in 1893 and lasting
roughly four years, a serious financial crisis swept the nation. The panic
resulted from a farm depression, a business slump abroad and a drain on
the U.S. Treasury's gold reserve. The downturn made investors wary and
tightfisted. Banks failed and people lost their savings. In St. Paul, the
German-American National Bank, the largest capitalized bank in Minnesota, with $2 million in capital, was forced to close its doors. When the
bank reopened, it had lost $1 million.

Luckily, Austin banks remained open but credit was tight and so was
cash. People were jobless and they bought less meat. Hormel's loan for
the new building at the packinghouse weighed heavily on him and

*The interior of the Hormel
Provision Market in 1902.
(Herman Hormel at far
right.)*

*George's younger brother,
Herman Hormel, joined
the company in 1892 as
manager of the Hormel
Provision Market.*

The Panic of 1893 brought the failure of many banks and the loss of life savings by many depositors. (1893)

pressure from the bank to make payments did not help his digestion. When his banker again requested a loan payment, Hormel dropped the keys to his plant and his meat market on the president's desk. "You're a meatpacker now," Hormel declared. "I can't stand any more harassment over money. Pay me enough to live on and I'll run the business for you." The bank president wisely invited Hormel to sit down and talk things over. "When he agreed not to press me about my obligation," Hormel wrote, "I picked up my keys and left."

With repayment pressure somewhat abated, Hormel faced two other pressing problems. The first was simple: Hormel needed to open two new retail outlets to sell his products. But cash was unavailable. Everything Hormel owned was mortgaged and the banks would not lend him more money. That was clear. The second problem was even more formidable: the larger meatpackers in Chicago were selling their products directly out of improved refrigerator cars which could be switched to any siding in almost any town in America. This competition, combined with the on-going depression, was devastating. Several hundred smaller meatpacking operations between Chicago and South Dakota went out of business faced with the direct, skip-the-middleman competition.

SAUSAGE TO THE RESCUE – Hormel was undaunted by the competition. He simply decided that he had to sell more product, and a better product, than his big-city competitors. Hormel created a better sausage which he variously called a "Superior Sausage" or "Hormel's Wonderful Sausage." The new product was so delicious that people were willing to pay a premium for it. To sell more sausage, Hormel packed his own bags and began traveling from town to town. His brother, John, moved to Austin, rode a bicycle over the countryside and proceeded to take orders for sausage. One day, John ended up in Preston, Minnesota, 50 miles from Austin, a testimony to Hormel's quality product and John's endurance and persistence.

"I think it was the sausage," Hormel said many years later, trying to explain how he had remained solvent during the Panic of '93.

Hormel was probably right – it was the sausage – and his foresight and luck that guided his decision to build the brick processing building one year before the financial panic when he could still borrow money. This daring move – when the company was less than a year old – enabled Hormel to increase his business at a time when competitors were watching volume diminish and were struggling to survive. Few did. After the panic, only four of the smaller meatpackers west of the Mississippi remained in business.

In the years to come, Hormel's farsightedness and good timing would guide and support the company through two formidable challenges, an insidious one from within in 1921 and the crash of 1929. But, according to Hormel, no single year would be as difficult as 1893, "the hardest year I ever faced."

As for those much-needed retail outlets, Hormel opened them in 1894. He went to his attorney friend, Russell Shepherd, and told him, "I need working capital. I have no collateral to offer you. Can you help me?"

Shepherd, like Hormel's former boss, Crandale, loaned him the money on a personal note. Buoyed by his friend's trust and faith, "I went back," Hormel wrote, "determined to make the business a success in spite of all the hurricanes out of Wall Street and all the refrigerator cars out of Chicago."

THREE, TWO, ONE, BLAST-OFF – Its worst year over, George Hormel's company began an exponential growth spurt. In the eight-year period between 1894-1901, which ended the company's first decade in business, the number of hogs processed jumped from 2,500 to nearly 33,000.

By 1899, Geo. A. Hormel & Company produced a wide variety of top-quality pork products.

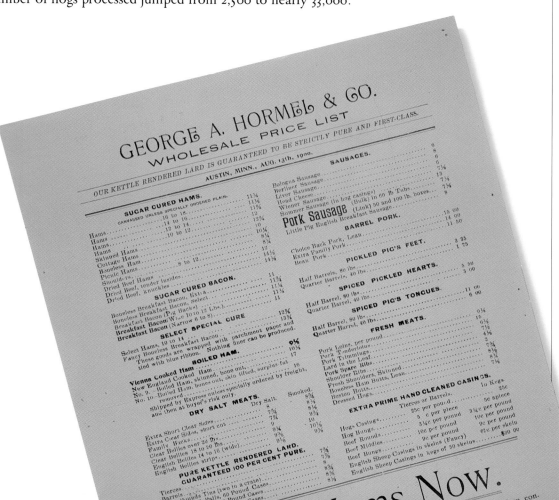

1903 PICNIC

In 1903, George A. Hormel and his family joined with other Hormel families for a picnic in Austin. (George A. Hormel, center, with a bow tie; Jay Hormel, lower left, leaning on elbow)

Hormel named its pork the Superior Brand in the 1890s.

To accommodate this growth, Hormel worked overtime and learned how to delegate authority. In 1894, he hired Elihu B. "Gid" Smith to buy livestock for the company. Smith was a man who, like his boss, thought big. For his first purchase, he obtained a herd of 63 hogs which he helped slaughter and dress because plant personnel couldn't handle the load.

To distribute the ham and bacon, Hormel hired Sam Jacobson to lead the Hormel Transportation Department which, in 1895, consisted of a mule and wagon. That same year the company received its first carload of hogs by rail. Soon animals arrived regularly via this route, snorting through the streets to the plant.

THE FIRST OF MANY FIRSTS – Hormel's father often reminded him that he should "originate, not imitate." For years Hormel tried to find ways to make fresh pork loins more appealing and profitable. In 1895, he removed the backbone, cured the remaining meat and produced "Hormel's Sugar-Cured Pig Back Bacon." Not the catchiest name for a new product (it's called Canadian bacon today), yet it sold immediately to customers who loved lean bacon. There were so many of them, the plant could not keep up with demand.

A YEAR TO REMEMBER – Eighteen ninety-five was a good year for George Hormel. His company and family were flourishing. His father had retired and moved to Austin next door to his son. Once there, John Hormel immediately became the plant's bookkeeper, as well as a source of philosophical, emotional and financial support to the plant's busy owner.

Hormel Provision Market delivery wagon in 1897.

George Hormel's brother, Henry, was also in town. He was minister of the Central Presbyterian Church where Lillian had played the organ. Henry would play a role in the company's transatlantic growth in the near future.

No doubt his mother's presence as a next-door neighbor helped George maintain his high standards of quality. She had taught him the lesson of doing the job right the first time and of wasting not and wanting not. As the company grew, these lessons were in constant need of reiteration. When Hormel spotted a piece of meat lying on the floor, he rebuked his workers for wasting the still-useful product. When he came into the plant and found the lights on while the sun shone outside, he asked his foreman, "What are the windows for? Why do we keep them clean? Why waste electricity?" And when it came to the appearance of his ham and bacon slabs, he was exhaustingly fastidious. For many years, Hormel trimmed every ham himself. Behind his back, some workers joked, "He looks over his hams the way most men look over a pretty girl." Hormel would demonstrate proper trimming techniques; then, holding aloft a ham, he would remind the crew, "If you can do one right, you can do them all right." The idea was uniformity of excellence. He recalled his own childhood lesson: like polished shoes, all the products should be perfect — not some fine and others, in his mother's word, phooey. Hormel's attitude toward waste, his unerring eye for detail and his unflinching stand on cleanliness were attitudes that became part of the company's culture. They meant not only profits for the company and decent working conditions for the employees but also distinction — not extinction — when the Meat Inspection Act became law in 1906.

CHARRED HAM FOR LUNCH – If 1895 was a good year for George Hormel and the company, 1896 was an extremely bad one. In the spring, Hormel's father contracted pneumonia and died soon afterward. George counted on his father for encouragement and moral support and his death left a void in his life. In the fall, a fire in the creamery spread to one of the smokehouses and threatened the entire complex. Luckily, a worker who lived near the plant spotted the fire early. Firefighters formed bucket brigades and set up a hose and pumped water from the river. The fire was eventually brought under control.

George A. Hormel (far right) supervises work on the hog cut floor in 1896.

The next day, can you guess what the crew ate for lunch? The salvageable ham. But more than 4,000 pounds of fire-damaged ham and meat were unsalvageable and inedible. Fortunately, Hormel had insured his property and out of the ashes arose a new smokehouse, hog slaughterhouse, poultry house and cold storage plant. This huge brick structure, 60' x 40' with 17-inch thick walls, was guaranteed to maintain a constant temperature of 36° F. during the warmest weather.

Viewing the new building, an Austin newspaper editor told Hormel, "You're wasting your money. There just aren't enough swine or cattle in this area to fill that thing." Did Hormel reply that he could see the future and the future was filled with vast herds? Probably not, but he was willing to take a risk and the future paid him big dividends. Over the next three decades, the number of herds of milk-fed hogs steadily increased and new strains of hybrid corn soon transformed the region into one of the most productive in the world.

RETIRING THE CLEAVER AND OVERALLS – At the beginning of 1897, Geo. A. Hormel & Company had processed 4,500 hogs and boasted a crew of nearly 20 men, including the three Hormel brothers. By the end of that same year, the hog operations nearly doubled, soaring to more than 8,000. To sell that product, Hormel hired his first full-time salesman, 41-year-old Sam Moe. It was Moe's priority — one that Hormel entirely endorsed — to get a check for "last week's delivery before talking about the next order." Soon, Hormel hired a second full-time salesman, William "Bill" Yelland.

Business was booming and expansion came rapidly in 1899, including $40,000 worth of new smokehouses, a pork processing facility and a storage unit. "The Hormel Company," the *Austin Herald* said in a glowing report, "has been at work several months making great changes. The work on a new, big refrigerator is now underway. New pumps and engines have been put in. There is a fine flowing well of the purest water, used for all cleaning and curing purposes. It is worth a trip to the place to see what a big institution Austin possesses."

In 1899, the hog operations nearly doubled again to more than 15,000 and Hormel installed an elevator to move hog sides from the first to the second floor. That was an improvement over the backbreaking labor of hefting sides by hand. But the most important change came when George Hormel, 39, hung up his cleaver and his overalls. By this time the com-

The main office of Geo. A. Hormel & Company in Austin. Pictured (from left) are Edgar Terry, Mr. McWane, George A. Hormel and others. (1901)

Only 10 years after its founding, the Austin plant was greatly expanded. (1901)

In 1901, more than 32,000 hogs moved through the company stockyards.

The company incorporated in the State of Minnesota in 1901.

pany needed someone to act as steward and guide. Hormel was the man. His two salesmen, Moe and Yelland, were traveling as far north as Duluth, Minnesota, to spread the word about "Hormel Good Foods." Ben Hormel and newly hired full-time salesman, Frank Sump, were building new business in the Twin Cities. They were so successful that the company opened its first branch office in 1901 on Central Avenue in Minneapolis.

By the end of its first 10 years in business, Geo. A. Hormel & Company had weathered the hurricanes of Wall Street and the refrigerator cars of Chicago as George had promised. The company was incorporated with capital of $250,000, selling 1,250 shares of preferred stock and an equal amount of common stock. The first directors and officers were George Hormel, president; Herman Hormel, vice president; A. L. Eberhart, who had been hired in 1900 as sales manager, secretary, and John Hormel, treasurer. Ben Hormel was also a director but not yet an officer. Bill Yelland was managing the new Hormel branch in Minneapolis with the assistance of John Hormel. Ben Hormel pursued new business in Rochester while Herman Hormel ran the extremely profitable Provision Market. Even Henry Hormel, now the minister at the East End Presbyterian Church in Ottumwa, Iowa, had divine inspiration and hatched business strategies for his brothers. On the threshold of a new era, the company's assets exceeded $118,000; its liabilities were $25,000, and its net worth totaled roughly $93,000.

Pork processing operations also increased to an all-time high. To transport the animals, the railroad ran a spur line into the plant. Hormel was now connected to the world by rail. The company was here to stay. Or was it?

UP, UP AND AWAY – Between 1901-20, America began emerging as a world power after defeating the Spanish in the Spanish-American War of 1898. Rough and ready Vice President Teddy Roosevelt succeeded President William McKinley after his assassination in 1901 and immediately began building America's armed forces. Under the aegis of the Monroe Doctrine, Roosevelt, in 1902, forced Germany, England and Italy to withdraw from their trade blockade of Venezuela. Roosevelt dug the Panama Canal in 1903 and, two years later, America took over the treasury of the Dominican Republic to maintain its monetary stability and protect it from European intercession. Between 1914–16, America's economy blossomed while World War I raged in Europe; the economy boomed when America joined the war in 1917.

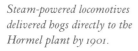

Steam-powered locomotives delivered hogs directly to the Hormel plant by 1901.

During the same two decades, Geo. A. Hormel & Company began to emerge as a force to be reckoned with in the meatpacking industry. Expansion was the modus operandi. During the first three years of the new century, Hormel made his future intentions clear by purchasing three parcels of land adjacent to the existing plant. With room for growth, he employed a specialist from Kansas City to develop plans for remodeling and expanding the packing plant. The company built a three-story pork processing facility, a two-story beef operation, an engine room, machine shop and casing processing room. He acquired a new ammonia compressor for refrigeration, although ice was still hauled out of the river to augment cooling.

The Provision Market, which by this time had moved to Main Street, was running out of room for its eagerly sought ham and bacon. When the Post Office next door moved to larger quarters, the market expanded into its quarters and became a supermarket in size long before they were commonplace. Profits from the market continued to increase yearly and so did the company's overall profits. Total sales at the end of 1903 reached $859,000, up from $711,000 the year before.

THE MORRELL CONNECTION – Despite impressive sales figures, Hormel found himself, as usual, critically short of cash. The reason? Growth drained cash. Here's where brother Henry's connection helped. One of his parishioners, Thomas Foster, managed the John Morrell & Company plant in Ottumwa, Iowa. Foster had a problem. His firm, part of the old English company, could not provide enough products for its sales territories. Hormel could provide sufficient product and wanted to produce more, but needed cash to do it. It was a marriage of convenience or relatively close to it. Hormel doubled its capital stock to $500,000, and Morrell paid Hormel $75,000 in cash. In turn, Morrell received 750 shares of preferred stock, a bonus of 750 shares of common stock and three seats on the Hormel Board. Hormel, on the other hand, received free access to Morrell's formulas for meat processing and, more importantly, the right to distribute products at Morrell's distribution centers.

As for its own operations, Geo. A. Hormel & Company expanded far beyond Austin. It opened a distribution center in Duluth in 1904, headed by H. B. VanName. In 1905, the company opened a branch in St. Paul, later managed by H. G. Cuneo. In 1908, the company built a new, elegant Austin office complex of gleaming white limestone cement blocks and, in 1911, began movement into the south with an office in San Antonio, Texas, managed by Ben Moore. Hormel opened a new outlet in Minneapolis in 1912 at 225 Fifth Street North and, the following year, inaugurated a branch office in Chicago, the city of Cudahy, Armour and Swift. It was undoubtedly a happy day for George Hormel to challenge the giants of the industry. The southerly expansion continued in 1916 when Paul Rice, a Hormel salesman, opened a branch in Dallas, Texas, and W. A. Perkins opened another in Atlanta, Georgia, in 1918.

Dairy Brand bacon was a customer favorite in the early 1900s.

Before refrigeration, workers harvested ice from the Red Cedar River in Austin.

While opening distribution centers and branch offices, George Hormel also cast a glance toward Europe. Through his contacts with Thomas Foster and after a trip to England in 1905, Hormel examined the feasibility of exporting product overseas. As a result of this visit, the company began an export business. It reached a high point during and just after World War I, generating as much as one-third of the company's sales volume.

A CLEAN, WELL-LIGHTED PLACE – We all know the pen is mightier than the sword. In 1906, many meatpackers discovered it was mightier, too. In that year, Teddy Roosevelt read *The Jungle*, Upton Sinclair's exposé of the meatpacking industry. He assigned federal investigators who soon produced what the President called a "sickening report." He threatened to publish it if Congress failed to correct conditions in the meatpacking industry. Congress that year passed the Meat Inspection Act, which doomed many companies engaged in interstate commerce. Those were the firms that Uncle Jacob Decker abhorred, companies that allowed the meat to get thick with flies and thought nothing of adulterating their products. "Clean food doesn't spoil in a hurry," Decker had said. "Dirty food spoils while you're looking at it." Of the sanitary conditions at Geo. A. Hormel & Company, the federal agents told the *Austin Herald's* reporter, "The Hormel plant ranks among the most perfect in the country from sanitary and inspection standpoints."

BIG ADS, SCARCE MONEY – In 1910, the company, now one year shy of its 20th birthday, went to the Chicago advertising agency of Long, Critchfield Corporation. Thinking nationally, Hormel signed a contract for monthly advertisements in *Ladies' Home Journal* at a cost of $7,500. The advertisements began in 1911 and pictured hogs on the farm and a

Hormel opened a St. Paul, Minnesota, branch in 1905. (16 East Third St.)

Employees at the Atlanta, Georgia, branch in 1921.

parchment-wrapped **Dairy** ham and side of bacon. The headline announced, "Here's the ham and bacon that your mouth has watered for." The advent of company advertising would make a lasting impression on 17-year-old Jay Hormel when his turn came to manage the company.

Unfortunately, national advertising did not bring immediate relief from Hormel's nagging cash flow problems. Even with vast increases in the yearly hog slaughter — 43,000 in 1902 to 480,000 in 1917 — and, despite comparable increases in sales over the same period, Geo. A. Hormel & Company suffered from a now perplexing shortage of cash. The company was always profitable, yet cash was always short. To raise needed funds, the officers increased the capital structure from $500,000 to $1 million in 1906; to $3.2 million in 1916; to $3.7 million in 1918, and to $4.2 million in 1920. Still, there never seemed to be enough cash. The company's "rapacious maw" continued to devour money, energy and ideas. "But always money," George Hormel had written, "it lived on gold!" Or did it?

A MISPLACED TRUST – Ransome J. "Cy" Thomson struck a chord in George Hormel. Although Cy had not performed satisfactorily in the plant, Hormel took a liking to him because he wanted to better himself. Cy had asked for an office job, but was turned down by Hormel because he lacked the training. Offered financial assistance instead, Thomson enrolled in Mankato (Minnesota) Commercial College, graduating one year later. He returned to his benefactor. Hormel was impressed because the young man had initiative, persistence and potential. He hired him in 1908 as a bookkeeper.

"Cy Thomson was born and brought up near Austin and lived in a house built by his grandparents, Minnesota pioneers," Hormel wrote. "His family was highly respected in the community. I was filled with admiration for a youngster who had gone back to school to better himself." Cy Thomson embodied the American dream. Anyone could become president of a company if he had the ambition. Thomson did. With his aptitude for finance, organization and efficiency, he rapidly moved through the ranks and in four years became assistant comptroller, responsible for the general ledger and the transfer of funds.

Thomson married, had a son and became a pillar of the community, serving as superintendent of the Sunday School, contributing to various benefits, charities and lending money to needy friends. From a wealthy

Dairy ham and bacon were featured in the company's first national advertisement in 1911.

aunt, he allegedly inherited a farm near LeRoy, Minnesota, which he immediately, with her investment funds, began to rehabilitate. The complex became the Oak Dale Farms. Cy spared no expense. The poultry operation, for instance, specialized in prizewinning Single Comb White Leghorns. Thomson paid $10,000 for a prize rooster. He was lavish with his friends, too. He built a dance pavilion large enough for 1,000 couples, decorated by famous artists and lit by 2,000 electric lights. For the children, he built a fully equipped 10-acre playground. To protect the premises, he installed a fire station and hired a full-time crew of firefighters. Thomson conceived big ideas, he worked hard and ideas led to more ideas — all of them bigger and better. Tourists flocked to his LeRoy farm as did the governor and state deputies. Ever accommodating, Thomson built a 50-bed hotel with dining room for 75 people.

Cy Thomson's lavish Oak Dale Farms attracted tourists throughout the region.

In addition to people and leghorns, Thomson liked cattle and swine. He bought a farm near Blooming Prairie where he raised prize Holstein cattle and Duroc hogs. The Holstein herd was worth $300,000, he claimed. He paid $25,000 for one-half interest in a Holstein bull and $6,000 for a Duroc boar, which sired a swine herd worth $30,000. Both herds lived in comfort. The swine barns were steam-heated and the cattle barns were equipped with fans that blew the ubiquitous flies into killing chambers.

Hired hands lived in comfort, too. At a time when working as a hired hand might mean sleeping in the barn on a bale of straw, working at any of Thomson's farms was "a hired man's heaven." For them, Thomson built a dormitory furnished with rugs, draperies and expensive lighting fixtures. There were billiard rooms, sunrooms, even dancing rooms. Thomson's was an enlightened management scheme for both livestock and men.

He was obviously a great entrepreneur and never had cash flow problems. People wondered about him, but not maliciously or suspiciously. He was so highly regarded and so well liked, no one suspected anything amiss.

George Hormel's only worry was for Thomson's sake. "Cy," he said one day, "wouldn't it be better if you gave up your job and devoted yourself exclusively to your farms? Hobbies are fine things but I think it's time you decided which is the hobby, the packinghouse or the farms?"

"Isn't my work satisfactory?" Thomson asked.

"Yes, it is," said Hormel, "but I wonder how long you can continue to divide your attention between the two enterprises."

"Nothing is more important to me than my job here," said Thomson. "Actually, I'm only a stockholder in the farms. My cousin operates them. My aunt asked me to invest her money and, of course, I recommended livestock . . ."

Nothing was more important than Thomson's job at Hormel because that's where his money was made. Some of it he worked for; the rest he made the easy way. He stole it. Thomson began stealing small sums in 1911. In 1917, he embezzled $28,000 and, in 1918, $88,000. Between Nov. 1, 1920, and July 7, 1921, an eight-month period, Thomson stole a whopping $606,000. In total, he defrauded the company of $1,187,000. He did it simply. He transferred funds from Hormel to the Oak Dale Farms which the bankers at Austin Farmers & Merchants State Bank believed belonged to the company. To cover the shortage during an audit, which was conducted regularly, Thomson withdrew money from Hormel bank accounts in Boston, Atlanta or Dallas. Deposits were made in the Austin Farmers & Merchants State Bank. Funds moving from Boston to Atlanta to Austin to San Antonio were funds in transit. Thomson kept them in transit for five years. A perpetual float of this type was common among large

Cy Thomson.

Thomson routinely transferred funds from Geo. A. Hormel & Company to Oak Dale Farms.

CY THOMSON

One of eight children of a well-respected Minnesota family, Cy Thomson attended high school in LeRoy, Minnesota, and graduated in 1905. After teaching school for a year, he moved to Austin and worked briefly in the Hormel plant where his father was employed as a beef buyer. Thomson returned to Hormel as a clerk/stenographer in 1907 after completing a business course in Mankato, Minnesota, and earned several promotions through hard work and dedication. His first embezzlement occurred in 1911 when he stole $800 enclosed in an investor's letter requesting stock. Over the next 10 years, Thomson boldly embezzled large sums from Hormel and avoided discovery by keeping the funds in perpetual transit. "Why I did this I can't tell you," he later wrote from his Stillwater, Minnesota, prison cell. "I have lain awake many nights trying to figure this out." By the time Jay C. Hormel discovered the embezzlement in 1921, Thomson had stolen more than $1 million in company funds. "Crime does not pay," Thomson later wrote in prison memoirs.

News of the embezzlement by leading citizen Cy Thomson shocked the company and the community. Over a number of years, Thomson stole more than $1.1 million from Hormel.

companies with branch offices located on both coasts. It was easily explained and never closely checked by the auditors.

There was only one drawback to Thomson's juggling act. It required constant attention. He never dared take a vacation for fear someone would uncover his scheme or fail to transfer the proper funds at the right time. Of course, the fact that he was always on the job worked in his favor. People believed he was diligent and dedicated.

On July 9, 1921, the juggling act came to an abrupt end. The notation "transfer of funds" on a canceled company check for $5,000, payable to Austin Farmers & Merchants State Bank and credited to Oak Dale Farms, caught the attention of Jay Hormel. It was a Saturday morning, Jay was searching for some operating figures in the Accounting Department and, with that bit of serendipity, Thomson's jig was up and with it, possibly, the entire Hormel company.

AFTER THE DARKEST DAY, THE PROUDEST – Nineteen twenty was not a good year for Geo. A. Hormel & Company. Hog prices, which had risen steadily between 1900-17, from $4.50 per hundredweight to $14, skyrocketed during World War I and then fell like a rock the following year to $12 per hundredweight. Meatpackers with large inventories were hit hard, Hormel among them. In addition, sales were down and the stock market was in a temporary skid. Hormel was $3 million in debt, not an unusual sum for the company, but in a bad year with a depressed market and a yet undiscovered embezzlement, there was a chance that the banks would seek liquidation. The bankers called a meeting.

"The night before I went to Chicago was a bad time for all of us," Hormel wrote. "I thought I had known my friends in prosperity – our lives had touched at many points and out of our united efforts had come success. But, in adversity I was gaining knowledge of them and of myself I had never had before. I had a good share of self-confidence but one gets a different concept of it on an occasion like this which tends to cut a man down to size."

The meeting was held July 20, 1921, at First National Bank of Chicago, the company's principal banker. George Hormel was 61 years old. His son, Jay, 28, accompanied him to lend support. The mood in the committee room was somber. The chairman explained the purpose of the meeting – whether to extend the loan or liquidate – and then called on Hormel. "I tried to put into words what the company had tried to put into practice for 30 years," Hormel wrote. He discussed the high standards of uniformity and quality that had been company hallmarks. He described how the salesforce had grown from three men to a group selling $30 million worth of products with only $3,000 in credit losses. "Consider this," he said, "if you liquidate the company, you will probably realize one-half of your investment. And the effects on Austin will be devastating. Once the full news is made known, there will be a run on the bank. Many will lose their life savings. The bank will probably not recover. In addition," Hormel said, "1,000 people will lose their jobs and $1.5 million in payroll will disappear. However, if you choose to extend our loan, I give you my word that nothing will be left undone to justify your continued confidence in the company. I pledge as collateral my home, insurance, stocks and everything I own. I ask you for two years' time to make up the loss."

In 1922, the John Koberstine Market prominently displays an array of Hormel products.

Women in gleaming white caps and neat frocks package bacon in the Austin plant in 1925.

E. E. Brown, First National Bank's vice president, stood and said, "Gentlemen, I move that we grant the extension." The motion carried unanimously, a creditors' committee was set up to oversee the affairs of the company and the bank loaned Hormel an additional $1 million.

Hormel later wrote that this personal act of tribute to his character and integrity was the proudest day of his life. But a day only lasts 24 hours and there was much work to be done. "I went home to clean house," Hormel wrote, "and that caused me more grief than any previous act in my business career."

OF GOING SOFT, MILLSTONES AND BONDS – Upon his return to Austin, George put H. H. "Tim" Corey in charge of Thomson's assets. Corey, who had joined the company in 1920 in the Time Department and later became its manager, recovered nearly $188,000 over the next four years. As a result, the company's net loss was slightly less than $1 million. Ironically, the $25,000 purebred Holstein bull, like Thomson's entire financial scheme, was sterile and ended up in the tallow tank.

While Corey liquidated the Thomson assets, George Hormel asked for the resignation of A. L. Eberhart, secretary, and several other long-time executives. Hormel did not believe the embezzlement was the fault of any of these men, but he could see that the crime reflected the course the company had taken. Hormel had grown soft, inattentive, and its management along with it. The great demand for food during World War I made selling easy. The salesforce had lost its aggressive edge and management had become less insistent on efficiency and quality in performance and production.

While analyzing the company's present and past dilemmas, Hormel gave himself a portion of the blame. Like his father who had trusted his first partner, "I had put my trust in a system," he wrote, "forgetting that no system is any more foolproof than the people who operate it and I had failed to evaluate, in terms of my associates, what I knew to be true of human nature in general."

Some members of the company's Board of Directors rightly looked outside the company for blame. Hormel's oldest friend, S. D. Catherwood, believed that by suing the auditors and the Austin Farmers & Merchants State Bank, they could recover much of the lost money. But Hormel's response, especially in light of the litigious 1980s, was remarkable. Hormel could wisely see that a public suit would ruin the accounting firms and damage the banks involved. But he also foresaw that ". . .while we carried expensive litigation through the courts, business would stand still. The company's strength and time and thought would be consumed in an essentially noncreative activity. A year's effort invested in the business, however, might go a long way toward paying off the lost money, produce results for years to come and harm no one."

The company would not sue, the principled Hormel concluded. It would work hard with its now streamlined management. But there was an immediate problem. The creditors' committee, also called the advisory committee, established to oversee the company's affairs, was an albatross. If the roof in the packinghouse plant leaked, the advisory committee had to be notified and the purchase of new shingles had to be cleared before the leak was stopped. Also, many of Hormel's long-time suppliers were shut out in favor of suppliers the advisory committee members favored because they had a vested interest in them. That meant higher operating costs at a time when the company wanted the best margins it could obtain. Most irritating of all, every aspect of corporate policy had to be approved by the committee. This meant the company was barred from taking the normal and advisable risks it needed to take in order to grow and prosper.

Unused to fetters, Hormel sought a way out. He went to see Lyman Wakefield, then associated with Wells, Dickey & Company, an investment house in Minneapolis. Hormel told Wakefield he needed the creditors off his back and Wakefield suggested he float a bond issue — a $1.5 million bond paying 6.5 percent over a 12-year period.

Hormel wondered, Would anyone buy such bonds? Wakefield said they would. He promised to take his salesmen to Austin where they could meet Hormel and tour the plant. Hormel decided to take the risk.

In November 1922, Hormel floated a $1.5 million bond issue to cover the loss incurred by Cy Thomson's embezzlement.

HORMEL COMPANY REFINANCES HUGE ISSUE OF BONDS

$1,500,000 Underwritten By Twin City Banks And Trust Companies

ALL DUE PAPER PAID

$75,000 Paid In Austin Alone To Banks And Individuals Here—Will Pay All Back Dividends With Accrued Interest

The George A. Hormel Company announced today that it had completed arrangements for the refinancing of the company by which it is to be relieved of the strain brought upon it by the Thomson defalcation of a million and a quarter dollars.

The company this afternoon issued its checks to pay every outstanding account whether due to band or individual and on the third Tuesday in November will, at its annual meeting, pay all dividends. The dividends of last year which were not paid will be paid also with accrued interest.

The Hormel company, by this deal passes out from under the supervision of the creditor banks, who put a committee in charge, following the crime of Cy Thomson, which nearly wrecked our greatest manufacturing institution.

Issue $1,500,000 Bonds.

The company has completed arrangements to issue the company's bonds to the amount of $1,500,000. The bonds are to draw six and a half per cent and are to run twelve years. The trustee of the bonds is the Merchants Trust and Savings Bank of St. Paul. The underwriters of this bond issue are Wells Dickey and Co. of Minneapolis, the Merchants Trust and Savings Bank of St. Paul, and the Minneapolis Trust Company of Minneapolis.

Austin banks and individuals held $75,000 worth of the company's paper which was all paid this afternoon.

93 Pct. S

The bonds were dated Nov. 1, 1922. They sold out that very day. With the money, the company paid its outstanding debts and the advisory committee was disbanded. In recognition of his work on behalf of the company, Lyman Wakefield was elected to the Hormel Board of Directors.

A COMPLETE RECOVERY ... AND A NEW LEADER – Free to steer its own course, Geo. A. Hormel & Company did so with alacrity. In 1924, the company redeemed not only the $100,000 due for payment but an additional $500,000. Two years later, the company completed the job by repaying the entire $900,000 it owed the bank, eight years ahead of schedule. Business was once again on track and booming. By 1924, the company was slaughtering more than 1,000,000 hogs each year, nearly a 200 percent increase over 1922. To move the products, the company stopped selling ham and bacon from refrigerated railroad cars and began delivering products in trucks. Salesmen driving a fleet of refrigerated vans called "sausage trucks" sold Hormel products and collected receipts. Some ambitious salesmen sold as many as 5,000 pounds of sausage and other high-priced specialty items in a single week.

The 1920s were roaring and the stock market was climbing daily to new heights. People had money. Many families were buying their first radios, refrigerators and automobiles. Herbert H. Hoover, in his political campaign, dared to say, "We in America are nearer to the final triumph over poverty than ever before."

It was a time of heady dreams and rapid change, a time to look to the future. By 1927, Geo. A. Hormel & Company had expanded nationwide with processing plants or distribution centers in Chicago, Illinois; Duluth,

Upon moving to California in 1927, George and Lillian Hormel donated their Austin home to the YWCA.

The Hormel retirement home in Bel Air, California.

Minnesota; Atlanta, Georgia; Dallas and Houston, Texas; New Orleans
and Shreveport, Louisiana; Los Angeles and San Francisco, California;
Seattle, Washington; Detroit, Michigan; Montgomery, Alabama;
Winston-Salem, North Carolina; Chattanooga, Tennessee; Tampa,
Florida; Newark, New Jersey, and New York, New York.

Looking ahead, George Hormel thought it was time to retire. In 1927,
the company's founder was 67 years old. He had been managing the
business for 36 years and felt it was time to turn over daily leadership
to younger men. Hormel also knew that if he continued to live in Austin,
it would be difficult to transfer power completely and properly to the
next generation of company leaders. Hormel and his wife decided to
build a home in Bel Air, a suburb of Los Angeles, where they had often
vacationed. They donated their Austin home to the YWCA and moved
to California during the winter of 1927-28. Their son, Jay, became acting
president and George continued as chief executive officer, receiving weekly reports on the activities of the enterprise. In the years to come, Jay
Hormel's leadership would be characterized by innovation, a flair for the
dramatic and the unusual and a roster of new products, including **SPAM**
luncheon meat.

George and Lillian Hormel.
(1940)

Which came first, the stew or the can? In the case of **Dinty Moore** beef stew, it was one-half million cans that inspired Jay C. Hormel to experiment with a ''poor man's dish'' that has since become an American favorite.

The Depression years challenged the Roosevelt administration to stimulate the economy and feed the unemployed. As a partial solution to the problem, the government underwrote a plan to buy livestock from farmers at a fair price and turn it over to Geo. A. Hormel & Company and other meatpackers to produce a canned roast beef and gravy product for the nation's urban poor.

However, in 1935, after only nine months, the program ended abruptly, leaving Hormel with 500,000 cans valued at $25,000. Jay C. Hormel, with his keen eye for innovation, decided to test the market with a canned beef stew. He began production of **Hormel** beef stew in a 24-ounce can that sold for $ .15. It soon became a phenomenal success and before

Geo. A. Hormel & Company cooked up a beef stew with only the freshest ingredients.

long, Hormel was purchasing unused cans from other meatpackers to help satisfy the demand.

Dinty Moore beef stew emerged in late 1935 after Hormel purchased the rights to the Dinty

---

PECTED AND
DEPARTMENT
LTURE. EST. 199

DINTY MOORE

NET WEIGHT OF CONTENTS 1½ LBS.

BEEF STEW

A Depression-era product created to feed the nation's poor quickly became a commercial success, selling for just $ .15 a can.

Convenient, affordable, just-like-homemade Dinty Moore beef stew turned fathers into culinary heroes.

"The big meal in the big can" has become an American classic.

Today Dinty Moore beef stew is a leader in its product category.

Moore name from C. F. Witt & Sons, a large wholesale and retail meat and grocery firm in Minneapolis, Minnesota.

Questions of copyright infringement arose, however, when King Features Syndicate, Inc., and George McManus, creator of the famous comic strip, "Bringing Up Father," informed Hormel that the character, Dinty Moore, along with Jiggs and Maggie, had been appearing in his strip since 1913. Because the two parties were not in direct competition with each other, the problem was soon resolved. Also, as a result of the negotiations with McManus, Hormel was able to secure the rights to feature Jiggs, Maggie and Dinty Moore in point-of-sale marketing efforts.

But the company's problems were not over. A New York City restaurateur, claiming to be the Dinty Moore of the comic strip, brought suit against Hormel. McManus came to the defense of Hormel by stating he derived the Dinty Moore name from a bellhop in a St. Louis, Missouri, hotel, not from the New York restaurant. Hormel was finally granted clear title to the Dinty Moore name. And, "the big meal in the big can" was born.

Today, **Dinty Moore** beef stew is an American classic. Although it competes with scores of national and regional brands nationwide, it remains the number one product in its category, making the **Dinty Moore** name synonymous with beef stew.

"**Dinty Moore** beef stew has endured the test of time," says Robert F. Patterson, group vice president, Prepared Foods, "because it is nutritious and convenient and gives consumers value for the dollar."

Through innovations in packaging, Hormel has extended that convenience to a wider spectrum of consumers. The product is currently available in four varieties (beef stew, chicken stew, meatball stew and vegetable stew) and five different sizes (40-ounce can, 24-ounce can, 15-ounce can, 7½-ounce cup and 10½-ounce bowl for microwave cooking). According to Eric A. Brown, vice president of the Grocery Products Division, future plans for the product will focus on new variations in packaging to make the product even more convenient. Extensions of the **Dinty Moore** line, utilizing new packaging techniques, will also evolve.

While convenience is the wave of the future, recent marketing efforts have appealed to health-conscious consumers. **Dinty Moore** beef stew, fast approaching its 60th year, meets the standards of the contemporary shopper by offering no preservatives and only 240 calories per eight-ounce serving.

Touted in recent advertising promotions as "America's Best Kept Secret," the truth is — there is no secret. Consumers know **Dinty Moore** beef stew as a contemporary, convenient and nutritious product.

More than 50 years later, Dinty Moore beef stew is still in step with the times.

Dinty Moore hits his stride in the 1970s.

CHAPTER THREE

The Master

of Invention

1927-1946

"The idea that an employer is the lord and master of his own business is an antiquated notion. . . . Give labor the fair treatment which is its right and labor's right to organize will never harm you."

Jay C. Hormel

1927

In 1935, Dinty Moore beef stew was introduced to consumers as "the big meal in the big can."

DINTY MOORE
NET WEIGHT OF CONTENTS 1½ LBS
BEEF STEW
LOOK FOR THE BIG BLUE AND WHITE CAN

Jay C. Hormel in 1945.

It was Jay C. Hormel who brought a penchant for daring new products and dazzling promotions to his father's company. No one had ever seen ham in a can, "sausage trucks" rolling across the Midwestern countryside or a women's drum and bugle corps that toured, sang and sold Hormel products. Nor had anyone ever considered a guaranteed annual wage in the meatpacking business.

1927-1933

1927-33   Sales branches, or distribution centers, as they are now known, are established in 14 cities.

1928   The company reincorporates under the Delaware charter.
■ First manufacturing outside Austin is done in Los Angeles, California.

A strike by Austin plant workers on Nov. 10, 1933, shook the company.

1929   George A. Hormel becomes chairman of the board; Jay C. Hormel is named president.
■ Austin office triples in size and production areas are modernized.
■ The stock market crashes, initiating the Great Depression.
■ 979,692 hogs are processed.

1931   Guaranteed annual wage is established.
■ Hormel Credit Union is organized.
■ In addition to hogs, the company processes sheep, cattle and calves.

1932   Franklin D. Roosevelt is elected president of the United States.

1933   Austin employees unionize, forming the Independent Union of All Workers No. 1.

1934-1936

1934   The company files for registration of its common stock on the Chicago Stock Exchange and applies for registration on the New York Curb Exchange, later named the American Stock Exchange.
■ **Hormel** vegetable soup is introduced.

1935   **Dinty Moore** beef stew and **Hormel** chili are introduced. Advertising includes a 20-member Mexican song-and-dance troupe called the Hormel Chili Beaners.

President Franklin D. Roosevelt.

■ Average company employment is 3,587.
■ Hog processing drops to 866,453 due to extreme shortage of hogs.

1936   Ice making machines are installed to replace annual ice harvest.

AUSTIN DAILY HERALD
STRIKERS TAKE CONTROL OVER HORMEL PLANT
Company Will Remain Shut Down Indefinitely

1937 **SPAM** luncheon meat is introduced and achieves an 18 percent market share within the year.

1938 The company establishes a Joint Earnings Plan.
- The company processes 964,845 hogs.

1939 Hormel sponsors its own national network radio program, "It Happened in Hollywood."
- Biggest pig comes to market — 1,105 pounds.

1940 The company contracts with George Burns and Gracie Allen, "Spammy" the pig, and Artie Shaw and his 23-piece orchestra to promote **SPAM** luncheon meat, **Hormel** chili and **Dinty Moore** beef stew.
- The company processes 1,149,308 hogs.
- Annual sales reach $65,512,881.

National advertising in the late 1930s quickly made SPAM luncheon meat an American family favorite.

1941 Japan bombs Pearl Harbor; United States enters World War II.
- The Hormel Foundation is created.
- Ben Hormel retires as senior vice president.
- The company doubles its canning production lines and hours of operation to supply 15 million cans weekly for the Lend-Lease program.
- The company processes more than two million head of livestock for the first time.

1942 The comedy team of Abbott and Costello holds a bond rally at the Austin Band Shell and sells $110,000 in bonds.
- A shortage of tin forces the company to discontinue production of the **Dinty Moore** line, chili con carne, canned hams and other products.

1943 The company hires 448 women to replace men serving in the war.

1944 The company institutes employee Profit Sharing Trust.

1945 By April, more than 100 million pounds of **SPAM** luncheon meat are shipped abroad.
- The Hormel Institute is founded in Austin.
- President Roosevelt dies and is succeeded by Vice President Harry S Truman.
- World War II ends.
- Jay C. Hormel gives a dinner for 100 returning company war veterans; 67 others die during the war.

1946 Lillian Belle (Gleason) Hormel dies at age 78.

- George A. Hormel dies at age 85.
- Jay C. Hormel is named chairman of the board and H. H. Corey is elected president.

Hormel products sustained Allied troops in both Europe and the Pacific throughout World War II.

The packaging of Hormel products was redesigned by George Switzer in 1941 to achieve a uniform and colorful appearance.

ON THE AIR

1946

Hormel chili was introduced in 1935 with the help of the Hormel Chili Beaners, a Mexican song-and-dance troupe.

In a bold marketing move, Jay C. Hormel established the Hormel Girls, a traveling troupe of 60 musical women, to promote Hormel products after World War II. The Girls traveled by caravan to cities throughout the country and starred in their own national radio show, "Music with the Hormel Girls."

Ⅰn the United States, 1927 was a banner year. Charles Lindberg soloed the Atlantic nonstop in the *Spirit of St. Louis*; Minnesota's own Ole Rolvaag published *Giants in the Earth*; Babe Ruth hit 60 home runs and the stock market began its climb to unprecedented heights. In Minnesota, far from Wall Street and Yankee Stadium, Jay Hormel had become acting president of Geo. A. Hormel & Company, the multimillion-dollar firm his father founded in 1891. Meanwhile, 2,000 miles away in Bel Air, California, George kept his finger on the company's pulse.

HEIR APPARENTLY – At age 35, Jay Hormel was no novice when he took over the company. For many years, he had a hand in a variety of company endeavors. For example, in the early 1920s, Jay masterminded a recruiting campaign by distributing brochures entitled "Where Do We Go From Here?" at colleges and universities around the country. With the help of H. H. "Tim" Corey, former college football star who later succeeded Hormel as company president, Jay recruited a number of promising college graduates.

In addition, Jay had uncovered the near-fatal embezzlement at Hormel, seeing anew what insiders had overlooked dozens of times. Jay Hormel had also stood by his father through the difficult and trying period when the creditors' committee from First National Bank of Chicago oversaw operations at the company. Jay shared in arranging the $1.5 million bond issue, and its timely repayment, that freed the company from debt and the millstone of outside supervisors.

CANNED HAM AND SAUSAGE TRUCKS – As part of his apprenticeship, Jay Hormel had overseen the development of three other significant projects that would characterize his tenure as president. He began work on the first project in 1926 – preserving ham in a can.

Although Hormel cured ham kept longer than a fresh ham, a canned ham was a pioneering stroke because it would keep indefinitely. For at least three years, from 1923-26, the company's embryonic research and development team tried to create an efficient, dependable canning process and, more importantly, a tasty ham. But the right combination of cure mixture, cooking time and vacuum seal eluded them. Either the ham balked the can or the can balked the ham.

Geo. A. Hormel & Company produced the first canned ham in 1926.

On June 21, 1926, Jay sent his father a note saying it might be a smart investment to invite Paul Joern of Hamburg, Germany, to Austin. Joern was hailed as an expert canner and, upon arriving in Austin four months later, he proved it. One by one, the company's vexing canning problems disappeared. Proper cooking temperatures and curing procedures emerged and the company soon began production of "Hormel Flavor-Sealed Hams."

Despite a laborious packaging technique that involved hand soldering the can lids, the product was test marketed in Seattle, Washington, and the "sweet, tender and highly palatable" canned ham became an immediate success. Orders arrived from as far away as Alaska and Japan and a new Hormel entity, the Flavor-Sealed Division, was born. It was headed by E. N. Sturman, a former Trinity College divinity student attracted by one of the company's early recruitment campaigns. The timing of this new venture was fortuitous because canning would play a vital role in the company's growth during the turbulent years ahead.

In 1927, Hormel initiated a second project upon recognizing the need to distribute the company's products, including canned ham, more widely. He conceived the idea of the "sausage truck," a van driven by salesmen who traveled short routes to sell and deliver products along the way. This distribution technique was much more convenient than the old method that relied on product distribution by refrigerated railroad car. At last, Hormel salesmen had ample inventory and more than enough mobility. Soon, 250 Hormel sausage trucks were rolling across the Midwest. Nearly 20 years later, Hormel would use a similar idea, plus 60 musical women, to promote the company's products nationwide.

While Jay Hormel was establishing this new system, he also recognized the need for an extensive marketing campaign. He started an intensive advertising program that exceeded one-half million dollars. When Jay's

*Advertising for **Hormel** Flavor-Sealed ham touted the revolutionary new product.*

Distribution of Hormel products was improved in 1927 with the advent of the Hormel sausage truck.

father heard the news, he exploded, "Half a million? That's a handsome year's profit. I can't imagine spending my father's money that way!"

"I'm sure you can't," Jay answered, smiling. "But you didn't have a rich dad like mine."

THE ONLY SON OF AN ENTREPRENEUR – When Jay Hormel was born in 1892, his father was not rich and the fledgling company would soon be confronted by the dual blows of a major financial panic and the advent of refrigerated boxcars.

Although he was an only child, Jay was not coddled and his father insisted early on that he earn his own spending money. Jay Hormel needed little encouragement because he was a born entrepreneur. In one of his early jobs, he demonstrated his willingness to be a leader and take responsibility. While he worked as a janitor at the church his family attended, someone in the congregation interfered. Jay vowed to his father, "I'm going to straighten this business out right now. If I'm going to be janitor, I'm going to janit [sic] and nobody else."

At the suggestion of his father, Jay also learned to profit from resourceful thinking. He persuaded a number of housewives in his Austin neighborhood to put traps in their sinks to catch grease. With the help of his friend, Ralph Daigneau, who later became a company director, Jay paid the women $.02 a pound for the grease. With entrepreneurial acumen, they turned around and sold their "recycled" grease to Hormel for $.04 a pound.

Working together, Jay and Ralph also learned about beating the competition. That occurred in the early 1900s when a city ordinance required that all gasoline cans be painted red so the fire department could spot them easily. The two hard-working buddies went to work. They knew that anyone who wanted gas had to fill up his own can from the tank on the outskirts of town. Stationed right there, the boys seized a perfect opportunity and charged $.15 to paint each can on the spot.

PACKING PLANT BORN – The formal packinghouse education of Jay Hormel began at a young age, although it is safe to assume he grew up breathing, eating and drinking the meatpacking business and its culture. (Jay's father, three uncles and grandfather were all meatpackers and,

At age 14, Jay Hormel took his first job in the Austin plant, working in the lard room at $.10 an hour.

at one time or another, each was involved in the Austin business.) After school and on Saturdays, Jay worked for Uncle Herman in the Provision Market and, at age 14, began working during the summers in the Hormel lard room at the less-than-princely sum of $.10 an hour.

Unlike his father who, at 14, went to work to help support his family, Jay attended Shattuck School for Boys, a private high school in Faribault, Minnesota. After graduation, Jay enrolled at Princeton University, Princeton, New Jersey. George Hormel hoped his son would study to become an attorney like his old friends Catherwood and Shepherd. But Jay had other ideas which were triggered by his entrepreneurial instincts. He saw a niche and wanted to fill it. Jay needed operating cash and requested seed capital from his father. Perplexed by his son's demands, Hormel called the Princeton dean to inquire, "How's Jay doing?" There was a considerable pause and then the dean replied: "After four years, Jay's going to have a poor scholastic record . . . but he should have a dandy laundry service."

Intent on seeing this phenomenon firsthand, George Hormel arrived at Princeton to find that Jay had taken over management of the college laundry. George and Jay exchanged words. The two men were impatient and angry with each other, but it was now clear to the elder Hormel that his son was not barrister material. He was a businessman with an eye for innovation, niche marketing and profits.

For his part, Jay thought of himself as a manager. After finishing his junior year at Princeton, he appeared unannounced in his father's office in a business suit ready to start work. "I'll learn from you what's to be done," Jay declared, "then I'll go and do it."

George Hormel, who had started his career in the pits of the hide cellar, knew better. "You can't learn a business from the top down," he told his son. "You've got to learn by working with men on the production line. There you'll see for yourself how to turn out a quality product. First, watch the most efficient men at work. Then ask yourself, 'Can you get the same result with greater economy? Can the same man accomplish more with better equipment, with a different setup?'" In addition, George passed on his father's maxim, "Originate, don't imitate." And he encouraged Jay to strive continually for higher standards of quality. "Can you learn all that by sitting behind a desk and pushing papers?"

Jay went home, put on a pair of overalls and returned to the plant where he began work unloading cars and trucks of hogs. During the next two years, he took his father's suggestions to heart. Jay Hormel learned

Jay Hormel in military uniform at Shattuck School for Boys. (1910)

While serving in France during World War I, Jay Hormel met Germaine Dubois and the two were married in 1922.

the meatpacking trade, scrutinized every aspect of the business and took sheaves of notes. He worked as a foreman, supervisor and plant superintendent before being named first vice president of the company in November 1916.

LOVE AND WAR – On April 6, 1917, the United States declared war on Germany. George Hormel hoped Jay would be deferred because he was involved in an essential food industry, but Jay was eager to serve. Although his draft number came up early, there was a delay in the enlistment procedure. Jay took matters into his own hands and set out for Camp Dodge, Iowa. Finally, on September 5, he was inducted – the first drafted man from Minnesota to report at Camp Dodge and the first enlisted man in the 351st Infantry, 88th Division, to mobilize against the Kaiser.

Jay Hormel rose quickly through the ranks, becoming a second lieutenant. He was shipped overseas and, on Jan. 13, 1918, stationed at the Quartermaster Depot in Gievres, France. There, his experience in the meatpacking business came in handy, because it was his job to provide clothing and food to the Army.

It was not his intention to fall in love while in France, the nation of lovers, but he did. He met Germaine Dubois of La Vernelle, France, and courted her until leaving the continent. The courtship continued long distance and they were married in 1922. Jay and Germaine settled in Austin where they built a home in the style of a French chateau and raised their three sons: George A. II, Thomas Dubois and James Catherwood.

Following their wedding in West Kirby, England, in 1922, Mr. and Mrs. Jay C. Hormel returned to Austin and built a home in the style of a French chateau.

BEFORE THE FALL – In the years between 1918, when Jay Hormel returned from the war, and 1929, when he became company president, he was rapidly becoming the man who could step into his father's shoes. Jay had managed numerous innovative programs. He had served as acting president and had been an essential player in saving Austin Farmers & Merchants State Bank when it was on the verge of failure in 1926.

But few things Jay Hormel did were as important as the work he oversaw in 1928. That year, Geo. A. Hormel & Company dissolved the old Minnesota corporation and reincorporated under the more favorable laws of the state of Delaware. The company authorized the sale of 500,000 shares of no-par common stock and 50,000 shares of par 6 percent preferred stock. It was a timely decision. Needing additional capital for a large building program in 1929, the company sold 60,000 shares of common stock at $55 per share, netting $3.3 million. With these funds, the company began construction of eight new structures, including an eight-story, Flavor-Sealed manufacturing plant. At the same time, Hormel headquarters facilities were remodeled and tripled in size. The new space was light and airy and filled with desks from wall to wall and front to back. Hormel believed that every person in the office should be accessible, from the chairman to the receptionist, so there were no private offices.

Now Hormel was ready to plunge into the fourth decade of its century. New buildings were erected or under construction. Capital was in hand and the organization restructured for greater efficiency and economy. Hormel had three separate divisions with H. H. "Tim" Corey, vice president of the Packing Division; Ralph H. Daigneau, vice president of the Abattoir Division, and E. N. Sturman, vice president of the Flavor-Sealed Division. Each division became an individual operating unit responsible for all phases of its business, from buying to processing to selling.

And there seemed to be a great deal of selling to be done. The present looked bright and the future brighter still. Hormel sales increased from nearly $35 million in 1925 to more than $40 million in 1929. The company boasted more than 2,000 employees.

THE RIGHT MAN IN THE WORST OF TIMES – But one of those 2,000 employees was taking another major step in his departure from the company he founded. In 1929, George A. Hormel became chairman of the board and his son, Jay, assumed the presidency.

In his farewell address, Hormel was optimistic about the company he had founded 38 years before. "The management," he said, "is young, compact and energetic. Each averages 13 years of service and experience while the

At Hormel headquarters in 1929, private offices were replaced with one bright, desk-filled space designed for ultimate accessibility.

Beginning in 1929, the Austin plant and office facilities were remodeled and expanded, thanks to a major building and development effort by Jay Hormel. (1935)

management boasts an average age of 35. The company is comfortably financed with no funded debt. The facilities are excellent and the brands well known. New accomplishments," he predicted, "and new successes will carry us beyond anything the past has seen."

Even in view of the recent stock market crash of 1929, George Hormel was confident: "A business in an essential and basic industry such as food," he assured everyone, "should not suffer materially."

Like so many other events at Geo. A. Hormel & Company, the change of leadership was propitious. George Hormel had built the company and placed it on a firm footing. "George was certainly the right man to get in there and dig out the beginnings of a business and make it work without money," Robert F. Gray, a Hormel chief executive officer, later observed. Jay, on the other hand, was the idea man and innovator. If George gave the company firm footing, Jay gave the enterprise wings to fly.

There would be only one obstacle to an immediate takeoff. The Oct. 29, 1929, stock market crash ushered in the worst and longest period of high unemployment and low business activity in modern times. Stockholders lost fortunes overnight. Banks, factories and stores closed, leaving millions unemployed and their savings wiped out.

Hormel grew and prospered through the Depression which was ushered in by the stock market crash of 1929.

FORESIGHT AND LUCK TO THE RESCUE – Despite the devastation of the Great Depression, Hormel paid quarterly dividends each year between 1929-33 when the economic collapse reached its nadir with 13 million unemployed and 9,000 bank failures. How did the company manage to survive when so many others didn't?

In this case – as in 1893 – it was sausage, Flavor-Sealed ham, canned chicken and several dozen other products that made the difference. It was also a testimony to George Hormel's foresight and good luck. In 1892, before the nation's financial panic, he borrowed money to build an improved processing facility that later allowed him to increase margins and business volume, and carry the company through the downturn. Once again, in 1929, the Hormel trait for anticipating trouble bolstered the business at exactly the right moment. The company completed a successful stock issue and building program just in time. Instead of going out of business, volume increased substantially. Between 1928-33, tonnage rose from 226 million pounds to 325 million pounds.

While the Depression continued, Hormel, still relatively unscathed, opened branch offices in a business-as-usual manner. In 1931, James F. Unicume opened an office in San Francisco, California, and Dewey Wengert another in Mobile, Alabama. In that same year, the company joined other business partners in a joint venture providing the capital for a pork processing plant in Mitchell, South Dakota. Dressed carcasses were shipped from Mitchell to Austin where they were processed and sold. In fall 1932, Hormel established a sales office in New York supervised by three men – Charles Hornburg, J. H. Heineman and A. R. Schneidewind. In 1933, Unicume established a branch operation in Seattle while, at home, Hormel completed construction of a new $1 million beef processing house. Benjamin F. Hormel advanced to manager of the Beef Division, the company's fourth and newest operating unit. Herman Hormel, still manager of the Provision Market and member of the Board of Directors, was nearing retirement.

THIS AAA WON'T TOW YOU, IT'LL TAX YOU – Regardless of the company's good fortune, the Depression continued to hit hard. By 1932, Hormel stock sank to a low of $11 a share, down from $55 three years earlier. In the country, among those farms still solvent, pork prices dropped to $3 per hundredweight compared to $20 per hundredweight in 1919. It was definitely a buyers' market and farmers were reluctant to sell at such a loss. Men were selling apples on street corners and people were starving. Yet, on the farms there was meat on the hoof everywhere, but not a bite to eat.

To close the gap between production and consumption, the Roosevelt administration passed the Agricultural Adjustment Act (AAA). Under the aegis of the AAA, five million hogs were slaughtered. Meat processors were paid for their work and farmers received a fair price for their hogs. To further balance supply and demand, the administration paid a bonus for reducing corn acreage by 20 percent and hogs by 25 percent. To finance the project, the government collected a processing tax from meatpackers that increased as the need for financing grew. The tax

The younger brother of George A. Hormel, Benjamin F. Hormel, assumed the management of the company's new Beef Division in 1933. (1940)

Consumer demand for Hormel canned chicken and other Hormel products kept production lines busy throughout the Depression. (1930)

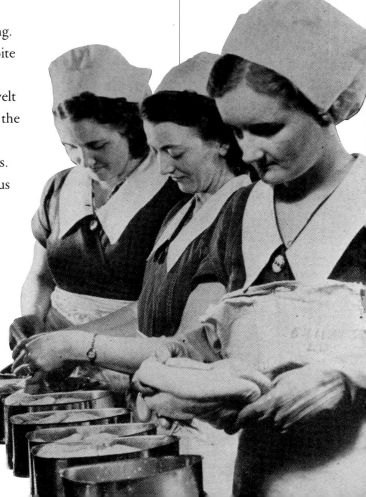

graduated from $.50 per hundredweight in 1933 to $2.00 by 1934 and to $2.25 in 1935, when it was finally declared unconstitutional by the U.S. Supreme Court.

The court's decision came at the right time. Paying $2.25 per hundredweight, the majority of meatpackers, particularly those specializing in pork, made little or no profit. During fiscal 1934-35, Hormel paid more than $8 million in taxes for hogs it slaughtered and processed. Not surprisingly, the volume of pork at Hormel dropped from 82.1 million in 1929 to 71.5 million in 1933. At the same time, veal, beef and lamb tonnage rose from 13.1 million to 74.4 million. In a pragmatic move, Hormel focused on meat not taxed by the AAA.

PAY ME MY MONEY DOWN – While meatpackers struggled with costs of the AAA, another problem was brewing at Geo. A. Hormel & Company. In 1931, Jay Hormel decided to experiment with an annual wage which, in those days, was called "straight time." Men were paid a weekly wage instead of an hourly wage in two departments. These men were considered permanent employees and were assured an average of 40 hours of work per week throughout the year. During the fall rush season, they might work more than 60 hours a week; however, in the slack spring period, they often accumulated less than 20 hours a week for the same pay.

Although the plan protected Hormel workers from layoffs and guaranteed a wage, they were suspicious. They were accustomed to an hourly wage, a system of payment that worked well in the early 1900s and provided considerable flexibility. For example, after the harvest, when farm animals were at market weight and ready to be shipped, field workers became processors at the plant. Later, as plant activity slackened and the spring growing cycle on the farm began, they returned to the farms. In the late 1920s and the early 1930s, however, farmers were becoming more diversified and packinghouses — with access via rail to the south and west — could work a crew in almost any season. Both workplaces required full-time employees.

By 1933, many Hormel employees were suspicious of management in general and wary of "straight time" in particular. They considered the new system an attempt to avoid paying the minimum wage and urged a pay hike. Employees also feared that more ambitious production quotas would lead to a work speedup.

Roosevelt's Agricultural Adjustment Act (AAA) gave farmers a fair price for hogs but placed a heavy tax burden on Hormel and other meat processors.

I'M A UNION MAN – Into this atmosphere of suspicion and promise of a salaried job stepped Frank Ellis. He was a union man who had witnessed membership in the American unions decline throughout the 1920s and 1930s until it reached a low of 2.7 million members in 1933. Ellis had been a general organizer for the Industrial Workers of the World (IWW), also known as the "Wobblies," a radical organization that sought to unite all workers, regardless of their skills or trade, and used strikes, boycotts or sabotage to accomplish its goals. Ellis believed there was, in his words, "an irrepressible conflict between the capitalist class and the working class. If there are any profits to be made," Ellis said years later, "they should go to the people who produce them. The workers produce every darn thing that you've got today."

Ellis joined Hormel in the Casing Department. In 1933, the federal government encouraged the creation of unions to help protect labor. Ellis needed no prompting. With his experience as an organizer for the Industrial Workers of the World, he quickly organized the Independent Union of All Workers (IUAW) at Hormel. The IUAW used as its model the IWW but did not seek a charter because, as Ellis said, "Working under the IWW, carrying credentials for the IWW, I was afraid to put the IUAW in the IWW. Having been wrecked so many times, I decided to come as near to the IWW as possible, follow the same pattern and see what happened."

What happened was probably a surprise to Ellis. Although one inevitable issue in the organization of any new labor union was assurance of the union's legitimacy, the IUAW was quickly recognized by Hormel management. Further, management endorsed the principle of seniority and, in its words, "agreed that no issues shall be permitted to lead to a strike . . . without first being submitted to arbitration."

AN INNOVATION STRIKES OUT – On Friday, Nov. 10, 1933, arbitration with management was not the first item on the agenda of the IUAW. A meeting had been called that evening. It was payday and "half the guys," says Frank Schultz, who was 16 at the time, "came tanked up.

Union organizer, Frank Ellis, joined the Hormel ranks in 1928 and later organized the Independent Union of All Workers (IUAW) at Hormel.

That's a hell of a time to have a union meeting, but Ellis' meetings were chaos anyway and nobody knew what they were voting on when they voted." Schultz later became president of Local P-9, the CIO-affiliated union of the Amalgamated Meat Cutters and Butcher Workmen of America.

Union members were voting on "straight time" which the company wanted to extend to all departments. Behind the scenes were two other issues — a newly installed Old Age Retirement Plan that had reduced paychecks by $.20 a week and an industrywide demand for a $.10 hourly increase.

In that stormy meeting, Schultz recalls, "We voted down the annual wage plan. Jay Hormel was a guy of real imagination, but we spent all our time tearing his plan to pieces." Union members then passed a motion to leave the strike decision in the hands of the executive board. The board wasted no time. "The strike vote," Schultz recalls, "carried by an overwhelming majority." The procedural niceties were overlooked and the men on the night shift began the strike at 10 p.m. that Friday.

Armed with clubs, strikers forced the company's officers to leave the plant. They shut off the plant's refrigeration, which endangered meat valued at $3.6 million. With meat spoilage forcing the issue on one side and the illegal takeover of the plant squeezing on the other, Jay Hormel was under intense pressure to resolve the conflict quickly.

The two sides arbitrated briefly and came to no agreement. Jay Hormel's options seemed limited to brute force — storm the plant, retake it, throw the strikers out and turn on the refrigeration. The Mower County sheriff assembled deputies and Floyd B. Olson, governor of the state of Minnesota, brought in the state's National Guard. The law was on the company's side, but Jay Hormel bided his time. He told strikers it would be impossible to meet their demands for a $.10 pay raise unless all other meatpackers did likewise. But those meatpackers were against a pay hike.

The situation seemed impossible. Then Governor Olson arrived in Austin. Fortunately, Olson was seen as a friend of labor. He was a member of the Farmer-Labor Party and had tremendous support in the 1930 and 1932 elections. He arrived in Austin on Sunday, November 12, and a settlement soon materialized. The union and company agreed to refer wage issues to the Minnesota State Industrial Commission. Subse-

Striking workers seized the Hormel plant on Nov. 10, 1933, demanding a wage hike.

quently, the commissioners ordered an increase in hourly pay from $.40 to $.45 per hour. The company agreed to rehire all strikers and drop the annual wage plan. The union agreed that its members would return to work in a cooperative spirit. The refrigeration was turned back on and the plant went into full operation Monday.

The company's first strike ended after three and a half days. To Jay Hormel, Governor Olson said, "I think you've got a lot of poise." In the *Austin Daily Herald*, a reporter described a scene that would hardly engender poise: "With the plant in control of the strikers, the refrigeration system turned off and a call made for National Guard and federal troops, the people's anxiety reached a pitch Saturday night that was probably never equaled in the history of the city." That reporter could not have foreseen the 13-month strike that ripped Austin apart in 1985-86.

Strikers guarding the Hormel plant shut down the company's refrigeration, risking spoilage of meat worth $3.6 million.

STRIKING OUT FOR NEW PRODUCTS – Within a year of the strike settlement, the improbable happened. The union committees asked Hormel to pay a guaranteed annual wage and, over the next several years, the entire plant operated on "straight time." An annual wage in 1934 for all plant workers meant a company obligation of $59,000 per week. To keep every employee busy, to pay them and to turn a profit, Jay Hormel believed a stellar product was needed that would become a household word. He turned to his inventory. **Hormel** whole chicken in the can, introduced in 1929, had been an immediate success but lagged behind during the Depression. **Hormel** canned ham, on the market since 1926, was a

Minnesota Governor Floyd B. Olson negotiated with Jay C. Hormel and strike leaders to end the shutdown.

Hormel onion soup, introduced in the mid-1930s, offered an innovative "double-your-money-back guarantee."

favorite of hotels and restaurants but was too bulky for the household shopper. In addition, Cudahy, Swift, Wilson and Armour were all producing ham in cans. The competition was fierce.

Jay Hormel decided to market ham in smaller cans, but the pork shortage of the early 1930s quashed the idea. Spiced ham was another innovative product that competition quickly copied. As a result, the company failed to create the brand name recognition it desperately sought. In another streak of product innovation, Hormel went far afield and developed vegetable soup with a hearty beef stock. Despite tremendous competition from Campbell and Heinz, the company expanded its line to include onion soup formulated to please discriminating diners on the East and West Coasts. With ambitious advertising campaigns and a "double-your-money-back guarantee," Hormel entered the market.

Then luck threw a slow curveball, waist high. In 1935, the U.S. government abruptly ended a food relief program for urban families hard hit by the Depression. Hormel, one of several meatpackers producing canned roast beef and gravy for the program, was left with $25,000 worth of 1½-pound cans and nothing to fill them. Hormel experimented with "a poor man's dish," a beef stew that sold for $.15 a can. Like many important births, this one in no way suggested the product popularity that was to come. But the **Dinty Moore** line was, in fact, born and **Dinty Moore** beef stew was soon followed by corned beef & cabbage, spaghetti & meat balls and Irish stew.

The popularity of SPAM luncheon meat exploded following its 1937 introduction.

In that same year, Hormel was inspired by "south of the border" Mexican fare and soon developed chili con carne in a can. The product triggered a sense of the dramatic in Jay Hormel with a 20-member troupe of song-and-dance women, named the Hormel Chili Beaners, singing the praises of the hot new product. Hormel soon became the largest producer of chili in the nation.

Jay Hormel created the Hormel Chili Beaners, a 20-member Mexican song-and-dance troupe, to promote Hormel chili.

In the following year, 1936, Jay Hormel and his company invented the product that would win the brand name recognition he sought. Hormel had been exploring ways to revive its spiced ham product which had innumerable imitators. He wanted the new 12-ounce canned product to contain ham and shoulder meat. What could it be called? The company offered a $100 prize for a winning name and it wasn't long before Kenneth Daigneau, actor brother of Vice President Ralph Daigneau, tossed out the name **SPAM** luncheon meat.

SPAM luncheon meat ignited, then exploded. By 1937, production lines were rolling and so was the advertising campaign that broadcast the product's versatility nationwide. Guided by Jay Hormel's flair for the dramatic, the world soon learned of **SPAM** luncheon meat through a variety of innovative media campaigns.

THE MAN AHEAD OF HIS TIME – While the company's development teams created new products to boost revenues, Jay invented new methods of rewarding company employees for personal initiative. In 1937, his introduction of incentive pay solved one persistent problem — how a worker is paid when the work load rises above the normal range stipulated by the annual wage. With incentive pay, Hormel employees were given a year-end bonus for work performed above and beyond the expected level.

In addition to incentive pay, Hormel also launched a Joint Earnings Plan giving employees a stake in company performance and a share in

*Jiggs (with and without Maggie) was featured in early advertising campaigns for **Dinty Moore** beef stew. The famous couple appeared daily in George McManus' nationally syndicated comic strip, "Bringing Up Father."*

HORMEL GIRLS

At one of their count-less public appearances, in 1948, the Hormel Girls paraded through downtown Eau Claire, Wisconsin.

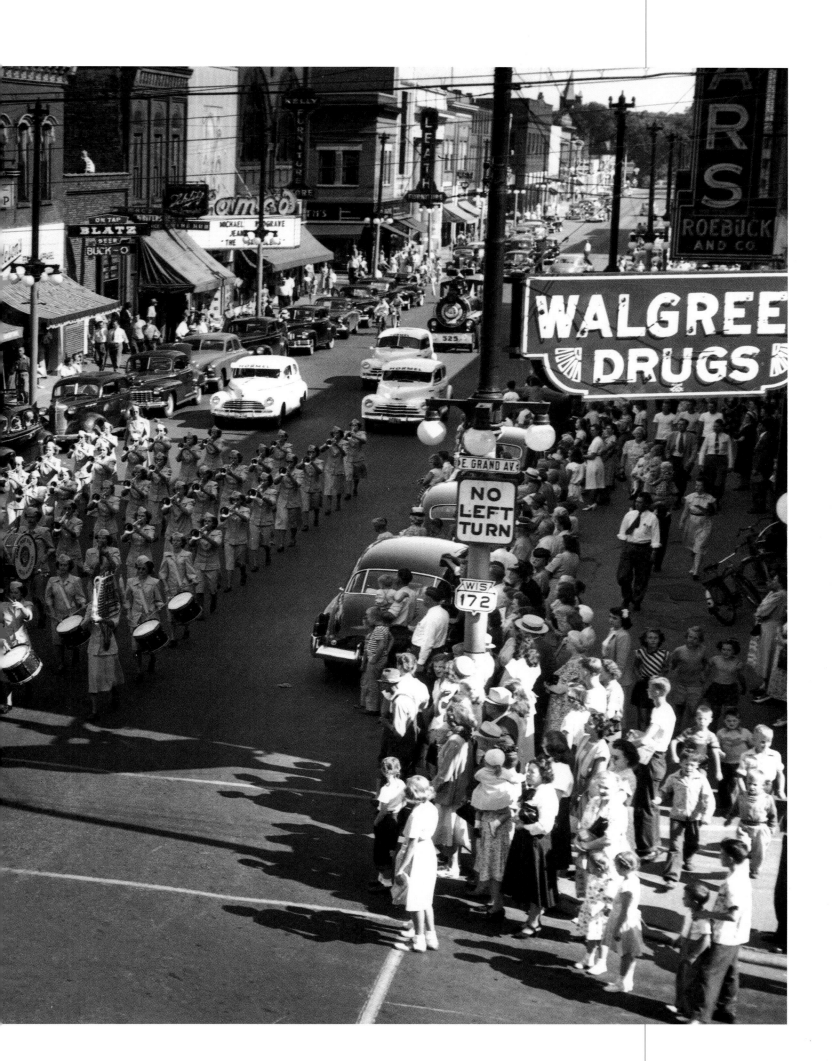

Jay Hormel initiated a company Joint Earnings Plan in 1938, giving employees a share of company profits.

Hollywood stars sang the praises of SPAM luncheon meat in the Hormel-sponsored radio show, "It Happened in Hollywood." Stars of the program, shown left to right, are John Hirstad, Helen Troy, Eddie Dunstetter, John Conte and Marsha Mears.

profits. In the program's inaugural year, the Joint Earnings payment amounted to one and one-half times an employee's regular weekly paycheck. By 1944, at the height of World War II, a typical Joint Earnings bonus payment totaled more than eight checks.

During his tenure as president of the company, Jay Hormel followed his grandfather's advice. He did a lot of originating and very little imitating. In fact, he developed Hormel market strategies that were 30 years ahead of their time. He organized a burgeoning employee credit union that today manages assets close to $50 million. He developed a personnel policy that operated on the principle of the Golden Rule. He encouraged workers to be loyal to their union. He stressed good workmanship, attention to the job and regular attendance. He was equally clear about grounds for discharge — intoxication, misconduct, incompetence or unauthorized absence for three consecutive days. And, to prevent a foreman or manager from firing an employee without cause, Hormel insisted on three warnings in writing, stating the date, hour and nature of the infraction.

While a cynic of today might smirk at an employment policy based on the Golden Rule, an editor of *Fortune* magazine in 1937 had another name for its proponent. Surprisingly, he called Jay Hormel "a Red Capitalist," suggesting a curious blend of free enterprise and socialism.

"Jay Hormel is an inventive man," the reporter said, "with an almost ingenuous enthusiasm for new stunts or schemes whether anyone else thinks them practical or not. He never lets his mistakes inhibit him from trying again when a hunch possesses him. He once promoted a marketing plan in which any retailer who contracted to make all his purchases from Hormel was guaranteed a 4.5 percent net profit over and above his operating cost and salary. He cooked up a traveling girl song-and-dance show called the Hormel Chili Beaners which barnstormed the Midwest advertising chili con carne. By far the most significant explorations by Mr. Hormel have been those programs in relation to his own employees, particularly in his so-called 'straight-time' plan . . . ."

LISTEN! "It Happened in Hollywood," Hormel's new idea in radio entertainment. Every afternoon, Monday through Friday, Columbia Network.

*By the late 1930s, demand for **Dinty Moore** beef stew, **SPAM** luncheon meat, **Hormel** chili and other Hormel Flavor-Sealed Division products kept production in full swing.*

But, in his review of Hormel employee policies, the *Fortune* reporter was hard-pressed to pinpoint flaws. "The employee plan has worked out well on both sides. The company has gained greatly by a stabilized supply of skilled labor. The employees have absolute security. However," he said, "union officials find in the plan one glaring evil: namely, a form of work speedup. Last year, the dry sausage department completed its 5.3 million pound budget in 39 weeks. Theoretically, the workers could have taken the next 13 weeks off with nothing to do but work in the garden, drink beer and collect paychecks. Instead, the company persuaded them to work the remaining time for nine extra paychecks as a bonus."

The *Fortune* article also quoted from a speech Jay Hormel made to the Rotary Club of Owatonna, Minnesota. Hormel exhibited an enlightened approach to labor relations rarely found in the 1930s.

"It is my belief that labor troubles would not occur if business could understand labor and the fundamental rights which labor demands," Hormel said. "If you will resist this whole trend toward labor organization, if you will deny its principles, I believe you will some day find yourself in labor difficulty. The idea that an employer is the lord and master of his own business is an antiquated notion. If you are an employer, you have a job and a trusteeship. It would be asking too much to expect to have a good union unless you also have a good employer. Give labor the fair treatment which is its right and labor's right to organize will never harm you."

According to the reporter, one Owatonna businessman was so upset by Hormel's speech that he asked the local newspaper to omit the more "inflammatory passages" from the article. And the newspaper obliged.

Creative, dynamic and in-
novative. These are but a
few words to describe Jay
C. Hormel, the market-
ing genius who launched
so many of the com-
pany's most successful
products. Jay's passion
for discovery included an
interest in
scientific re-
search begin-
ning in 1928
when on-site
experimentation
by a young bac-
teriologist solved
a perplexing prob-
lem in the Hormel
curing cellar.

In 1938, under Jay's
leadership, the company
Board of Directors found-
ed the Hormel Research
Foundation, an unusual
grant program created to
support postgraduate
research in areas related
to the meatpacking in-
dustry. One early success
was the breakthrough
discovery of NDGA, a
natural lard preservative
that contributed to the
Allied effort during World
War II.

During the war years,
company founder George
A. Hormel and his son,
Jay, formed The Hormel
Foundation—an organiza-
tion holding controlling
interest in the company
and dedicated, among
other goals, to the sup-
port of scientific research.
Through foundation fund-
ing, the company's long-
term commitment to
scientific research was
secured.

Four years after the
founding of the Hormel
Research Foundation,

continued on next page

FULL STRIDE AT FIFTY – Jay Hormel was a friend of labor and was also a dedicated capitalist. "The company," he said once, "must make a profit for without profit the business cannot function. The company needs profit to buy materials, to build buildings and to employ men."

The company Jay Hormel ran did profit. Between 1933-41, while the nation suffered through the worst Depression in its history, net sales at Geo. A. Hormel & Company rose from $25.2 million to $74.6 million, representing between 2.5 and 3 percent of the volume of all packing businesses in the United States. By 1941, the company was operating in six divisions with Ralph H. Daigneau, Jay's childhood friend, head of the Pork Division; Arthur A. Dacey in charge of the Beef, Lamb and Veal Division; Robert F. Gray, head of the Packing Division; Park Dougherty, manager of the Flavor-Sealed Division; T. H. Hocker, supervisor of the Service Division, and R. D. Gower, manager of the Office and Comp-troller's Division. The first five divisions reported to H. H. "Tim" Corey, board member, vice president and general manager; the sixth reported to M. F. Dugan, board member and company treasurer.

For its 50th anniversary in 1941, the company hired George Switzer, commercial artist, to redesign its product packages to provide a uniform and colorfully attractive look. Hormel boasted 4,495 employees and the company was braced for another 50 years of growth. The effects of the Depression were beginning to ease. The Rural Electrification Act of the 1930s brought electricity to farms and rural homes. Gone were most of the kerosene lamps, lanterns and outdoor privies. Electric lights, telephones, refrigerators, milking machines and cooling tanks were now either installed at farms and homes or the new gadgets occupied engineers' drawing boards. Tractors were replacing the horse and oxen in the fields. Geo. A. Hormel & Company was part of a brave new world. Unfortunately, a portion of that world was already at war.

THE UNLEASHED STORM – When Germany invaded Poland on Sept. 1, 1939, many Americans wanted to stay out of this second war in 25 years. Isolationism was the operable term. "This ain't our war!" was the common slogan. Jay Hormel was one of those Americans adamantly opposed to American participation in World War II. In fact, he used his marketing savvy to try to shape public opinion by creating a popular song he hoped

HORMEL INSTITUTE

continued from previous page

The Hormel Institute was born. It was created on Nov. 30, 1942, through an agreement between The Hormel Foundation and the University of Minnesota. The Institute, which is part of the Graduate School at the University of Minnesota, serves as a biological and chemical research organization funded, in part, by The Hormel Foundation and staffed by University scientists and faculty.

Located in a facility completed in 1960 adjacent to company headquarters in Austin, Minnesota, it is, today, one of the nation's preeminent lipid research centers focusing not only on the study of fats and oils but also on the role of more complex lipids in biological membranes. Alterations in lipid metabolism are often linked to human disease such as cancer, heart disease, diabetes and obesity. Therefore, much of the research performed by The Hormel Institute is significant to the study and treatment of these diseases. To continue this study, The Hormel Institute receives major financial support from the National Institutes of Health.

would sweep the country. Hormel engaged Harry Harris who had collaborated on a recent hit, "Baby Me," to write the lyrics and music for a song entitled "This Ain't Our War":

Not unless they come a-knockin' at our door!
If they want to fight each other, well, it's none of our affair;
We haven't any mothers with an extra son to spare;
Let's sing "God Bless America" instead of "Over There."
This ain't our war!

Despite the song and Hormel's strong opinion, the U.S., led by Franklin D. Roosevelt, moved slowly toward involvement in the growing conflict. On Nov. 1, 1940, No. 158 was the first draft number drawn under the Selective Training and Service Act. Ironically, it belonged to Leonard Hughes, a Hormel sausage truck salesman working in Georgia. Five months later, in March 1941, Congress passed the Lend-Lease Act, providing all possible aid to the Allies short of a declaration of war. For the Hormel Company, this meant shipping canned meat, especially **SPAM** luncheon meat, to Britain and Russia. **SPAM** luncheon meat would be a godsend. In the words of one English soldier after the war, "We couldn't possibly have survived without it."

By mid-1941, the Federal Surplus Commodities Corporation (FSCC) had informed meat canners it wanted four million cans of meat weekly for Lend-Lease. Like some government organizations, the FSCC was often impractical. For instance, the FSCC wanted meat shipped in round cans, although this style required 25 percent more shipping space and the canning industry had almost no facilities to produce and fill round cans. Hormel prevailed on the FSCC to change its policy from round to oblong cans which the industry had facilities to produce. In September 1941, the FSCC increased its quota to eight million oblong cans a week and, in November, raised its quota to 15 million. Not by accident, **SPAM** luncheon meat was packaged in these handy oblong tins.

YOU'RE IN THE ARMY NOW – Soon after the Japanese bombed Pearl Harbor, Hormel became a war facility. Plant tours were canceled. Bright lights and a steel fence were installed. As at a munitions plant, guards were posted to protect the company and its products. Every employee was photographed, fingerprinted and required to wear an identification badge.

When the United States entered World War II, Hormel adopted the security measures required of all war facilities. All employees were photographed, finger-printed and required to wear identification badges to enter the plant.

*As part of the Lend-Lease Act, Hormel shipped millions of pounds of **SPAM** luncheon meat and other canned meats to Russia and Great Britain.*

To the various military branches, Hormel supplied a variety of foods — from fresh meat to canned, from ham to whole chicken, from English-style stew to combat rations like pork & apples, beef & pork and ham & eggs. Hormel products for the Lend-Lease program, destined for civilian use abroad, consisted mainly of canned goods because fresh food could not be refrigerated while crossing the Atlantic. Millions of pounds of "Tushonka" were dispatched to Russia in 28-ounce tins, containing pork from the Boston butt packed in lard and seasoned with salt, black pep-pers, onion and bay leaves. Hormel also produced dehydrated pork shoulders for Lend-Lease — a tremendous space saver when shipped over-seas. To reconstitute one pound of pork, a soldier simply added three cups of water and soaked the product for 25 minutes.

Between 1941-45, shipments of Hormel products to the armed services or to the Lend-Lease program represented hundreds of millions of pounds and, by 1944, more than 90 percent of Hormel canned foods were des-tined for Uncle Sam's operations.

Meanwhile, the government instituted massive regulations on the pro-duction and price of many products, including metals, food and rubber. Tin, for example, was a top-priority item because, without it, the com-pany could not can its products. Early in the war, however, Japan had overrun Southeast Asia, the world's leading tin supplier. While Hormel was able to secure tin for products made for the armed services, restric-tions banned canning for domestic consumption, including **Dinty Moore** beef stew, chili con carne, canned ham, corned beef hash, canned chicken and many others. These were the products Hormel had spent millions to advertise. Now they were not available to consumers because Hormel had no ready replacement for tin.

Sugar was another necessary product used in canning. Because of the war, the company had to cut its use by 20 percent, although it qualified for more sugar if the cured meat was destined for servicemen.

Rubber was also regulated and even that scarcity affected Hormel. While the government desperately sought a synthetic substitute, it rationed gas to reduce travel, tire wear and rubber use. Ironically, gas was abundant during the war. Car owners were told to restrict their speeds to 45 mph, avoid fast starts and stops, keep their tires inflated properly and rotate them every 5,000 miles. Of course, these regulations restricted the Hormel salesforce and, no doubt, dampened their characteristic enthusiasm.

While sales territories coalesced, prices for meat fluctuated with supply and demand until the Office of Price Administration (OPA) stepped in and placed a ceiling on primal pork cuts. In April 1942, the ceiling was established on live hog prices as well as what packers could charge for their pork. Conditions were tough – efficient packers were able to make a small profit while inefficient ones failed.

Thanks to a longstanding focus on efficiency, the company achieved excellent profits. Ration demands from the armed services were insatiable and the production crunch at Hormel was mind-boggling. Hogs were processed in ever-increasing numbers. In fact, one day in 1942, there were 10,000 more hogs in Hormel stockyards than the plant could handle. Luckily, the government announced a price ceiling of $13.25 on hogs weighing from 240-270 pounds and farmers kept their smaller animals in the pens that year. The next year, however, produced the greatest "hog run" in company history. During the third week of October 1943, 47,000 animals filled Hormel stockyards compared to 20,000 the year before. Consider the momentum of change. In 1892, Hormel processed a total of 610 hogs. In 1924, that number reached one million for the first time. And, in 1944, the company dispatched one million hogs in little more than four months.

"I marvel," George Hormel wrote to his son, from California, "that it was possible to put that much tonnage through the house. I am sure it is an achievement you will not equal again even though you enlarge your facilities."

For once, farsightedness had eluded George Hormel.

CUSTOMERS? WE'VE GOT ONE CUSTOMER—UNCLE SAM – By February 1945, 65 percent of all products Hormel produced were devoured by Uncle Sam's troops in the two war theaters – Europe and the Pacific. The government purchased between 60-80 percent of Hormel beef production,

As Geo. A. Hormel & Company grew into the 1940s, farmers had a solid customer for their hogs. (1940)

Those visiting Austin in the 1940s found colorful postcards of the Hormel plant to send to friends and relatives.

View of Geo. A. Hormel & Co. on Cedar River at Austin, Minn.

*Customers at Peoples'
Meats in St. Paul lined up
to receive weekly meat rations during wartime.
(1945)*

*Geo. A. Hormel & Com-
pany produced informa-
tional materials to help consumers cope with war-
related food shortages.*

50 percent of its veal, lamb and pork and 80 percent of its lard. By 1943, meat rationing became law and, with it, Hormel did some serious planning. The future of the company's civilian customer base was at stake. Company directors decided that Hormel customers, whether large or small grocers, should get a fair share to sell to their consumers. Sales territories were reorganized and condensed and every retailer received some meat each week. Each sales area received a proportionate share of the total supply reserved for civilians and each salesman reserved meat for his customers. What a far cry this was from the days when George Burns and Gracie Allen with "Spammy," their pet pig, extolled the goodness and plentiful supply of **SPAM** luncheon meat to millions of American radio listeners.

YOU'RE NOT BEHIND A PLOW . . . OR AN IRON – While the war ground on, it swallowed up men and women from America's workforce in vast numbers. At Hormel alone, 1,961 employees who had received a two-week vacation with pay and assurance of a job upon return, went off to serve. Sixty-seven men did not return. To replace employees-turned-GIs, Hormel hired women and, by 1944, nearly 1,300 women were working the production lines.

The company's financial performance was nothing short of phenomenal during the war years. In 1939, Hormel tonnage totaled 436.8 million pounds of product and net sales reached $60.3 million. The company's net worth was $10.7 million.

By 1942, volume climbed to 576.8 million pounds and net sales leaped to $119.4 million. In that year, annual pork processing reached an all-time high of 1,665,570 head. The company's net worth had risen to $12.9 million.

And, in 1945 – although production and net sales had fallen off from the 1944 wartime, precedent-setting peak – Hormel was in a financial position envied by any company. It had no debt beyond its current operating costs and the capital stock and surplus totaled a healthy $15.3 million.

By 1945, Joint Earnings fell to 2.4 times the weekly check, still a tidy sum for Hormel employees but a sign of the future. The war was coming to an end. By August 1945, both Germany and Japan had surrendered and government regulations of the marketplace rapidly dwindled away.

American servicemen began returning to the jobs Hormel had promised them. While they fought, Jay Hormel confirmed his assurance to them in writing: "We have in our file," he wrote, "94 projects, each of which is an idea for more business or new business. Thirty-four of these projects are ready to go — whenever we can get the equipment, the manpower and the nerve enough to take the business risks involved. In any case, your old job will be here for you. The person who has taken your place will have to find the next best job."

BRAVE NEW WORLD – Luckily, there were plenty of jobs, at least at Hormel. As wartime restrictions lifted, Americans began purchasing food that had long been rationed. That meant brisk business at Hormel. But what had Hormel become? The war had been profitable but it had altered the company's product focus and, more important, debilitated its prewar consumer marketing efforts. Before the war, those efforts included a passel of promotions from Burns and Allen testimonials to "**SPAM**wich" giveaways for 50,000 American Legionnaires to Chili Beaners performances by the Hormel song-and-dance troupe.

By 1945, however, only **SPAM** luncheon meat, the ubiquitous food staple of the war, had kept Hormel in the limelight. To broaden the company's image nationwide, to promote a closer relationship with the company's prime customer, the housewife, and to employ women returning from the service, Jay Hormel organized the Hormel Girls, a team of 20 ex-servicewomen, that later expanded to 60, all with musical ability. In groups of six, these talented troopers traveled to fairs and benefits spreading the musical word about Hormel and its products.

Apparently women had a corner on rhythm and musical talent because Jay Hormel also developed an all-woman drum and bugle corps to compete in the August 1947 National American Legion Convention in New York. Hormel handed the project to Dale Schamber, **SPAM** luncheon meat product manager, who managed the impossible. He found 74 candidates, ex-servicewomen with musical and sales abilities who were willing to begin an arduous five-week training session that included 11 hours a day of marching and practicing in preparation for the event. The team did not win, but they were the first all-woman drum and bugle corps to enter the national competition. As such, they garnered much publicity for Hormel.

Women joined Hormel production lines in ever-increasing numbers during the war years, replacing the 1,961 employees who had entered the service.

In an effort to employ ex-servicewomen and promote Hormel products, Jay Hormel organized the Hormel Girls, a 20-member musical troupe that later expanded to 60 members.

But Jay did not stop there. In a continuing quest for nationwide attention, he organized 20 members of the Hormel Drum and Bugle Corps
into a touring, singing and selling team that traveled to Cleveland, Ohio;
Dallas, Texas; and Shreveport and New Orleans, Louisiana, with additional success. Next, Hormel had prime-time radio in his sights. So he
dispatched his troupe to Los Angeles for on-the-air training. Louise
Mulvany became the group's choral director and, in March 1948, the
show, "Music with the Hormel Girls," aired over a single Los Angeles
radio station. By late May, the show had attracted 20 California stations.
From there, "Music with the Hormel Girls" went nationwide Sundays from
6:30-7 p.m. on the Mutual Broadcasting System. Soon "the Girls" graced
both ABC and CBS on Saturday afternoons and Sunday evenings.

Today, an advertising campaign like this might seem homespun, but
the program was packed with music and cleverly integrated with commercials. A typical half-hour radio drama carried three commercials, while
"Music with the Hormel Girls" featured five commercials as well as 15
mentions of the Hormel name between numbers.

When they weren't on the air, the Hormel Girls traveled with a great
deal of advance work orchestrated in each city. Radio stations and newspapers announced the Girls' arrival while Hormel salespeople bought
local advertisements in the newspapers. And because they rode in a caravan of 35 white Chevrolets, there were tie-ins with the local car dealer-
ship. Whenever possible, the governor of the state greeted the Hormel

*Traveling in a caravan of
35 white Chevys, the
Hormel Girls commanded
local attention wherever
they went.*

*The Hormel Girls per-
formed for audiences
throughout the country.
This trio sang a musical
number in Austin, Min-
nesota, in 1952.*

Girls with hype and hoopla. The crowds were guaranteed and many went
away with an armload of purchased Hormel products. It was a marketer's
dream.

For the next five years, this sophisticated and complex promotional
plan dreamed up by the "Red Capitalist" traveled the country and broadcast the Hormel name nationwide. By any measure, the caravan was a
success, although expensive. The traveling fleet included 35 cars and five
trucks. Each of the Hormel Girls earned $55 per week, plus $30 in expenses, hotel bills and gas. In addition, the performers earned 10 days off,
all expenses paid, every three months. But the caravan was a breadwinner
for the company. "Because of its national coverage," said Park Dougherty,
vice president of the Flavor-Sealed Division, "our division rapidly expanded its salesforce and our sales more than doubled. Directly or in-
directly, the Hormel Girls exercised a great influence on our operations
and on our financial results."

*In 1946, at age 85, company
founder George A. Hormel
died at his home in Bel Air,
California.*

THE SPIRIT OF AMERICA – By 1946, company sales had reached $129.3 mil-
lion with 5,728 employees. But, in that year, George A. Hormel, the company's founder and first employee, died. He was buried in Oakwood
Cemetery in Austin beside his wife, Lillian, who had passed away a few
months earlier.

At the annual stockholders' meeting in December 1946, Jay Hormel
eulogized his father. "That spirit which is America produced George A.
Hormel who, in turn, developed the business which bears his name. His
courage and purpose which drove immigrants and pioneers to new opportunity will inspire his people to strive for better opportunity for themselves. His character and basic religious conviction will inspire people to
those positive virtues which will make this community and this world a
better place in which to live."

Following the founder's death, Jay Hormel became chairman of the
board and H. H. "Tim" Corey became Hormel president, the first who did
not carry the family name.

With the war behind them, the company's business refocused, and with
a national advertising campaign launched by the Hormel Girls, Geo. A.
Hormel & Company was ready to begin a new cycle of growth that
would see sales skyrocket by almost 300 percent over the coming eight
years.

Advertising for Hormel chili in the 1940s tied the product to its Mexican heritage.

Hormel chili, introduced in 1935, is the top-selling canned chili in the country.

When it came to innovation, company president Jay C. Hormel accepted no limitations. In 1935, the same year the company introduced the now famous **Dinty Moore** brand, Jay Hormel ventured south of the border to bring **Hormel** chili to the American consumer.

Although chili enjoyed wide acceptance in the South, Southwest and far West by the early 1930s, it was virtually unknown in other parts of the United States and consumer acceptance of the spicy,

Mexican dish was untested. Weighing the risks, Hormel met the challenge with a high-quality recipe supported by an unprecedented "double-your-money-back" advertising guarantee. To market the hot, new product, Hormel also exercised his promotional flair by creating a 20-member Mexican song-and-dance troupe, named the Hormel Chili Beaners, to perform and offer product samples to consumers throughout the Midwest. "If you can get it in their mouths,

they're going to buy it," the ever-optimistic Hormel reasoned. And once again, his gamble paid off. In no time, Geo. A. Hormel & Company was the biggest producer of canned chili in the nation.

"Today, chili is considered an all-American food associated with leisure and fun times," says Robert F. Patterson, group vice president of Prepared Foods, "but in the 1930s, chili was a unique, ethnic product unfamiliar to most people. That's why Jay Hormel instituted a series of firsts in 1935. Not only

In 1935, Jay Hormel introduced the Hormel Chili Beaners, a 20-member Mexican song-and-dance troupe, that toured the Midwest promoting Hormel chili.

was Hormel the first major chili producer in the country but advertising and promotion strategies were industry innovations.''

Today, **Hormel** chili ranks number one in its category while competing against hundreds of regional brands that cater to a wide variety of tastes.

''Chili is a product with many variations in ingredients from region to region,'' says Patterson.

Hormel chili is made from the freshest of ingredients, including carefully selected beef, vine-ripened tomatoes and a special combination of spices.

Hormel chili is made with carefully selected beef, red Idaho beans, vine-ripened tomatoes and a special combina-

consumer concerns regarding convenience and nutrition. At the same time, it's a fun food popular among young people. We're a solid number one now and the popularity of chili is still growing,'' he says.

The company now produces **Hormel** chili in 18 varieties and sizes, more than any other canned food item in the Grocery Products Division. Choices include a low-salt version for health-

In the 1950s, Hollywood star Ray Milland and other celebrities shared their favorite Hormel chili recipes with magazine readers.

It's Chili Time - at Noon - at Night - at Midnight!

''For example, Texans never make chili with beans while in Boston they wouldn't consider chili complete without beans. In Cincinnati, the predominant chili recipe includes cinnamon while in some parts of the country they make it with macaroni. At Hormel, we produce chili with a 'flavor profile' that is readily accepted all over the United States.''

tion of spices. The ingredients are blended and simmered slowly in an open kettle to bring out the full flavor and aroma. The result is, according to company advertising, ''the next best thing to homemade.''

Although **Hormel** chili has led the market for more than one-half century, the company continues to refine the product, says Eric A. Brown, vice president of the Grocery Products Division. ''At Hormel, we're continuing to respond to

conscious consumers and convenience packaging in microwave cups and bowls for people on the go.

Today, Hormel chili is available in 18 varieties and sizes to accommodate the diversity of the American consumer.

CHAPTER FOUR

Tackling Business in Postwar America 1946-1955

"If I have developed any philosophy, it is that any person who works hard and applies himself will find success, happiness and the satisfaction of accomplishment."

H. H. "Tim" Corey

1946

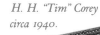
H. H. "Tim" Corey circa 1940.

President Harry S Truman, the postwar president.

- The company adds new, state-of-the-art medical facilities to its Austin plant.
- Tonnage reaches 644.8 million pounds.
- The company begins manufacturing gelatin, a meat byproduct.

1948 The Hormel Girls expand to 60 members, including a 24-piece orchestra and 36 voices.
- Employees number 6,957 with 4,815 located in Austin.

1949-1951

1949 Hormel introduces **Mary Kitchen** roast beef hash, **Mary Kitchen** corned beef hash and **Hormel** deviled ham.

1950 Hormel capitalizes on the trend toward convenience packaging with a host of new products.

H. H. "Tim" Corey, the husky college-athlete-turned-president, brought hard work and gridiron determination to Geo. A. Hormel & Company during an extraordinary postwar decade of peace and prosperity. Consumer appetites seemed insatiable and the company added plants and boosted production to keep pace. By 1948, total tonnage climbed to an astounding 696 million pounds sold — a record that would soon be broken.

1946-1948

1946 Hormel hosts the **National Barrow Show** for the first time.

1947 **SPAM** Post 570 Drum and Bugle Corps competes in the American Legion National Drum & Bugle Contest in New York City. Later to become the Hormel Girls, it was the first all-woman corps to compete.

Less than a decade after World War II, Hormelites went back to war in Korea.

In 1952, Hormel processed its 50 millionth hog.

50,000,000

- Tonnage breaks records at 796.7 million pounds and sales reach $249.8 million.
- Hormelites go back to war — in Korea.

*Beginning in 1946, Hormel has annually acted as host of the **National Barrow Show** in Austin.*

GEO. A. HORMEL & CO.

The patented Hormel hog immobilizer, developed in 1952, later earned American Humane Association seal of approval.

1951 First Hormel employee, George Peterson, dies at age 86.
▪ This marks the completion of the company's 60th year.

1952-1955

1952 Hormel introduces the patented "Hormel hog immobilizer."
▪ The company processes its 50 millionth hog.

▪ New plants open in San Francisco, Beaumont and Montgomery. Extensive remodeling and enlargement of facilities begins in San Antonio, Mobile, Winston-Salem, Houston and Atlanta.

1954 Jay C. Hormel dies in August; H. H. Corey is named chairman of the board in December.
▪ Ethiopian emperor, Haile Selassie I, visits the Hormel plant in Austin.

1955 Hormel begins manufacturing **SPAM** luncheon meat overseas through Lunham Brothers, Ltd., Cork, Ireland.

The 1950s was a decade of national growth and expansion for Geo. A. Hormel & Company.

Jay C. Hormel died on Aug. 30, 1954, at age 61.

1955

In 1950, Joan Sokolovsky took the first can of SPAM luncheon meat off the line at the Hormel plant in Fremont, Nebraska.

HERALD

Fair

Jay Hormel Dies of Heart Attack at His Home Here

Wife, 3 Sons Survive Noted Austin Packer

Wilcox Says His Cards Were Torn Off Truck

Open Trial

Like a sail without wind, America's wartime prosperity languished in the doldrums between 1946–48. Production in postwar America slowed because companies such as Hormel were busy converting from wartime to peacetime production. The nation's output diminished even though consumer goods like **SPAM** luncheon meat, snazzy Studebakers and televisions with eight-inch screens were in great demand.

Americans in 1946 found their country plagued with inflation, housing shortages and recession after the war, but they demonstrated their optimism by humming popular tunes like "Come Rain or Come Shine" and "Zip-a-dee-doo-dah" while flocking to William Wyler's hit film, *The Best Years of Our Lives.*

At Hormel headquarters in Austin, Minnesota, the company seemed to be a rubber band stretched between worrisome periods of "decontrol" and "recontrol" as the federal government tried to reestablish the free market's equilibrium. During "decontrol," a large volume of livestock came to market and Hormel customers deluged the company with unusually large demands for meat. During "recontrol," livestock stayed on the farm and tens of thousands of meatpackers were laid off.

"The employees in our plant had little work to do," new Hormel president, H. H. "Tim" Corey, told shareholders in November 1946, describing the effects of "recontrol." "Some departments worked only two days of the week and less than two hours each of those days. But it wasn't only our people without work. The plant was empty; our facilities were idle, our inventories and accounts receivable became merely money in the bank."

How bad was it? The chairman of a local picnic committee in Austin had underestimated the attendance at his event and called Hormel at the last minute for an extra 25 pounds of wieners. The conscientious Corey told him, "We simply don't have 25 pounds of wieners to give you."

Fortunately, Hormel had a solid financial footing during this unsettling period. The company had no debt and a nest egg of net working capital totaling $11.2 million. Despite the fluctuations in government controls, sales had increased an impressive 10.5 percent over 1945, reaching $129.3 million.

Work was sporadic at the Hormel plant between 1946-48 as postwar America struggled to readjust to a peacetime economy.

READY AND WAITING – True to Jay Hormel's promise in 1945, servicemen returning from the war had jobs waiting for them. By year-end 1946, 951 Hormel veterans had come back to the Austin plant and the company had hired another 121 ex-servicemen, newcomers to Hormel. The company hosted welcome-home dinners for the vets, but the atmosphere was bitter-sweet. "They are a fine looking bunch of boys," the *Squeal* noted. "In the groups around the tables, in their civilian clothes, were lads from all the beaches in the world. Guadalcanal, Hill 660, Normandy, Aachen, Bastogne, Guam, Iwo Jima." But 67 Hormel men never made it back to participate in the reunion dinner at Queen of Angels Church in Austin.

Demobilized servicemen were delighted to hear Hormel had extended its Straight Time Plan to most of the company's branch operations and had expanded its production and incentive payments. In addition, joint earnings, another Hormel innovation, continued to boost employee paychecks. In 1946, among the 5,531 employees on the Hormel payroll, 5,108 qualified for joint earnings and each received an average wage or salary plus a joint earnings bonus totaling $3,033, about $400 more than the previous year. In addition, employees enjoyed sick leave, group insurance plans and profit sharing after four years with Hormel. These benefits were rare or nonexistent at most companies in the late 1940s.

George A. Hormel and his son, Jay, had proven to be notable risk takers with an enlightened view of management. Now, in 1946, it was up to Tim Corey, the first nonfamily member, to perpetuate that Hormel leadership style as the company's third president.

TACKLING THE JOB – There was no question that Corey had muscle and stamina for the assignment. Born in Escanaba, on the Upper Peninsula of Michigan, Corey made headlines at age 13 when he pushed a rowboat out onto thin ice to rescue a struggling young man who had fallen into

In 1946, the Hormel Squeal reminded workers of the many benefits provided by the company and encouraged Hormel workers to do their best to keep it that way.

Jay C. Hormel hosted welcome-home dinners for the 951 Hormel servicemen returning from World War II. Sixty-seven Hormel men were killed in action during the war.

At age 13, H. H. "Tim" Corey rescued a young man who had broken through thin ice into freezing water. The Green Bay Gazette proclaimed him a hero.

The 1917 annual of the University of Nebraska Cornhusker listed Corey's many athletic honors.

the frigid waters. That demonstration of boyhood courage prompted the *Green Bay Gazette* to call him, "Harold Corey: A Young Hero."

Through high school, Ripon College and the University of Nebraska, Corey was both student and athlete. Big and strong, he played tackle for the Nebraska Cornhuskers, became captain of the team and ultimately was named an All-Missouri Valley Conference tackle and All-American. Corey kicked the extra point after Nebraska's first touchdown, securing the winning margin in a 20-19 cliff-hanger against the Fighting Irish of Notre Dame.

When World War I broke out, Corey served as captain on the front lines in France. After the war, he remained in Europe as a diplomatic courier for the World War Peace Conference in Paris until 1919 when his former football coach, Jumbo Stiehm, convinced him to become an assistant coach at Indiana University. When the season ended, Corey applied his brawn to the Omaha stockyards and flirted with staking a claim in the Wyoming oil fields.

At this point, Tim Corey's life intersected with Geo. A. Hormel & Company. On the invitation of Hormel employee, Richard S. Banfield, a friend who had served with him in France, Corey visited Austin in 1920 and met Jay Hormel.

The junior Hormel was probably impressed with Corey's athletic achievements that derived from personal discipline and hard work, not to mention his self-determined spirit. Any fellow who could heft hindquarters in Omaha and consider wildcatting on the Wyoming frontier had the right stuff for Hormel.

CORNHUSKER

HAROLD H. COREY, *Tackle*
Captain; High School, Four Years;
All-State Guard at Ryan College,
Wisconsin; Third Year Varsity.

In a tribute to Corey in 1965, the Hormel News *acknowledged some of his accomplishments before joining the company — All-American tackle for Nebraska, captain in the 88th Division during World War I and U.S. Army courier serving the peace conference in Europe following the war.*

And so he did. Corey's career began in the Time Department where the company cut checks for employees. He soon rose to manager. Corey then returned to the campus to recruit bright college graduates for Hormel. Next, he managed the export business when Hormel, in 1922, was shipping 100 carloads of Wiltshire sides, Cumberland middles, English bellies and Irish backs to the British Isles each week. Eventually, Corey became a plant superintendent, Packing Division manager, vice president and general manager, member of the Board of Directors and, subsequently, president, chief executive officer and board chairman of the company.

If the chief characteristics of George A. Hormel's business life were innovation and daring and Jay Hormel's trademarks were marketing ingenuity and employee relations, Tim Corey's stamp was hard, steady, uncompromising work. At age 43 and head of the Packing Division, Corey told a Nebraska group, "I can justly make the claim that the most particular thing in my life has been hard work. If I have developed any philosophy . . . it is this: Despite the general trend of the times, any person who works hard and applies himself will find success, happiness and the satisfaction of accomplishment."

I. J. Holton, later a Hormel chief executive officer, observes, "Corey's involvement with the business was his life. I never heard of him taking an extensive vacation. . . . His dedication to the company was 100 percent." And before it earned a popular business acronym, Corey practiced MBWA (Management By Walking Around). "Corey would walk through the plant every day," Holton recalls. "He had a presence with the people and knew what was going on. He kept his thumb on day-to-day operations."

BUSTIN' OUT ALL OVER – Tim Corey's familiarity with plant operations served him well in the late 1940s and early 1950s – a decade of expansion prompted by pent-up consumerism and the company's own development.

From 1946-48, Tim Corey oversaw a spate of expansion and acquisition projects. In 1946, Hormel added sliced bacon and pork sausage facilities at its Charlotte and Winston-Salem, North Carolina, and Montgomery, Alabama, plants and increased sausage manufacturing volume in Houston,

This group of Austin plant employees gathered for a photo in 1947. They are (left to right) Miriam Kermes, Helen Remington, Mary Kurth, Margie Bednar, Hazel Rice, Clara Hoff, Jeanette Arens and Muriel Peterson.

Geo. A. Hormel & Company purchased the Fremont (Nebraska) Packing Company plant in 1947 and added a new $5 million facility for processing hogs and cattle.

San Antonio and Dallas, Texas. In Austin, the company expanded its natural casings capabilities for sausage production. Hormel also acquired Mitchell Abattoir, Inc., in Mitchell, South Dakota, adding more capacity and closer proximity for its growing customer base.

In 1947, Hormel marched ahead with growth prompted by consumer demand that exceeded the Austin plant's ability to produce sufficient quantities. Hormel expanded its Dallas beef processing plant, purchased just two years earlier, and completed the new gelatin plant in Austin. The company also purchased a processing plant from the Fremont Packing Company in Fremont, Nebraska, a city served by two railroads and situated in a choice hog-growing area. Fremont became a model abattoir, a one-story operation conceived by Jay Hormel. Designed to streamline production, it moved products laterally instead of vertically. This was a far cry from the old "arm-strong" method employed at the turn of the century in Austin when a man stood on a barrel and hoisted a 75-pound hog side to a coworker reaching through a hole in the floor above.

Built at a cost of $5 million, the Fremont plant processed both hogs and cattle and took a huge chunk out of company operating funds.

In that same year, consumers were not the only beneficiaries of the growth of Geo. A. Hormel & Company. In Austin, the company built a new cafeteria and Medical Department for employees. "The new medical quarters include a large reception-record room and dispensary, examining rooms, private offices, x-ray, physiotherapy, medical lab, minor surgery, sterilizing room and two recovery rooms with two beds each," Tim Corey reported to shareholders. Ever mindful of the welfare of its people, Corey added, "It is now our belief that none of our people need suffer for lack of medical advice or care."

In 1948, the company improved its manufacturing facilities in Austin; added or improved livestock procurement outlets throughout its service area; beefed up processing operations at the Mitchell and Dallas plants; added canning capabilities in Dallas, and expanded manufacturing in Houston and San Antonio.

Financial stability made Hormel expansion possible and it occurred at precisely the right time. The company's total tonnage climbed steadily upward – from 524.3 million pounds sold in 1946 to 644.8 million pounds in 1947 and finally to an astounding 696.7 million pounds in 1948. This was an increase of 7.8 percent over the 1944 wartime peak that few believed could be matched. In 1948 alone, Geo. A. Hormel & Company sold more than $272 million in meat products.

SAYING NO TO J. J. HILL – As company operations reached well beyond Austin, Chairman Jay C. Hormel anticipated rumors and questions in his community and among investors. He addressed them with a story about his father and the Minnesota empire builder, James J. Hill:

"George A. Hormel never intended to be a small frog in a puddle," Jay told shareholders in December 1948. "However, his business had not progressed much beyond that point when he met J. J. Hill many years ago."

Hormel admired Hill and the feeling was soon reciprocated; Hill decided to create a huge livestock-marketing center in South St. Paul and invited George to do it.

"The offer was enticing," Jay said. "Mr. Hill agreed to provide adequate finances on a favorable basis. Here was an opportunity for Mr. Hormel to become an important pork packer.

"But he decided against it," Jay said. "Mr. Hormel was unable to turn his back on his neighbors – the community in which he had established himself. He felt both loyalty and responsibility to the people who worked with him in his little packing business. He was friends with the farmers whose livestock he had processed. Mr. Hormel decided to cast his lot and his future in the community of Austin."

To those investors who worried about the speed of Hormel expansion in the 1940s, Jay replied, "My father had many opportunities to acquire packinghouses at bargain prices – Midland at Sioux City, Skinner at Omaha, Iowa Packing at Des Moines and Farmers' Cooperative at Newport, to mention just a few."

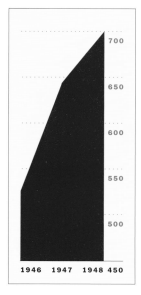

Tonnage sales at Hormel climbed steadily in the postwar years, surpassing the 1944 wartime peak.

The company added a new state-of-the-art Medical Department for Austin employees in 1947.

In 1949, Austin was a prosperous community of nearly 28,000 and home to Geo. A. Hormel & Company for more than one-half century.

In a 1946 article entitled "How to carve a $117 million roast pig," the Hormel Squeal *identified the numerous people and outside interests who shared the financial feast.*

But George Hormel refused because he did not want to take on more than could be handled. In every respect, quality products and performance were the elder Hormel's top priorities.

Ironically, however, it was Hormel quality, Jay said, that attracted consumers and literally forced the company to grow beyond Austin with additional processing, packing and distribution sites.

"Mr. Hormel's single purpose was to be known as the man who produced the best ham, the best bacon and the best sausage," Jay explained. "Quality attracts customers. And to take care of those customers, it is necessary to have more raw materials and more facilities.

"Mr. Hormel never wanted more than one plant, but long before he ceased his active management of the company, his insistence on quality had begun to force him into plant operations outside of Austin."

Jay told shareholders Hormel had gained 10,000 additional customers from 1945-48 and that "caused us to increase our production outside of Austin nearly twice as much as in Austin."

SLICES OF THE PIG – Nineteen forty-eight was surely a year of celebration for Hormel, but also one that underscored the high cost of growth for the conservative president, Tim Corey. Unlike other years when Hormel could boast no debt and cash surpluses in the millions, 1948 was different. "Our profits this year were not sufficient to pay for the new facilities and equipment we need in addition to replacing equipment that is obsolete and worn out," Corey told stockholders. "We have had to draw upon past savings."

In this modern era of highly leveraged American companies, the gravity of drawing upon past savings may seem misplaced. At least Hormel

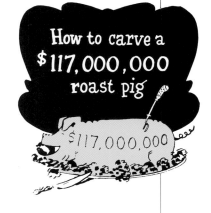

had savings. But, at the time, the notion of borrowing was anathema to this company that had successfully averted financial collapse from embezzlement and put a nest egg in the bank for safekeeping.

Rising costs also prompted Hormel to make a special effort to educate employees about how their company's financial pie or, in this case, roast pig, was carved up by operating expenses in the postwar years.

In a 1946 edition of the *Squeal*, David Owen, editor, used 1945 as an example of "How to carve a $117 million roast pig."

"That's what Hormel & Company took in during the year," he explained. "But it doesn't all belong to Hormel. Let's call it our roast pig, carve it up and see who shares in this feast."

Owen went on to explain that nearly 84 percent of the $117 million sum was handed back to farmers for livestock and vegetables, to suppliers for the spices, sugar and containers, to advertisers and insurers. The rest went for mail, telephone and other business expenses. For each Hormel employee that year, the nearly 84 percent "slice" equaled $19,760 in operating expenses.

Next, Uncle Sam and the state, county and municipal authorities were handed their share — property and other taxes, income taxes, social security and unemployment contributions. The total? 1.4 percent of the $117 million roast pig.

Hormel employees received a 10.8 percent slice in wages, salaries, joint earnings payments and profit sharing; railroads and express companies received 2.4 percent to carry Hormel products to market; replacement of worn-out machinery and buildings took 0.4 percent of the roast pig; 0.3 percent was put "on ice" for future growth and financial reserves, and 0.8 percent went to shareholders in dividends.

As time passed and Hormel moved into the decades following World War II, that roast pig would be carved up even more and the term "lean" would take on special meaning.

LAST RESPECTS

Friends and family gathered in Austin to pay their respects to Jay C. Hormel following his death on Aug. 30, 1954.

A PANOPLY OF PRODUCTS – Another cost of growth was new product development and Hormel picked up the pace in postwar America. Gelatin became a new product, along with **Hormel** deviled ham, deviled tongue, liver paté and **Mary Kitchen** hash, all introduced in the late 1940s.

Gelatin was a masterstroke. Over the years, the production of Hormel canned hams left a large volume of pork skins that the company shipped to 11 gelatin makers, most of them located on the East Coast. Gelatin, derived from the tissues of pork skin, is used in such diverse industries as food processing, pharmaceuticals and photography. But why, management reasoned, couldn't the company manufacture its own gelatin and make a profit? In fact, it could. Hormel hired an expert in the gelatin business, launched the new venture and, as demand and profit grew, even went outside for extra pork skins when its own supplies were exhausted.

In exploring the uses of byproducts, Hormel discovered that pancreas glands from hogs, cattle, calves and sheep were essential in the preparation of insulin for treating diabetics; pituitary glands from livestock were an ingredient in ACTH, a medicine for treating arthritis; beef bile was a basic component of cortisone, and hog and beef blood fibrin were useful in developing amino acids for intravenous feedings.

The postwar conversion from wartime to peacetime production also led to some surprising manufacturing applications. For example, **Hormel** deviled ham and other meat spread items were rolling off former K-ration production lines that had once turned out 275,000 cans of indelicate Army food each day. The meat spreads represented an approach to value-added processing that turned conventional meats into special consumer products with a niche all their own. Joining them was another new product, 4-ounce **Hormel** Vienna sausage.

"From foxhole to cocktail party is the conversion here," a Hormel wag observed. Introduced in 1947, these products, designed for entertaining, had a particular lifestyle statement: "They are promises of a postwar world to come," wrote a Hormel commentator. "Their daintiness and smallness give say-so to their role in promises of the future." America was ready to party again.

Mary Kitchen roast beef hash in a 15-ounce can was another new product debuted in 1949. Made from fresh cuts of beef, diced Idaho potatoes

Gelatin, a meat byproduct, was added to the Hormel line in the late 1940s. The product opened new markets in a number of diverse industries, including food processing, pharmaceuticals and photography.

Returning to Hormel after training military cooks during World War II, institutional sales manager Jean Vernet (right) was soon teaching the fine art of cooking to hotels and restaurants at a school in Minneapolis.

and a touch of onion and seasoning, it had a genuine and notable roast beef taste. Other competing products of the era tasted more like the boiled beef served at the front.

With characteristic fervor, Jay Hormel declared to shareholders at the 1949 annual meeting, "Our hash tastes as if it were roasted. Do you know how our people manage that?" He paused and smiled for dramatic effect. "They actually roast it!"

Preparing food the right way – whether by roasting, braising or broiling – was the domain of Jean Vernet, institutional sales manager for Hormel, who started a school to train cooks for hotel and restaurant duty in Minneapolis. Loaned by Hormel to the U.S. Army during the war to tutor cooks who prepared meals for the military, these veterans, with a flair for food, returned to their peacetime lives with skills they could apply. Vernet was there to coach them.

Reestablishing Hormel in the minds of consumers as a high-quality food company with innovative new products offered a smart way to expand that roast pig, making everyone's slice larger.

PRIZE PIGS – There was also plenty of attention paid to the pig's composition. How much muscle? How much fat? How heavy? What was the ideal age for a market-ready pig? What were the meatpackers looking for? What were America's consumers most likely to buy?

My deah! It's superb HASH!

Mary Kitchen ROAST BEEF HASH

All of these questions percolated through the **National Barrow Show**, hosted in Austin since 1946 with Hormel as its chief sponsor. It was an honor for the community and Hormel to plan and manage the big event which drew more than 2,000 prize hogs, along with owners, herdsmen and breeders from farms and processors in 13 states. At the show, experts in the business toured the hog pens, gathered for special demonstrations and discussed feeds, weights, raising techniques and market conditions. The objective of the **National Barrow Show** was to provide a common meeting ground where swine producers could study, compare and learn about the kind of market hog the meatpacker and consumer wanted. The hands-down winner was a hog with maximum muscle, minimum fat, weighing 200-225 pounds and ready for market in six months or less. This hog was likely to produce the most tender, succulent and palatable pork.

As hosts of the show, Hormel and Austin had a particular advantage. The agreement was that all prizewinning boars and gilts were sold at auction to allow a good number of the highest quality animals to find their way to farms in the Hormel livestock buying area. In 1946, the Grand Champion Truckload of barrows turned out to be Chester White, raised in Woodville, Ohio, on rolled oats, cracked corn, alfalfa hay, bromegrass, protein and mineral supplements and a tasty skim milk mixture called "slop." They oinked in satisfied splendor as photographers snapped away. The 1946 Grand Champion Barrow traveled only 100 miles north to Minneapolis. This Poland China hog, owned by Mancryco Farms in Manning, Iowa, was sold to Curly's Cafe for $8.85 per pound, the world's record price for a market hog.

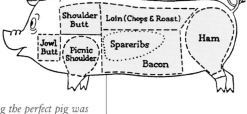

*Defining the perfect pig was the task of the **National Barrow Show**. Even in its inception, the event drew more than 2,000 prize hogs from 13 states as well as owners, herdsmen and breeders.*

Winners of the Grand Champion Truckload competition were proudly displayed in 1946.

ENTER THE NEW DECADE IN CELLOPHANE – As the 1950s began, Geo. A. Hormel & Company reported net sales of $258.8 million and an all-time sales tonnage record of 796.7 million pounds. In his letter to shareholders in 1950, Tim Corey was not shy about blaming new income taxes approved by Congress for lower net earnings. However, investors still realized a substantial increase in their common stock per share price.

Recognizing that America's population was both increasing and shifting to urban regions of the country, Hormel established new manufacturing facilities in Seattle and San Francisco, as well as an additional canning operation in Stockton, California. Mindful of transportation costs as Hormel grew into a national company, Corey told shareholders, "The products manufactured on the West Coast will be made from materials that are readily available and will be for sale there. The savings in freight will be substantial."

It was also in 1950 that Hormel demonstrated its readiness for a major consumer trend that would shape the American food processing industry for decades to come. Lacking the bravura of Jay Hormel, Corey simply but accurately described the shift in consumer interest. "Our people have been alert to the trend in consumer packaging with processed meat products," he said. "Our Research Department has been active in developing suitable products and packaging. During the year, we have introduced some 16 different items that have met with satisfactory acceptance in the trade."

Among those products were **Hormel** skinless frankfurters packed in cellophane and developed by the company's new Consumer Pack Department. "A Picture Historic," the company magazine exclaimed in December 1950, showing Violet Slowinski holding a package of the franks, flanked by dozens of them waiting to be wrapped up. "The package Violet is holding is the first attempt to meet the modern shift in consumer buying," the *Squeal* reporter explained. "Namely, the housewife's selection from the modern refrigerated self-service meat counter. It is the one-pound cello skinless frank. The eye-appealing cellophane package has printing and decorations on it in the red and yellow combination of the Hormel Company, colors that have proven to be attractive to customers and effective in sales."

Other Hormel products introduced in individual consumer packs and intended for self-serve counters at the new American phenomenon – the supermarket – included one-pound natural casing **Dairy** franks; one-pound roll chili con carne; one-pound Flavor-Saver sliced bacon; one-pound midget link sausage; one- and two-pound bag sausage; one-pound

In 1950, Hormel established the Consumer Pack Department in recognition of the new trend toward self-serve supermarkets and convenience packaging. Violet Slowinski, an Austin employee, displayed a newly designed cellophane package of **Hormel** *skinless franks.*

Hormel expanded rapidly on the West Coast following World War II, opening new facilities in Seattle, Washington, and San Francisco and Stockton, California.

country-style fresh and smoked sausage; 10-ounce braunschweiger, and several boxes or trays of pork cutlets, steaks and chops.

Proving that Hormel was truly a family organization, the *Squeal* editor noted that Violet Slowinski, featured in the "picture historic," had three other family members in the company's employ — her husband, a brother and sister.

LIFE ON THE OPEN ROAD – The blizzard of new products made life sunny for Hormel salesmen eager to meet their quotas, but the traditional road trip could be stormy and unpredictable in the Midwest, as Richard Kelly, Flavor-Sealed Division salesman, discovered in March 1950.

"When I left Minneapolis for my South Dakota trip, I could smell spring in the air," Kelly wrote to S. H. "Tate" Lane, his district manager. "The samples of **Hormel** ham & beans were a hit and I truly believed I'd win 20 new lifelong accounts.

"Tuesday morning I finished work in Madison and started for Brookings, a 60-mile drive. Before I could leave, however, I had to go to three different gas stations. The first two didn't have any electricity to run their pumps. When I finally got my gas, the attendant told me a winter storm was moving in, due at about 11 a.m."

Kelly figured he had about one and one-half hours to reach Brookings. He took to the highway, speeding along at 60 miles an hour, hoping to get in before the big blow started. He luckily avoided a collision with a car that came to a sudden stop in front of him. Kelly sailed past other drivers who chose to wait out the storm in a schoolyard.

Before long, the wind was blowing at gale force and visibility dropped to 10 yards. Kelly inched along at five miles an hour until hitting the brakes to avoid a semitrailer truck stranded in the middle of the road. When the windshield wipers failed, Kelly pulled over and saw a farmhouse just 30 feet away. Through winds that seemed to blow 100 miles per hour, he helped a young man and his aging parents, stuck in a nearby

In the 1950s, Hormel products were in great demand as American housewives sought to provide tasty, convenient and nutritious meals for their growing families.

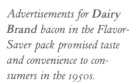

*Advertisements for **Dairy Brand** bacon in the Flavor-Saver pack promised taste and convenience to consumers in the 1950s.*

car, walk to the farmhouse. Kelly ventured out again to help a truck driver. Soon the farmhouse was filled with people, including a salesman for a New York publishing house, three farmers, a little girl who lived nearby, four college boys and a professor from Brookings.

"It was now about 5:30 p.m. and everyone was hungry. The lady of the house put on the coffee. That's when I remembered the ham *&* beans in my car. The other salesman and I started for my car. We couldn't see it initially, but finally found it and pried the frozen trunk open.

"Back in the house, I baked the samples in the oven. Believe me when I say that **Hormel** ham *&* beans found a spot in the hearts of every one of us and made an everlasting impression."

The tale was featured in the company magazine, an example of a Hormel salesman's true grit, resourcefulness and willingness to seize an opportunity to build consumer loyalty.

EXPENSES VERSUS INCOME – While Hormel salesmen braved blizzards, company leaders considered the sheer magnitude and corresponding demands of the enterprise.

In 1951, Hormel marked its 60th year. Now there were 8,000 employees – a sharp contrast to the original pair of George A. Hormel and George Peterson. The company processed three million head of livestock in one year, as compared to 610 hogs in 1892.

But size did not always guarantee economies of scale. In fact, Tim Corey pointed out, it was quite the opposite. While the prices of finished Hormel products had increased, they had not kept pace with the escalating costs of daily operations, equipment maintenance, replacement, facilities expansion and taxes. Contributing to the problems were price restrictions imposed by the Federal Office of Price Stabilization to restore market equilibrium after the war. Prices were not allowed to rise to normal free market levels which meant Hormel was caught in the squeeze between fast-growing expenses and slow-growing income. The result was shrinking profits.

Hormel posted an earnings decline in 1952 despite net sales which exceeded the previous year and sales tonnage that reached a new high. Regardless of the earnings decline, Hormel paid joint earnings equal to approximately 1.4 additional weeks of pay per person and contributed $1.1 million to the Employees' Profit Sharing Trust.

Hormel employee, Roberta Lohman, and Austin farmer, Dick Felton, posed with the 50 millionth hog processed at Hormel on Nov. 20, 1952.

In 1954, Ethiopian emperor, Haile Selassie I, visited the Hormel plant in Austin and toured with Hormel President H. H. "Tim" Corey (left) and Julius A. Zillgitt, superintendent of the Flavor-Sealed Division.

In 1953, Geo. A. Hormel & Company acquired the Tobin Packing Company of Fort Dodge, Iowa.

Helping reduce the severity of the earnings decline was the development of a new method of processing hogs that saved money by lowering labor costs, improving working conditions and producing a better product.

The patented process, called the Hormel hog immobilizer, was developed by the company's Mechanical Engineering and Practical Research Divisions coordinated by L. W. Murphy. *Food and Engineering* magazine applauded the breakthrough while the National Association for the Prevention of Cruelty to Animals and the American Humane Association gave Hormel special recognition. This innovative method was soon adopted by many industry competitors. Linked to the company's immobilizer technique was an improved system for efficiently removing beef hides and dressing more animals per hour.

By 1953, as dollar sales became more robust, sales tonnage set new record gains and with government elimination of price restrictions, Hormel returned to a positive earnings track. It was at this time the company purchased Tobin Packing Co., Inc., of Fort Dodge, Iowa. The decision was made to relieve pressure on existing plants already overloaded by consumer demand. Prior to this acquisition, Tim Corey explained to shareholders that Hormel had to manufacture **SPAM** luncheon meat at outside packinghouses for several years just to satisfy orders.

In 1954, earnings dipped again, largely because Hormel was paying a premium price for a more limited supply of hogs. In that year, the Hormel Board voted to borrow an unprecedented amount – $12 million – to retire its long-term debt and allow for more working capital to finance growth.

Fortunately, in 1955, pork supplies improved. Hormel reported sales tonnage in excess of one billion pounds for the first time in history. Net earnings bounced back markedly – from a weak $3.41 per share in 1954 to

$7.30 per share in 1955. Returning to active expansion, the company purchased the Cudahy Packing Company plant in Fresno, California, to ease processing pressure at other West Coast plants.

The first half of the 1950s had been unpredictable financially, but the commitment to steady expansion one decade earlier was confirmed. "Over the past 10 years," Tim Corey told shareholders in 1955, "the company invested considerable money in new facilities and in modernizing our Austin and outside plants. These investments proved to be justified . . . and they made increased volume possible."

The outstanding performance of 1955 was a timely tribute to Jay Hormel, the man who brought remarkable innovation, a flair for the dramatic and enlightened employee practices to the company for 35 years. "The indestructible Jay Hormel," as he had been called by the editor of *Fortune* magazine, died on Aug. 30, 1954, at age 61, after a series of heart-related illnesses.

The death of Jay C. Hormel marked the end of an era. He was the last family member to lead the company.

To consumers, Jay Hormel was the mastermind who created the Hormel Girls promotional entourage, the Chili Beaners song-and-dance troupe and two product bombshells, **Hormel** canned ham and **SPAM** luncheon meat.

Among employees and the nation's employers, Hormel was equally well known for his then-radical thinking about employment. His introduction of a guaranteed annual wage meant workers could rely on 52 paychecks a year rather than seasonal, and often unpredictable, employment.

Like his father, Jay Hormel was the steward of quality, uniformity and cleanliness in production and products. He was a gadfly when the subject was taxes or government policy. "The insidious thing about taxes and controls is that we get used to them," Hormel told stockholders in 1951. "Government rule soon learns to concern itself with the masses and to ignore and submerge the individual."

Finally, Hormel embraced corporate citizenship with an understanding that few of his peers exhibited in those days. "Business does not exist apart from humanity," Hormel told his salesmen in a homily-style speech in 1940. "Business is not a vehicle for just getting. Business is a vehicle for giving — a vehicle for getting by giving."

Countless tributes to Jay Hormel poured into Hormel headquarters in the hours and days after his death. But one of the most touching was marked by its simplicity in the company magazine: "The people felt deeply about Mr. Hormel; they were proud of him."

In the 1930s, advertisements for **SPAM** luncheon meat emphasized convenience as well as product quality and good taste.

"**T**his is London," Edward R. Murrow announced over the radio during World War II. "And the British people will have a nice Christmas. Though their tables will not be lavish, there will be **SPAM** for everyone."

Few food products can lay claim to a place in history. But **SPAM** luncheon meat does.

The story of **SPAM** luncheon meat began in 1936 when Geo. A. Hormel & Company devised a recipe for a 12-ounce can of spiced ham. Because the new product was quickly copied by competitors, Jay C. Hormel was determined to find a brand name with a distinct identity that would set it apart from the competition.

Hormel offered a $100 prize for the best name for the spiced ham prod-

uct. The hands-down winner was "**SPAM**," submitted by Kenneth Daigneau, actor-brother of Hormel Vice President Ralph Daigneau.

With the catchy winning name in hand, Hormel embarked on an extensive national radio advertising campaign to market the new product. In 1937, **SPAM** luncheon meat commercials were aired on the popular musical programs "Swing with the Strings" and "It Happened in Hollywood." Later, they were heard on "The Burns and Allen Show" which featured top-draw entertainers George Burns, Gracie Allen, Artie Shaw with his 23-piece orchestra and "Spammy," the group's mascot pig.

In March 1941, Congress passed the Lend-

Lease Act, providing aid to Allied forces, and Hormel shifted into wartime production. Soon **SPAM** luncheon meat was traveling to Britain and Russia to help meet quotas of 15 million cans a week.

As the war spread worldwide, so did **SPAM** luncheon meat. The "meat of many uses" soon achieved notoriety

In 1937, Austin plant workers inspected cans of SPAM luncheon meat as they rolled off the production line.

as "the ham that didn't pass its physical" and a "meatball without basic training."

Despite the ribbing it took, President Dwight D. Eisenhower set the record straight after the war in a letter to Geo. A. Hormel & Company. He said, "I ate my share of **SPAM** along with millions of soldiers. I will even

In their 1940 radio show, George Burns and Gracie Allen, along with "Spammy" the pig, put SPAM luncheon meat in the national spotlight.

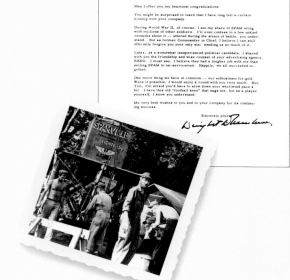

confess to a few unkind words about it — uttered during the strain of battle, you understand. But as a former Commander-in-Chief, I believe I can still officially forgive you your only sin: sending us so much of it."

No less a leader, Nikita Khrushchev even credited **SPAM** luncheon meat with keeping the Soviet Army alive. In his autobiography, *Khrushchev Remembers*, he said, "There were many jokes going around in the army, some of them off-color, about American **SPAM**; it tasted good nonetheless. Without **SPAM**, we wouldn't have been able to feed our army."

vividly remember that we opened a tin of **SPAM**," she wrote. "We had some lettuce and tomatoes and peaches so it was **SPAM** and salad."

The postwar popularity of **SPAM** luncheon meat continues to be enormous. In the United States alone, 3.8 cans of **SPAM** luncheon meat are consumed every second, making it the unrivaled number one product in its category. It is enjoyed by more than 60 million people in every corner of the U.S. and is sold in more than 99 percent of American grocery stores. But its popularity is not confined to American consumers. The **SPAM** luncheon meat trademark is registered in 93 countries, including the USSR and People's Republic of

SPAM luncheon meat continues to be the butt of jokes and tongue-in-cheek events. David Letterman proposed **SPAM**-on-a-Rope "for people who get hungry in the shower," and Monty Python developed one of its most well-known sketches around a couple in a restaurant trying to order a meal without **SPAM** luncheon meat.

Back home in Minnesota, several events surrounded the 50th Anniversary of **SPAM** luncheon meat in 1987, but all of them may have been eclipsed by Hormel President Richard L. Knowlton's personal presentation of a can of **SPAM** luncheon meat to Soviet President Mikhail

Soldiers in a U.S. Air Force unit during World War II named their camp "Spamville" in light-hearted tribute to the ubiquitous product. Years later, President Dwight D. Eisenhower acknowledged the product's importance in a letter to Hormel President H. H. "Tim" Corey.

Early advertisements for SPAM luncheon meat focused on the product's versatility.

In her reminiscences of the war years, British Prime Minister Margaret Thatcher describes **SPAM** luncheon meat as a "wartime delicacy." In 1943, as a young woman of 18 living in her family's grocery store, she feasted on **SPAM** luncheon meat on Boxing Day, a British holiday celebrated the day after Christmas. "We had friends in and I can quite

China, and it is manufactured in five foreign countries on three continents.

Consumers the world over clamor for the product. While it took 22 years to sell one billion cans of **SPAM** luncheon meat, a milestone achieved in 1959, the next billion cans were sold in half that time. Geo. A. Hormel & Company sold its three billionth can in 1980; its four billionth can came to market in 1986.

Despite evidence of its current popularity,

Gorbachev on his historic visit to the state on June 3, 1990.

To add a touch of variety to a versatile product, the **SPAM** luncheon meat family includes the original and low-salt varieties in 7-ounce and 12-ounce cans and a smoke flavored version in a 12-ounce size. New **SPAM** breakfast strips, introduced in 1990, add yet another healthful variation to the ubiquitous product which is one of the most treasured in American product history.

The SPAM luncheon meat family now includes smoke flavored and low-salt varieties.

CHAPTER FIVE

Battling the Giants 1955-1969

"I thought it was important to divide responsibility. The idea was to give people the leeway they needed to get their jobs done, on their own . . ."

R. F. Gray

1955

R. F. Gray circa 1962.

M. B. Thompson circa 1969.

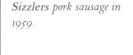

Hormel introduced Little Sizzlers *pork sausage in 1959.*

R. F. Gray, the champion of individual effort, and M. B. "Tommy" Thompson, the salesmen's salesman, were the fourth and fifth presidents of Hormel. It was an exciting era of plant and product proliferation as Hormel truly became a national brand with manufacturing and distribution sites hundreds of miles in all directions from Austin, Minnesota. The momentum would never wane.

1955-1959

1955 R. F. Gray is elected president in April.
- The company introduces **Hormel** delicut ham.

1956 Hormel establishes a new Research and Development Division managed by Julius A. Zillgitt.

- The company establishes a comprehensive health insurance plan for retired employees.

1957 Hormel introduces skinless pork sausage links, the forerunner to the **Little Sizzlers** brand, delicut smokies and delicut buffet ham.
- The state of Minnesota authorizes a swine testing station in Austin — the fourth such station in the nation.
- The Board of Directors meets in Fremont, Nebraska, on the 10th anniversary of the Fremont plant's purchase. This represents the first board meeting ever held outside Austin.

1959 The American Humane Association presents a plaque to Hormel for humane slaughtering achieved with the hog immobilizer.

- **Hormel produces its one billionth can of SPAM luncheon meat.**
- The company invests in new equipment and packaging for sliced luncheon meats and bacon.
- Hormel introduces **Little Sizzlers** pork sausage.

President John F. Kennedy.

1960-1964

1960 Hormel introduces "Famous Foods of the World."
- Benjamin F. Hormel dies at age 82; John G. Hormel dies at age 84.

In September 1959, the one billionth can of SPAM luncheon meat rolled off the Austin assembly line.

1,000,000,000

The civil rights movement of the 1960s, led by Dr. Martin Luther King, Jr., (center) changed the social and political balance of America.

■ December 4 marks the 100th anniversary of the birth of George A. Hormel.

1961   Hormel is the first meatpacker to use all-purpose, 50-foot refrigerator cars, 50 of which are delivered in three months' time.

1962   Brown 'n Serve sausage is introduced.

■ The company discontinues slaughter of lambs and calves.

■ Plans are developed to expand facilities in Austin, Los Angeles, Mitchell, Charlotte and Atlanta.

1963   Hormel introduces **Cure 81** ham.

■ A 75,600 square foot plant is constructed in Austin and leased to the American Can Company for the manufacture of cans.

1964   Hormel adopts a new corporate design for product packaging.

■ A new 25,000 square foot corporate office building is completed in Austin.

■ After 38 years, the Hormel Flavor-Sealed Division is renamed the Grocery Products Division.

■ Hormel introduces Deviled **SPAM** Spread and Re-Seal Pak, a new package for sausage and luncheon meats.

1965-1969

1965   H. H. Corey retires after 45 years with the company; R. F. Gray is named board chairman, and M. B. Thompson becomes the fifth president of Geo. A. Hormel & Company.

1966   Hormel purchases its 100 millionth hog. The company now processes more than four million head of livestock each year.

■ H. H. Corey dies at age 72.

Research gathered from meetings with nearly 1,000 homemakers in 16 American cities led to the development of Cure 81 ham, introduced in 1963.

✤Hormel✤

In 1964, Hormel debuted a new, updated company logo for use in advertising, product packaging and corporate identification.

Hormel teamed with the National Football League in a 1963 promotion identifying Hormel products as "Official Training Table Foods."

NFL SELECTED OFFICIAL TRAINING TABLE MEATS

In July 1957, the Hormel Board of Directors met in Fremont, Nebraska, to discuss such issues as increased industry competition and shrinking profit margins.

1969

The 1950s was an era of growth and prosperity in America, often typified by the traditional, nuclear family.

After World War II and the Korean War, after the Red Hysteria whipped up by Senator Joe McCarthy and his aide, Roy Cohn, Americans by the mid-1950s were ready for a time of repose and prosperity. The population increased substantially and so did the number of consumers. And everyone liked Ike. Dwight David Eisenhower, the former Supreme Allied Commander in Europe, was eyeing his second term as the nation's president, which he would win by a landslide, along with his vice president, Richard M. Nixon.

The 1950s was definitely the American decade. America set an example for the rest of the world and the American dream was a reality. But, under the placid surface, events were taking shape that would bring about substantial changes in our culture. For example, as early as 1953, President Eisenhower announced that the United States had loaned France $60 million to conduct its war in Indochina, better known today as Vietnam. By the mid-1960s, the young men of America would be engaged in that bitter and divisive struggle halfway around the world.

At home, the pot was also beginning to boil. In 1954, the United States Supreme Court unanimously ruled that segregation in the public schools was unconstitutional, but the nation moved slowly to effect this change. By the late 1960s, the demand for change became increasingly insistent: for civil rights, women's equality and an end to the war in Vietnam. When changes came too slowly for some and too rapidly for others, confrontation, civil disobedience, riots and assassinations erupted across the country. In his song of that era, Minnesota's own Bob Dylan was warning, "Get out of the new road, if you can't lend a hand, for the times they are a-changin' . . . "

DOWN HOME IN AUSTIN – The times were changing in Austin, Minnesota, too. Events in the nation and the meatpacking industry would have a significant impact on Geo. A. Hormel & Company during the 1950s and 1960s. The population of the nation, for example, was continuing to shift from rural to urban. In 1917, one-half of the population lived in the country and one-half in towns and cities. By 1959, 69 percent of the population lived in towns. The shift to urban centers, continuing throughout the 1960s, left smaller numbers of farmers on fewer farms with larger acreages. And those farmers specialized. While barnyards traditionally held cattle, hogs, chickens, sheep and calves, by the 1960s, farmers specialized in one animal — hogs or beef or dairy cattle. For Hormel, this meant more pork was produced by fewer suppliers who were able to extract higher prices that, in turn, cut into the company's already thin margins.

In 1955, Hormel earned a net profit of $1.14 on every $100 of sales. That was a good year. In 1958, the margin dropped to $.80 per $100 of sales. As Jay Hormel had said, "Getting a profit from meatpacking is like dipping a sieve into a bucket of water."

Competition, low margins, sluggish sales, the shifting farm economy and population, the incentive system, the annual wage, decentralization and expansion and the pressing need to shift from a slaughter-for-volume to a market-driven industry were all issues Geo. A. Hormel & Company would face and solve during this era rife with change.

THE FAMILY LEADERSHIP ENDS, A LEGACY REMAINS — A monumental change had already occurred in the company with the death of Jay C. Hormel in 1954. The founding father, George A., and his heir were gone and the third generation was neither old enough nor experienced enough to assume leadership. Jay's death had come very fast and so unsettled the Hormel Board composed of many longtime Hormel directors — Richard S. Banfield, Ralph H. Daigneau, Park Dougherty and M. F. Dugan — that H. H. "Tim" Corey was not named chairman and chief executive officer until December 1954. Corey continued as president until R. F. "Bob" Gray was elected to that post in April 1955.

Despite this awkward succession, many aspects of the company's corporate culture, including the values and ideals instilled by George A. and Jay C. Hormel between 1891-1954, continued to guide the business.

What was the Hormel legacy? Entrepreneurship was the heart of it. Both father and son were entrepreneurs who organized, operated and assumed the risks for their business ventures. They believed in the American ideals of taking responsibility and learning from their mistakes, working hard and persevering. They believed that strong selling formed the core of every business and that a dash of good luck was an important, but not necessarily guaranteed, ingredient in every successful enterprise. To his father's ideals, which he shared and nurtured, Jay Hormel brought

In cities and rural areas throughout the country, consumers relied on Hormel for high-quality foods. In Austin, the Herbert Kamp family (top) and the Howard Willis family (bottom) enjoyed Hormel products in the 1950s.

Under the leadership of R. F. "Bob" Gray, Hormel employees were granted greater autonomy and responsibility.

*In September 1959, R. D. Arney and Ruth Gibson take the one billionth can of **SPAM** luncheon meat off the Austin assembly line.*

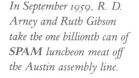

rare marketing instincts and a genius for innovation that surpassed his grandfather's maxim, "Originate, don't imitate." Jay also contributed fair and equitable management of employees that was far ahead of its time. Finally, both were strong, self-sufficient leaders, qualities Tim Corey perpetuated during his years as president.

R. F. GRAY: GIVE PEOPLE THE FREEDOM TO SUCCEED – Unlike his predecessors, Gray was a man who, by nature and persuasion, sensed the company's leadership needed to function in a new capacity. "Tim Corey," he recounts, "spent an awful lot of years behind Jay Hormel and, having done so, had little opportunity to make decisions on his own. Jay was a strong personality like his father. In meetings, he did not hesitate to make up his mind for all of us. We might all be against him, but he would win.

"I thought it was important to loosen the company up and divide the responsibility in those areas in which people operated. The idea was to give people the leeway they needed to get their jobs done on their own, the way they wanted."

"One of the most important steps Gray took," recalls David A. Larson, vice president of human resources, "was making Harold B. Butler manager of the Austin plant in 1958. There had never been a plant manager before. The idea was to coordinate activities at the plant and to give Butler responsibility for the entire operation. Once that happened, people had to go through Butler to get things done. Previously, the plant and headquarters were tied together and it was difficult to determine who was in charge. Now the two units acted as separate entities."

Butler, former group vice president of operations, now retired, recalls that "the idea was to spread authority around. With the plant operating on its own, separate from headquarters, we could even stir up some healthy rivalries between the divisions, making them more competitive."

UP THROUGH THE RANKS – Bob Gray, the delegator, was born in Vernon Center, a small town in south central Minnesota. He joined the company in 1927, the year Jay Hormel became acting president, working as a sausage truck salesman in Iowa. Three years later, Gray became assistant

manager of the Motor Truck Department. In 1932, Gray, with other
young Hormel salespeople, including M. B. "Tommy" Thompson, who
later succeeded Gray as president and chairman, was transferred into the
Market Plan Department. The Market Plan was Jay Hormel's farsighted
but short-lived strategy to provide meat retailers with all the provisions
they needed, to coin a modern business phrase "just in time." One year
later, Gray was managing the Transportation Department, coordi-
nating the rapid and economic movement of products by truck and rail
to the company's customers. In 1937, he took over as manager of the
Packing Division and, five years later, became a company vice president.
Elected to the Board of Directors in 1945, Gray assumed the executive vice
president's post the following year. Nine years later, in 1955, he became
the fourth president in the company's 64-year history following Tim
Corey's election as board chairman.

SERVING A NATIONAL MARKET – As president, Bob Gray not only dele-
gated authority and decentralized management of the company, he also
carried forward a rigorous program of growth. Expansion, of course, was
nothing new to Hormel. The company had been growing steadily since
1931 when the first hog processing facility outside Austin was established in
Mitchell, South Dakota. Growth continued in 1947 with the acquisition
of the Fremont (Neb.) Packing Company plant. In 1953, Hormel expanded
its processing capacity by acquiring the Tobin Packing Company plant in
Fort Dodge, Iowa.

The acquisition of the Tobin Packing Company in Fort Dodge, Iowa, along with new processing facilities in Mitchell, South Dakota, and Fremont, Nebraska, greatly expanded company processing capacity.

However, by the mid-1950s, company expansion really began to soar.
In the Northwest, West and South, Hormel increased processing and
distribution facilities by opening new plants in Seattle and San Francisco;
Montgomery, Alabama, and Beaumont, Texas, and by remodeling and
enlarging facilities in San Antonio and Houston; Mobile, Alabama;
Winston-Salem, and Atlanta.

To remain competitive and maintain its market share in a fast-growing
population, Hormel had to acquire and make improvements in existing
facilities nationwide. In the early 1960s, the company added to its production and distribution facilities at Fremont, Fort Dodge, Fresno and
Chattanooga. Subsequently, Hormel constructed a new smokehouse and
expanded operating space in Fresno and acquired property for a distribution

center in Charlotte, North Carolina. Substantial improvements in the Austin plant included new equipment installations, modernization of the hog kill and new sausage processing facilities. In Mitchell, renovated pork processing operations were completed.

Also in the 1960s, when M. B. Thompson, executive vice president, succeeded Bob Gray as president, the company made a host of improvements at multiple locations. They read like a flight navigator's map: Miami and Oklahoma City, Oklahoma; Los Angeles, California; Des Moines, Iowa; Springfield, Missouri; Houston, Dallas and San Antonio, Texas; Birmingham, Alabama; Atlanta, Georgia; New Orleans, Louisiana; Orlando, Florida, and Minneapolis, Minnesota. And, following the reassurances given by Corey and Gray, the Austin community was consistently part of the picture. In 1964, in Austin, Hormel began operation of a new factory for the production of cans by the American Can Company; installed a six-story hydrostatic cooker imported from Holland to increase output of **SPAM** luncheon meat, and completed a new 25,000 square foot Corporate Office building.

Hormel employees, who numbered more than 8,000 in the 1950s, possessed a wealth of diverse and specialized skills that fueled national growth and expansion.

RETURNING ABROAD – While Hormel was busy growing in America, it was also casting an ambitious eye toward foreign export business. As early as 1905, George A. Hormel had gone to England to set up a profitable trade that flourished for many years. At one point, overseas business accounted for nearly one-third of the company's profits.

After World War I, however, export business declined and was not revived until 1955 when Hormel established subsidiary arrangements for the production of **SPAM** luncheon meat in Cork, Ireland, which was the only way to introduce the product into England. Between 1955-62, Hormel made similar subsidiary arrangements with companies in Calgary, Alberta, Canada; London, England, and Cagua, Venezuela. At first these companies, under license, manufactured only **SPAM** luncheon meat; eventually they made other products and expanded international trade.

SWIM OR SINK – Hormel business in the late 1950s appeared good. Net sales and earnings climbed from $347.9 million and $3.3 million, respectively, in 1957 to $401.7 million and $5.8 million in 1959. Yet, like the era itself, the outer calm belied an inner tumult. In the words of Bob Gray, "Our competition in the late 1950s included some of the giants – Armour, Swift and Wilson – and a few companies about our size, including Rath Packing Company and Oscar Mayer and Company. I remember Mr. Rath saying to me, 'Bob, it will be interesting to see how your company and ours turn out down the road because you've elected to decentralize and we've elected to centralize.'

"Well, they went out of business and that's because they decided to centralize. They kept piling more stuff on their plant in Waterloo, Iowa. When they had labor problems, they had them all right there."

Decentralization and expansion programs at Hormel kept the company afloat and also provided protection for changes that lay ahead. Decentralization distributed responsibility and risk out of the hands of a few people and into the hands of dozens eager to lead. Expansion of the company's processing and distribution facilities also gradually and gently changed the focus of the company. Hormel was no longer just Austin, Minnesota. By the 1960s, in terms of its Packing Division alone, Hormel was Austin, Charlotte, Fresno, Los Angeles, Fort Dodge, Dallas, Seattle and Fremont.

A MAXIM INSTITUTIONALIZED – John Hormel, George A.'s father, had often told his son, "Originate, don't imitate." George took that maxim to heart by creating "Hormel's Sugar-Cured Pig Back Bacon" in 1895. Sixty-one years later, in 1956, the company took that maxim to heart by establishing a Research and Development Division. Julius A. Zillgitt, former

Between 1955-62, Hormel established agreements for the manufacture of SPAM luncheon meat with companies in Ireland, Canada, England and Venezuela.

Business was brisk at Hormel in the late 1950s, with sales increasing 15.7 percent between 1957-59. Jacqueline Garis, an employee in the Austin Flavor-Sealed Division, tallied figures in 1958.

*Hormel established a new
Research and Development
Division in 1956 to enhance
product quality and explore
new product development.*

*Using information supplied
by nearly 1,000 home-
makers throughout the country, Hormel developed "the
world's most nearly perfect
ham," Cure 81 ham, in
1963.*

production superintendent of the Grocery Products Division, became
R&D director with the assistance of Frank M. Brown, engineer; Wayne
E. Batterman, foreman; A. D. "Doc" Cipra, curemaster; Hillary Krause,
researcher, and Harry Louk, chemist.

The new division, set up in a corner of the old Austin plant, had 20
employees and an operating budget of $220,000. Zillgitt and his staff were
assigned to improve product quality and explore new product development, especially canned foods. By 1961, R&D also supervised mechanical,
structural and industrial engineering and had responsibility for smoked
and cured meat processing.

Zillgitt retired in December 1968 after more than 38 years at Hormel.
Among many assignments, he worked on **SPAM** luncheon meat. "We
spent years developing a 12-ounce canned luncheon meat," he recalls.
"Sterilization was always the big problem. Cooking 12 ounces of meat for
any length of time broke down the meat's cell structure. We would get
eight ounces of meat and four ounces of juice.

REACHING FOR THE TOP TEN – In 1963, Hormel introduced a new product
destined for long-lasting stardom. The **Cure 81** ham, a registered boneless
ham, was given a special cure known only to Doc Cipra, Hormel curemaster. To determine the market potential for this new product, company
researchers sat down with panels of homemakers representing a variety of
family sizes and economic backgrounds. The panelists told Hormel what
they wanted in a boneless ham. The company tailored **Cure 81** ham to
these specifications and the product soon became a solid gold hit. Sales increased dramatically and so did the number of people producing **Cure 81**
ham — from six in 1963 to nearly 200 by 1966.

"New product development is essential to any company expecting
to remain competitive," R.D. Arney, executive vice president, explained
to employees in a 1968 issue of *Hormel NEWS*.

"The roots of progress," he added, "lie in the fascinating area of
product development. This requires a high degree of teamwork from the
research, marketing, production and sales departments."

By 1968, teamwork was intrinsic to the Hormel culture and product
development began to accelerate. Hormel was producing more than 750
products compared to 375 little more than a decade earlier.

MORE OF A GOOD THING – Along with new products, there were ambitious line extensions in the late 1950s and early 1960s. Examples included **Hormel** delicut buffet ham; skinless pork sausage links; a new Canadian bacon, and delicut smokies. In addition, the company introduced a boneless buffet ham for smaller families; a cookout line consisting of smokies, ham treats, knockwurst and Polish sausage; **Little Sizzlers** pork sausage, and a precursor to microwave foods, the **Brown 'n Serve** line of fully cooked sausage products that were ready to eat in only four minutes.

LOSERS AND WINNERS – Naturally, not all of the products debuted by Geo. A. Hormel & Company were winners. Sometimes the reason for failure seemed arbitrary at best. Reflecting on some, Bob Gray recalls the "kottbullar and the stroganoff were marvelous, but the public didn't buy them. I can't say why. We marketed the heck out of them. I remember another product, an onion soup we made in the early 1930s. I've never seen one that good since. But nobody bought it. On the other hand, I can think of one or two Hormel products I thought were ordinary, yet they made it big in the marketplace. But this is a fickle business. Who would have guessed at the success of **Cure 81** ham?"

Or the continued success of **SPAM** luncheon meat, for that matter? By 1959, Hormel had sold its billionth can of **SPAM** luncheon meat and, in 1963, to meet increasing demand for the product, purchased a hydrostatic cooker from Stork Brothers, a manufacturer in The Netherlands. The huge device, requiring only one operator, processed 350 cans of **SPAM** luncheon meat per minute. That output equaled one-half million cans per 24-hour day.

MAY I HAVE YOUR ATTENTION? – The success of **SPAM** luncheon meat notwithstanding, the fickle nature of the meat processing business was on everyone's mind at the 1963 annual stockholders' meeting. Gray addressed the problem this way: "Mrs. Housewife is an independent thinker. The type of package, the size of the package, its retail price and many other factors have a bearing on her purchase. Oddly enough, it's not always the quality of the product that is the deciding factor."

*In 1962, M. B. "Tommy" Thompson and his secretary, Fern (Ellis) Giffin, sampled **Brown 'n Serve** sausage in celebration of the product's introduction.*

JOINT EARNINGS

Hormel employees received their 29th consecutive joint earnings check in 1967. The Joint Earnings Plan, in effect since 1938, gives eligible employees a share of company profits.

Product innovation and marketing savvy are a hot combination—and with **Little Sizzlers** pork sausage, Hormel once again blazed a trail to success. As the first skinless pork sausage on the market in 1957, the new product was introduced to meet growing consumer demand for time-saving, convenience foods. The tasty new breakfast sausage was first marketed under the name "Hormel skinless pork sausage links." Although the product was well received by consumers, Hormel recognized the need for a lively, eye-catching brand name — a name with pizzazz. Intense brainstorming produced the inspiring name **Little Sizzlers** — and cash registers started ringing. Initial advertising and merchandising substantially increased sales and the product has been sizzling ever since — making **Little Sizzlers** pork sausage the top-selling product in its category for over 10 years.

"After more than 30 years, **Little Sizzlers** pork sausage is an idea that has not grown old,"

continued on next page

The following year, to attract consumers to Hormel products and to hold their attention, the company created a new logo. The improvements included bold lettering for the Hormel name in red, black and green, and redesigned packaging. The new designs were meant to give Hormel products a more distinctive look and a stronger corporate image.

❄Hormel❄

FLUCTUATING SALES – The company's ability to consistently hold consumer attention was apparent by 1962. From 1954-59, sales increased from $344 million to $401.7 million. Although there was a $17.2 million sales dip in 1956, strong increases followed. Sales tumbled again in 1960 by $29.4 million; rose by nearly $12 million in 1961, and increased by only $597,000 in 1962.

Explaining the 1960 performance to stockholders, Gray said lower dollar sales were the result of low prices for dressed beef and unsatisfactory results in the beef operation.

To stockholders at the 1962 meeting, Gray offered this analysis: "Downward pressure on our profits came from three sources – costs of processing beef, particularly at our Austin plant; intense competition for available supplies of hogs, and the constant difficulty in maintaining adequate margins when marketing our products."

By 1963, sales had increased by almost $9 million over the previous year, but Gray's analysis signaled an impending change: "The continuous pressure on our margins by reason of increasing competition and industry improvements in production means we must carefully analyze all of our costs."

OF SALES AND SALESMEN – Careful cost analysis alone, however, could not account for the company's sudden sales upsurge in the years that followed. In 1963, sales began an eight-year ascent, fueled in part by Gray's dual program of decentralization and expansion and the company's move toward a marketing focus.

What factors specifically accounted for the eight-year gain? Certainly the new logo and packaging designs helped, as did the phenomenal success of **Cure 81** ham, **Little Sizzlers** pork sausage and **SPAM** luncheon meat. Also contributing to company successes was an all-encompassing promotional campaign with the National Football League in which

LITTLE SIZZLERS

continued from previous page

Hormel products were identified as "Official Training Table Foods." The company's promotion of the Re-Seal luncheon meat line offering homemakers "easy-to-see and easy-to-use resealable containers" provided another sales boost. Equally important, through expanded facilities, the company's ability to meet consumer demand continued unabated.

THE MAN WITH THE SHEEPSKIN – When M. B. "Tommy" Thompson became the fifth president of Geo. A. Hormel & Company in July 1965, he had precisely the right strengths for the era. Thomas J. Purcell, former director of marketing and advertising, called Thompson "the salesmen's salesman." Born in Webster, South Dakota, Thompson attended Indiana University where he was recruited by Hormel. With a Bachelor of Science in business, he joined the company in 1931 and soon began a successful career in sales. In 1936, Thompson advanced to manager of the Houston plant and, three years later, after he transferred to Chicago, Thompson was recognized as "Most Valuable Player" for consistently outselling his established quotas. He returned to Austin in June 1941 as sales manager for meat products, advancing to manager of the Meat Products Division in 1945. One year later, he was named executive officer of the Pork Division. In 1947, he became manager of the newly acquired one-story Fremont plant which Jay Hormel purchased to streamline labor and production costs. It was here that Thompson posted an outstanding record of growth and achievement. He was instrumental in developing the Fremont plant from an employee base of 50 people in 1947 to more than 650 people 11 years later.

In 1956, Thompson became a director of Hormel and, two years later, returned to Austin as executive vice president. When Corey resigned as chairman of the board, to be succeeded by Gray, Thompson became the first man with a college degree to hold the office of president. George A. Hormel had not ventured beyond elementary school; R. F. Gray graduated from high school, and Jay C. Hormel and H. H. Corey attended college but left before earning diplomas.

THE BUILDING BOOM GOES ON – His college degree notwithstanding, Thompson adhered to the course set by his predecessors and, like Gray, supervised the continued growth of Hormel.

In his first year at the helm, the company expanded and improved its sausage manufacturing facility in Houston; purchased a major interest in Purveyors, Inc., Hopkins, Minnesota, a supplier of processed meats; signed a two-year agreement with I.D. Packing Co. in Des Moines for the

says **Stanley E. Kerber,** group vice president, Meat Products Group. **"The strength of this famous brand is truly amazing when considering the large number of food manufacturers producing breakfast sausage and the wide variety of competing brands found in refrigerated meat cases nationwide."**

Little Sizzlers pork sausage is available in a number of varieties and sizes: patties (10-ounce package); old-fashioned links (10-ounce package), and both regular and hot and spicy varieties of skinless links (12-ounce package).

"Nothing Else Stacks Up to SPAM," a Hormel advertising campaign claimed in the early 1960s.

A 1963 promotion with the National Football League identified Hormel products as "Official Training Table Foods." Carl Eller, star defensive end with the Minnesota Vikings, made public appearances in support of Hormel products to the delight of young football fans.

As part of its aggressive building and expansion program, Hormel completed a 194,500 square foot plant in Atlanta, Georgia.

custom processing of 750,000 hogs per year, and entered into a similar arrangement with Rod Barnes Packing Co. of Huron, South Dakota, the following year.

In 1966-67, company construction and acquisition forged ahead. Hormel remodeled dry sausage manufacturing facilities in Austin; installed additional refrigeration at the Springfield plant, and completed a new distribution center in San Antonio. In Oklahoma City, Hormel purchased Hereford Heaven Brands, Inc., a frozen meat plant catering to both retail and institutional customers. In Orlando, Hormel acquired the equipment and inventory of Gertner Meat Packers, Inc., a meat supplier to central Florida.

At the Austin corporate offices in 1967, management also inaugurated departmental expansion by creating two new divisions — the Foodservice Division and the Industrial Products Division. The former was staffed by specialists who marketed Hormel products to the foodservice trade, including hotels and restaurants, hospitals, colleges and universities, and in-plant feeding operations. Sales, promotion and development of new products for both the vending and manual feeding trade also came under the aegis of this division. The Industrial Products Division was created to move the company into new areas of the food business. Gelatin and gelatin-based products became an important and lucrative segment of the new division along with products for the pharmaceutical industry.

Companywide expansion continued apace in 1968. Hormel opened a new distribution plant in New Orleans and gave **SPAM** luncheon meat production a boost by installing a hydrostatic cooker at the Fort Dodge plant. Hormel also expanded canning operations in Austin and Stockton. In the following year, Thompson's last as president, Hormel realized one of its most ambitious building goals with the completion of a new 194,500 square foot meat products/grocery products plant in Atlanta.

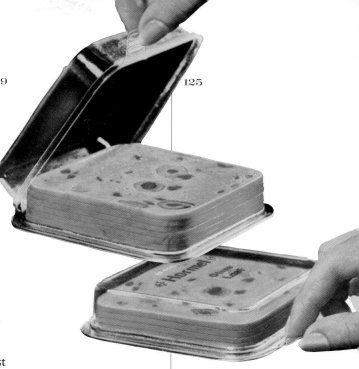

AN EXPANDING GLOBAL VISION – Along with its domestic growth, the company also developed new overseas operations. In 1964, Hormel arranged a joint venture with Britain's N. Kilvert & Son, Ltd., establishing the Kilvert-Hormel Import Agency, Ltd., Manchester, England. In 1965, the company formed a new partnership, known as Lloyd's Industries, Inc., to expand its international presence.

The fruits of this initiative were slow to ripen. By 1969, however, Hormel had established another joint venture, this one with Hormel-Cerebos Pty. Ltd., which marketed **SPAM** luncheon meat in Australia. In 1970, the company started two joint ventures. One was set up in Okinawa to introduce Hormel products to Japan. It was named the First Enterprise Corporation and, by 1971, doubled its production of **Mary Kitchen** corned beef hash. In the Philippines, a joint venture relationship with Pure Foods Corporation resulted in license agreements for processed meats and other items.

Because Hormel had always been oriented to its domestic business, international operations developed slowly. That attitude began to change in the late 1960s.

UPWARD SALES — BY LEAPS AND BOUNDS – Changing, too, was the Hormel sales focus. "We sought to develop a sales program that would transform us from a commodity, volume-oriented operation into a marketing and sales-driven business," M. B. Thompson recalled in 1988.

Thompson's approach helped dollar sales grow from $393.7 million in 1963 to $626 million in 1969. The growth during that six-year span was considerable when compared to earlier years. Between 1954-63, a 10-year period, Hormel sales increased by $49.7 million, from $344 million in 1954 to $393.7 in 1963. But, in the following five years, between 1965-69, sales expanded by $184.4 million, from $441.6 million in 1965 to $626 million in 1969. Also significant was the leap in net earnings. Between 1961-66, income hovered between a low of $3.1 million and a high of $3.5 million. But, in 1967, net earnings jumped to $8.7 million and, by the end of the decade, reached $9.2 million. A corresponding increase in margins also occurred, rising from $.80 per $100 of sales in 1961 to $1.58 per $100 in 1967.

TO MARKET, TO MARKET – Nineteen sixty-seven was a turnaround year for Geo. A. Hormel & Company, a fiscal year to remember. A look at the records reveals sales, tonnage, net earnings and working capital all climbing upward. Describing the company's marketing success in a 1967 issue of

In its quest to provide high-quality, convenience foods to American consumers, Hormel introduced the Re-Seal luncheon meat line in the early 1960s.

Benefits to Hormel employees were valued at an impressive $25,138,477 in 1968.

In 1965, R. F. Gray was named board chairman following the retirement of H. H. Corey and M. B. Thompson became the company's fifth president. Under Thompson, Hormel continued its course of expansion and acquisition. Pictured (clockwise around the table) is the Hormel Board comprised of F. W. Sherman, Harold B. Butler, James C. Hormel, Gordon Murray, M. B. Thompson, R. F. Gray, George W. Ryan, I. J. Holton, R. D. Arney, Bruce Corey and O. L. Marquesen. (1967)

Hormel NEWS, M. B. Thompson wrote, "We plan a full year in advance. We know how much and where each product has been marketed during the past several years. We assess population growth trends along with the growth of our competitors, alternate methods of distribution, the availability of personnel and production facilities as well as our funds for advertising. We set our corporate marketing goals and, when the plans are complete, each sales territory, district, branch and plant is assigned sales targets for the coming year."

BUT THE TIMES THEY ARE A-CHANGIN' – To Thompson's discussion of sales and marketing, an executive vice president added these thoughts about change. "Nothing is permanent in the marketing of our company's products," he wrote. "We must be aware of market changes and anticipate them before they occur. Increased wages, continued dividends and money to expand the business must come from future profits. We can expect profits if we adapt to the changes taking place within the food industry. I use the term 'food industry,' because Hormel is operating – and must operate – beyond the original concept of a meatpacker."

Clearly Hormel had come a long way from the days when growth was measured in the numbers of hogs processed. The industry was changing, mergers and acquisitions were making strange bedfellows of once-fearsome competitors and the small, but efficient, independents were stealing market share from the giants.

THE COMPANY'S MOST IMPORTANT ASSET – Although change was the trademark of the mid- and late 1960s, one aspect of the company's corporate culture did not change – the way the organization treated its people. Each year, eligible employees continued to receive as much as two

or three times their weekly paychecks from joint earnings, the innovative profit sharing program initiated by Jay Hormel in 1938.

Furthermore, employee pay increases occurred yearly and, on occasion, twice each year. At that time, pay raises were negotiated on a national basis by the meatpackers' unions. Between 1955-69, union pay scales, including cost-of-living adjustments, rose every year. Typical raises had been $.075 to $.13 per hour but, in 1968, cost-of-living provisions increased wages by $.06 per hour on January 1 and $.06 again on July 1. Base rate increases of $.11 per hour and a job classification adjustment, averaging $.03 per hour, became effective in September. In 1969, the total hourly increase was $.26. During the same period, 1955-69, total raises had increased workers' base pay by $1.65 per hour.

THE HINT OF CHANGE – Despite pay hikes and the company's excellent profits in the late 1960s, trouble involving the annual wage and incentive system was brewing beneath the surface. Problems first came to light in March 1954. "Geo. A. Hormel & Company has felt the first strain of the annual wage since 1934," the *Squeal* reported. "The cause was a 25 percent cut in production of hogs by farmers." There was less to do at the packinghouse and workers would have been laid off if not for the annual wage commitment.

"The annual wage will work – and not become a string that strangles us – if men can be shifted to other work areas. Otherwise," the *Squeal* warned, "management will run out of money to meet the payroll."

The company's willingness to meet the payroll received nationwide attention in *Business Week* magazine but the article hinted at change. "The guaranteed annual wage at Hormel," a reporter wrote, "has been considered a model for two decades. Hormel experiences in adverse times may be cited when management makes decisions at the bargaining table."

In the mid-1950s, workers across the country wanted the comforts of a guaranteed wage. The Independent Union of Electrical Workers had asked Westinghouse Electric Corp. to guarantee a minimum of 2,080 hours' pay annually to all employees with one year of seniority. Walter Reuther, president of the United Auto Workers, affirmed the union was "dead serious" about its annual wage demands. The innovative idea spawned by Jay Hormel had become a national issue and would stir debate for years to come.

continued on next page

LOGO EVOLUTION

continued from previous page

The first uniform logo design emerged in 1941 when commercial artist George Switzer developed a style featuring rounded block letters for the Hormel name, along with illustrated silhouettes of a hog, sheep and cow for product packaging.

A revised corporate identity, featuring the Hormel name in red, green and black, a parsley sprig and the tag line ''Fine Food Products,'' was instituted in 1964 after extensive research and testing. It was the first and most comprehensive effort to introduce a consistent corporate symbol into all aspects of Hormel identification. That logo was further refined in 1978 with a change in type style and by enclosing the Hormel name in color bars.

More recently, the company has placed still greater emphasis on the Hormel name to capitalize on the longstanding reputation for quality. Although major brands continue — **Dinty Moore** beef stew, **SPAM** luncheon meat, **Cure 81** ham and **Little Sizzlers** pork sausage — the Hormel name has become larger and more prominent in product packaging. This step has contributed to greater consumer recognition, awareness and acceptance of the company as the nation's leading independent meat and food processor.

But Hormel assured *Business Week* that "we haven't revised our thinking on the long-term value of a guaranteed wage just because we had a little test of it the past year."

That "test" cost Hormel approximately $650,000 in additional wages or approximately 1.5 percent of the total wages paid. If the company had laid off employees, its unemployment tax, under Minnesota's merit rating system, would have increased $350,000. Moreover, the annual wage eliminated costs involved in recalling laid-off workers or hiring and training new ones.

INFLEXIBILITY IN A CHANGING ERA – By 1969, the guaranteed annual wage and incentive system had become essential parts of the company's corporate culture. But would the incentive system be flexible? According to Bob Gray, "The incentive system was the problem that led to troubles in later years. We didn't know how to produce a proper work schedule."

David A. Larson, vice president of human resources, recalls, "The incentive plan was a good idea on paper. It was designed to pay employees for hard work and for exceeding production quotas. But nothing is static in this world. Manufacturing improvements developed, making old quotas too low and obsolete. However, nobody wanted to revise the quota upward."

"When the pay rate was $.35 an hour," said Gray, "an inaccurate quota didn't make much difference, although our margins were always low. But, when we started paying hourly wages of $4-5 an hour and, finally, $10-12 an hour, plus all the fringe benefits, the inflexibility of the quota system began to hurt."

DISAPPEARING GIANTS – While the problem festered, the quota system remained in effect. But pressures in the late 1960s began to build against it. The meatpacking industry, like everything else in this era, was undergoing significant change with new low-cost operators entering the industry. "The independents," Larson says, "had several things in their favor. First, some were nonunion; others worked out special union contracts to get established and operating. Second, these company plants were newly built, modern and efficient. They could process in volume and their operations were not as labor intensive. Third, they began packing beef in boxes which made their products easier to transport and helped reduce distribution costs. With all these advantages, the independents could easily underprice larger producers."

Soon the independents were taking a big bite out of profits. In 1969, Swift, Armour, Wilson, Morrell, Hormel, Oscar Mayer, Hygrade, Cudahy and Rath had combined sales of $7.9 billion while sales for the independents totaled $11.2 billion. The independents, with their numerous advantages, eventually drove many of the giants out of the beef business.

TOWARD THE NEW DECADE – In spite of new competition, the future for Geo. A. Hormel & Company looked bright in 1969. "We're changing from a slaughterer-for-volume industry to a marketing industry," Hormel President M. B. Thompson told *Business Week* in 1968, "and there are profits to be made by the innovators."

However, these innovations would not be made through diversification or merger, Thompson declared. Hormel had numerous segments of its own business to develop and had no intention of merging with anyone. Furthermore, Hormel could resist an unfriendly takeover, thanks to The Hormel Foundation which was established in 1941 and controlled 58 percent of the company's stock in 1968.

Thompson told *Business Week* that Hormel would innovate by applying the marketing strategy first propounded by Jay Hormel who believed the company could achieve national distribution with certain items. "Consider this," added Thompson. "Ten years ago, our economic forecasting was informal at best. Now the company has strict cost controls, long-range sales planning and a five-man executive committee replacing one-man rule. We don't expect to compete with the independents on cost, but we're ahead in overall marketing ability and, unlike them, we haven't put all our eggs in one product basket."

By 1969, Hormel had many baskets. Decentralized, expanded and enriched by acquisitions, the company was ready for a new era with a new president and a new chairman.

Hormel saluted Austin and its hometown workers in a 1968 advertisement in Fortune *magazine.*

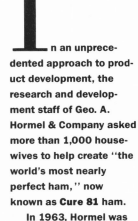

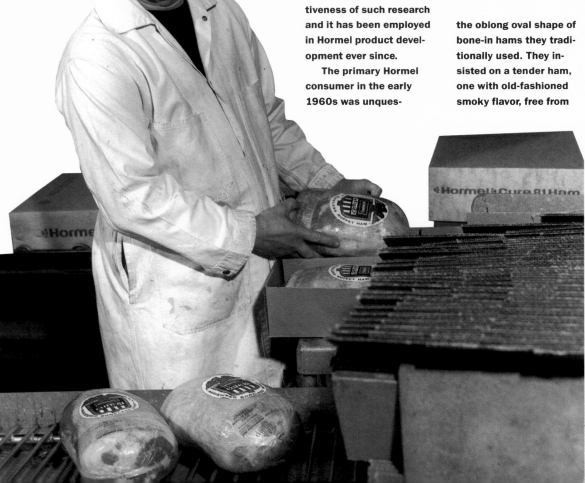

Early advertisements for Cure 81 ham pictured the product against brick ovens in the old packinghouse to emphasize Old World quality.

I**n an unprecedented approach to product development, the research and development staff of Geo. A. Hormel & Company asked more than 1,000 housewives to help create "the world's most nearly perfect ham," now known as Cure 81 ham.**

In 1963, Hormel was just beginning its transition from commodity-based meatpacker to marketing-driven food producer. The company sought consumer attitudes toward product taste, name, package design, labeling and advertising in an ambitious effort to develop a boneless, premium ham for buffets, holidays and family meals. The immediate success of **Cure 81** ham proved the effectiveness of such research and it has been employed in Hormel product development ever since.

The primary Hormel consumer in the early 1960s was unques-

tionably the American housewife, so R&D staffers interviewed homemakers in 16 areas of the country. These discriminating women generated a list of strict requirements they believed Hormel would have to meet in order to call its boneless ham "the world's most nearly perfect ham." Homemakers said it must be completely boned with the shank off and skinned to take the work out of preparing and serving it, but it must have

the oblong oval shape of bone-in hams they traditionally used. They insisted on a tender ham, one with old-fashioned smoky flavor, free from

fat inside and out and available at a reasonable cost.

Hormel product developers accepted the challenge of creating the first successful boneless ham and vowed to meet every last specification provided by consumer panels. They started by selecting the best hams and trimming excess fat with sharp, curved knives specially made for the task. The handcraftsmanship of expert meat carvers was employed — rather than automation — at the request of consumer panels.

№ 49607

Each Cure 81 ham is individually registered, inspected and guaranteed.

These panels were asked to test many variations of the product until one met the standards for flavor, shape and serving ease no other ham on the market could match. The task then fell to Hormel marketers to promote the product's high-quality image. They developed a clear package to show off

Individual craftsmanship is retained in every phase of Cure 81 ham production, from trimming and shaping to packaging.

cure|81®
celebrating 25 of doing it right
years

the leanness of the product and created a label sporting a gold eagle to symbolize early American craftsmanship. A second label across the bottom carried a registration number for the **Cure 81** ham and an unprecedented quality guarantee: if the product did not meet customer satisfaction, it would be replaced. The guarantee was signed by the Hormel curemaster who personally inspected each ham.

At first, Robert F. Gray, then president, was pleased with the new product and the packaging, but he was concerned that the early American design would make it appear "too old-fashioned." After all, Hormel was a progressive food producer. Joe C. Swedberg, former group product manager, Meat Products Group, later remembers that the name **Cure 81** was chosen to project the company's forward-thinking image. Jokingly, he says, "Most people think the name means Hormel got the product right on the 81st try, or that 81 is the name of a curing solution. Well, **Cure 81** ham actually

meant 'the ham of the future.' In 1962, the year 1981 was far away. It's almost ironic that 30 years later the product is still going strong."

When it came to advertising, Hormel captured a nostalgic mood

Hormel pays careful attention to every detail of Cure 81 ham production, including its unique gold embossed and foil stamped label.

that projected traditional quality and values of **Cure 81** ham. In early advertisements, the ham was photographed against brick ovens in the old packinghouse. Signaling the importance consumer panels placed on craftsmanship, headlines

emphasized the product's registration and guarantee.

Even though 1981 has long since passed, **Cure 81** ham is among the top-selling, premium hams in America and demand for the product continues strong.

"Just as Hormel listened to consumers to develop the product, the company has also made improvements to meet changing tastes," noted Stanley E. Kerber, group vice president of the Meat Products Group. "Although still tender, juicy and naturally smoked, today's **Cure 81** ham is leaner than ever to meet preferences of health-conscious consumers." **Cure 81** ham comes in a variety of sizes: a whole ham weighing up to 9 pounds; a one-half ham between 3½-4½ pounds, and a 2-2½ pound size for smaller families and single-person households. Recently, Hormel added "spiral-slice" bone-in **Cure 81** ham prepared in the old-fashioned way with slow cooking and curing.

Despite many technological innovations at Hormel and production in ever-increasing quantities, each **Cure 81** ham is still inspected and trimmed the old-fashioned way — with handcrafted care.

Cure 81 ham is boneless with excess fat removed, making it perfect for special holiday occasions, buffets and family meals.

Advertisements describe Cure 81 ham as the premium ham homemakers depend upon when entertaining.

"For important occasions, I depend on Cure|81 Ham...
in 9 years, I've never been disappointed!"

Dependability worth paying for.

CHAPTER SIX

People, Products and New Plants 1969-1979

"Basically, it's the people who make the organization work and get the job done."

I. J. "Jim" Holton

1969

I. J. Holton in 1982.

To serve the growing number of health-conscious consumers, Hormel voluntarily introduced nutritional and ingredient labeling on Hormel meat products in 1973.

- The company reorganizes into three groups: Prepared Foods, Meat Products and Operations.
- Sales reach an all-time high of $626 million.

1970 Hormel introduces **Curemaster** ham.
- The company builds an 85,000 square foot dry sausage plant in Algona, Iowa.
- A new advertising character named Dinty Moore first appears in national advertising for the Hormel brand.

1971 The company launches the largest advertising and promotion campaign in company history for **Cure 81** ham.
- Hormel builds a 66,000 square foot distribution plant in Seattle, Washington, and begins construction on new facilities in Shreveport, Louisiana; Oklahoma City, Oklahoma, and Fremont, Nebraska.

- Construction begins on a multimillion dollar canning and warehousing plant in Beloit, Wisconsin.
- Hormel markets **Leoni Brand** pepperoni.
- Hormel markets three new **Brown 'n Serve** sausage products.

As the world watched, Americans Neil Armstrong and Edwin Aldrin, Jr., made history in 1969 as the first astronauts to walk on the moon.

- The company's international subsidiary changes its name to Hormel International Corporation. Expansion continues in the Philippines, Okinawa and Western Europe.

1973 Hormel is the first company in the meatpacking industry to introduce nutritional and ingredient labeling on meat products.
- OPEC imposes an oil embargo on the U.S., Western Europe and Japan.

As a student, I. J. "Jim" Holton consumed countless cans of **Hormel** chili but knew nothing about the meatpacker in Austin, Minnesota. Nevertheless, he landed his first job in the company's Law Department and, 22 years later, became the sixth president. During his tenure, Holton guided Hormel through a decade of unprecedented growth and investment in equipment and facilities.

1969–1971

1969 Hormel Board Chairman R. F. Gray resigns and M. B. Thompson succeeds him as chairman of the board and chief executive officer.
- I. J. "Jim" Holton is named the sixth president of Geo. A. Hormel & Company.

President Richard M. Nixon.

1972–1974

1972 Hormel introduces **Wranglers** smoked franks.
- The company doubles the size of the Austin-based Corporate Offices.

- The Hormel vending products line, which includes 19 items, is introduced to grocery stores to meet the growing demand for convenience foods.

1974   Delicatessen sections start to appear in supermarkets, boosting Deli Department sales and paving the way for new products.
- President Richard M. Nixon resigns from office in the wake of the Watergate scandal.
- The company completes a 32,000 square foot research and development building in Austin.
- Spiraling inflation drives food prices up sharply.
- Sales reach $943 million.

Hormel met growing consumer demand for high-quality convenience foods by offering a 19-item vending products line in a 7 ½ -ounce size to grocery stores across the country.

1975-1977

1975   The company completes construction of a 90,000 square foot distribution plant in Houston, Texas.

1976   Jimmy Carter is elected the 39th president of the United States.
- Sales top $1 billion for the first time in company history.
- **Hormel** chunk ham is introduced.
- A 345,000 square foot pork processing plant is opened in Ottumwa, Iowa.

1977   A 110,000 square foot Knoxville, Iowa, dry sausage plant begins operation.

Hormel introduced Wranglers smoked franks in 1972.

- Hormel discontinues beef operations at the Austin and Fremont plants.

1978-1979

1978   Hormel and Local P-9 reach agreement that leads to the ultimate end of the incentive pay system provided for 41 years to union workers.
- Hormel introduces a distinctive new corporate logo, assuring a significant improvement in consumer recognition and product family brand identification.

- Hormel announces plans to construct a 1,089,000 square foot replacement plant in Austin.

1979   Hormel President I. J. Holton is elected chairman of the board and R. L. Knowlton succeeds him as president.
- The company begins Phase I construction of a $100 million Austin plant.
- A 100,000 square foot Davenport, Iowa, gelatin/specialized proteins plant opens.
- Sales reach $1.4 billion.

In 1979, Geo. A. Hormel & Company began Phase I construction of a $100 million state-of-the-art Austin, Minnesota, flagship plant.

In 1978, the company modified the corporate logo developed 14 years earlier by enclosing the Hormel name in black and green color bars.

In June 1978, Hormel and Local P-9 ratified an agreement that ensured construction of a replacement plant in Austin.

1979

AUSTIN DAILY HERALD

WAITING, WONDERING FINALLY ENDS

P-9 ratifies pact; new Austin plant assured

Appliance energy use to be labeled

On July 20, 1969, United
States astronauts Neil Armstrong and Edwin Aldrin, Jr., became the first
men to walk on the moon. As the Stars and Stripes waved against the
lunar landscape, America's technological superiority was visible to the entire world.

At home and abroad, however, the nation's wealth and strength could
not win the war in Vietnam. America's confidence was further shaken by
mounting evidence that President Richard M. Nixon, his staff and campaign aides were involved in a coverup of the Watergate break-in. In October 1973, the Arab oil-producing nations imposed a total ban on exports
to the United States and inexpensive, easy-to-obtain gasoline and heating
oil became a fond memory. Ten months later, in August 1974, Nixon
became the first U.S. president to resign from office.

America's distrust of the political system helped elect Democrat Jimmy
Carter to the presidency in 1976. Carter put on a sweater, turned down
his thermostat and declared the ongoing energy crisis the moral
equivalent of war. Meanwhile, America's fortunes continued to tumble.

Throughout the 1970s, inflation, unemployment and falling industrial
productivity, the decline of presidential authority, the growth of Soviet
military power and the loss of control over energy supplies plagued
the nation. Still, there was reason to hope. During America's Bicentennial
celebration, tall ships sailing into New York harbor, and a cleaned and
refurbished Statue of Liberty, reminded the country of its inimitable
heritage.

Despite troubles elsewhere in the nation and abroad, the 1970s was a
productive and profitable period for Geo. A. Hormel & Company. The
population was growing and, whether hawk or dove, Republican or
Democrat, labor or management, people needed and wanted nutritious
and convenient food products.

Culminating a 42-year career, Board Chairman Robert F. Gray resigned
in August 1969 at age 64. President M. B. Thompson succeeded Gray as
chairman of the board and chief executive officer and I. J. "Jim" Holton,
executive vice president and secretary, became the company's sixth president. Hormel also reorganized into three distinct groups and named three
new group vice presidents: Raymond J. Asp, Prepared Foods Group;
Harold B. Butler, Operations Group, and L. D. Housewright, Jr., Meat
Products Group.

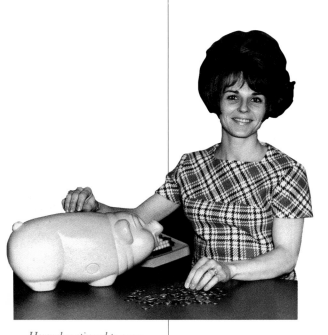

*Hormel continued to grow
and prosper despite severe
economic troubles plaguing
the nation. The company's
financial philosophy of pru-
dent saving and spending
was characterized by Diane
K. Merritt, an Austin-based
employee.*

With its newly reorganized operating groups and a new management team, Hormel set its sights on the 1970s bolstered by an excellent financial performance in 1969. In that year, net earnings reached an all-time high of $9.2 million on record sales of $626 million, a surge of $40.1 million over 1968. For the 31st consecutive year, qualified employees shared joint earnings, receiving $2.5 million. The Employee Pension Trust increased by $6.3 million, bringing the total trust to $54.2 million, and capital expenditures reached $10.5 million.

By decade's end, 1979, net sales would more than double and net earnings more than triple. Yet, the 1970s would not be without its problems. Inflation, a government-imposed price freeze, stiff competition and high labor costs topped the list. Solving them fell to the company's new president.

At age 12, Jim Holton was a member of Boy Scout Troop 12 in his hometown of Cedar Rapids, Iowa.

THE GENTLEMAN FROM CEDAR RAPIDS – Educated in the Iowa public school system, an Eagle Scout and president of his senior class, I. J. "Jim" Holton attended the University of Iowa, graduating in 1941 with a Bachelor of Arts degree in economics and a Phi Beta Kappa key. Following his military service, which included the Normandy invasion, he resumed his studies at the University of Iowa Law School and received his law degree in February 1947.

"In the spring of that year," Holton said, "I was walking across campus when a fellow asked me, 'Hey, Jim, whatcha gonna do now?' I told him I didn't know yet and he said, 'I hear they're looking for a lawyer at Hormel.'

"'Who's Hormel?' I asked.

"'A meatpacking company in Austin, Minnesota.'

"That didn't exactly charm me. But then he said, 'They make that chili in the yellow can.'

"'Boy, if they make chili that good,' I said, 'maybe I ought to check into it!'"

In May 1947, Holton joined Hormel. He was impressed with the company's concern for people. "It was demonstrated in so many ways," he says, "through their labor policy, profit sharing, employee pensions and an absolute insistence on quality manufacturing and products." As a new employee, Jim Holton observed various plant operations and helped out in sales for vacationing sales representatives. Holton was then assigned to

Holton joined Geo. A. Hormel & Company in 1947 as an attorney in the Law Department.

the Law Department under veteran George W. Ryan, secretary and assistant treasurer. Holton was elected secretary of the company in 1956 and a director in 1961. He became an executive vice president and a member of the executive committee in 1968.

Over the years, Holton gained broad experience and distinguished himself in legal work related to contract negotiations, real estate transactions, labor relations and legislation. He represented Hormel in Washington, D.C., when price controls and other new legislation affected his industry. He supervised Hormel purchasing, transportation, industrial engineering and market research. And Holton took a particular interest in corporate organization and governance, making sure that the Hormel Board of Directors included more experienced outsiders to ensure a balanced perspective on business decisions.

In August 1969, Holton says, "Thompson and Gray took me aside and said, 'Jim, we've got to do something about the next president. We thought you might try it. What do you think?'"

Holton, the master of understatement, said, "I'll give it a whirl."

EIGHT THOUSAND STRONG – A modest man with a wry sense of humor, the new Hormel president presided over a company with 8,000-plus employees working in 17 processing plants; 10 distribution plants; scores of district sales offices, and operations in several foreign countries, principally Australia, the Philippines and Okinawa. These Hormelites, as

Employees throughout the organization, including these prosciutto ham packers, contributed to company growth during the Holton era.

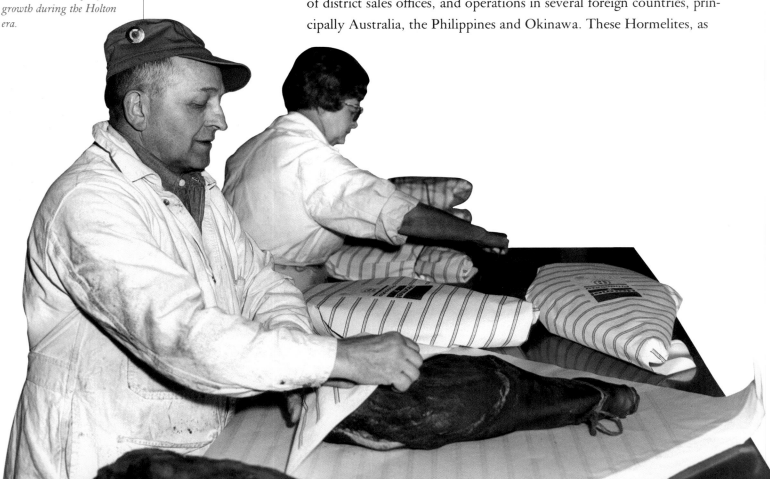

they were called, produced more than 750 meat and food products, including boneless hams, sausages, sliced bacon and luncheon meat products which were fresh, frozen, cured, smoked, cooked or canned and sold through aggressive marketing, promotion and advertising campaigns. Over the years, these same Hormelites introduced dozens of new eye-catching and taste-appealing products and took part in a decade-long surge in construction, expansion and acquisition.

Jim Holton is quick to point out that the company's success during the 1970s depended upon the efforts of many people. The days of George A. or Jay C. Hormel, entrepreneurial leaders who would "make up their minds for everyone," were long gone. "I think there is very little," Holton says, "that a person does solely on his or her own initiative. It's easy to overestimate your accomplishments. Basically, it's the people who make the organization work and get the job done."

Who were these people and why had they joined Hormel? Had they, like Jim Holton, been attracted by the chili? To find the answers, the editor of the May 1972 *Hormel NEWS* interviewed a number of representative Hormelites.

Among them, Howard L. Sewick, production employee in Austin, responded, "Hormel offered me 36 hours of work each week and guaranteed 52 paychecks a year with paid holidays and paid vacations after one year. You can't beat that. The people at the plant are always ready and willing to give you a hand when you change to a new job in a different department."

Robert L. Halvorson, Jr., a foreman in the Austin plant Sanitation Department, proved he was thoughtful about his decision: "After discussing employment with approximately 10 major companies, I chose to work for Hormel. An established company such as this offered future security. It also offered the chance to learn a great deal about the meat-packing industry."

Others told the *NEWS* they were impressed with the company's insurance coverage and retirement benefits — but, most of all, the people. As one Hormelite observed, "I thought it would be a pleasure to work with every one of them. Each person I talked to showed such enthusiasm for his job."

During Holton's tenure as president, job security, excellent wages and benefits and a friendly environment contributed to making Hormel an attractive workplace.

Growing consumer demand for Hormel products kept people employed around the clock as evidenced in this scene of the Night Shipping Department at the Los Angeles, California, distribution plant.

WORKING THE GRAVEYARD SHIFT – Hormel was also a good place to work at night. In the early 1970s, 15 percent, or about 1,300 of the company's workers, were night owls who finished their jobs at midnight or as late as 7 a.m. One such worker was LaVerne L. Michels, who had worked the graveyard shift in the **SPAM** Luncheon Meat Department at Austin for nearly 16 years.

"I like night work," Michels told *Hormel NEWS*. "The hourly rate is somewhat higher and there are advantages to being home during the day." In 1956, Michels joined the 4 p.m. to 2:30 a.m. shift as a utility man. "Sometimes," he said, "I haul cans for the bulk line from the American Can Company. Other times, I'll work on the filling machine line at the hydrostatic cooker or on the box forming line. As a utility man, I need to know every job in the department."

Utility man, chuck boner, fireman, house washer, tail cutter, stripper, secretary, president, chemist, engineer, driver, mechanic, salesperson — these Hormelites and many thousands more created the team that kept the hydrostatic cooker cooking, the products flowing and the plants and equipment running smoothly.

RUNNING WIDE OPEN – Overseeing the efficient operation of Hormel plants was the job of plant managers. At the Austin plant, R. L. "Dick" Knowlton took over that responsibility in October 1969, succeeding Harold B. Butler who advanced to group vice president, Operations. Like so many Hormel employees, Knowlton's father had worked at the plant weighing hogs. "He weighed the hogs that came in from buying stations," Knowlton recalls. "He figured the average weight so when they were processed we could compute the yield per hog."

At age 16, Knowlton started working summers at the Austin plant. After graduating from high school, he studied at the University of Colorado in Boulder, majoring in geography and economics. During the summers, Knowlton sold for Hormel. "I would relieve salesmen and take over their territories while they went on vacation," he says. "I graduated from Colorado on a Saturday and, true to the work ethic even then, I reported for my first day with Hormel on Monday morning." Knowlton started as a meat products sales representative in Denver in 1954. In 1959, he was transferred to the Austin plant as sales manager of Minnesota meat products. He later was named sales manager of the Midwest Division and, subsequently, assumed responsibility for the six sales divisions assigned to the Austin plant. He moved to the Corporate Offices in June 1967 as sales manager for the companywide Meat Products Division.

In August 1969, Knowlton became general manager of the Austin plant. "We realized the only way to make the plant profitable was to run it 'wide open,' " said Knowlton. "By building volume up, it was possible to operate profitably. This was accomplished by bringing together a team combined of sales and management professionals who, along with a great plant employee force, allowed us to take advantage of and maximize every opportunity."

Pork was profitable and so was beef — at least for a period of three years. "We wanted to save the beef operation," Knowlton remembers. "We started producing choice boneless beef, a product ahead of its time. We sold it to restaurants and retail accounts where improved margins were possible. For two years, we patched up an operation that had been un-profitable for a number of years. However, it cost about $67 a head to produce this product which ultimately was vulnerable when low-cost in-dependent operators started production with substantially reduced labor costs. We couldn't compete. Our plant was also inefficient, our product flow was poor due to the multistory design of the facility and the costs of maintenance, sanitation and refrigeration were all high. In addition, we had allowed an incentive pay system to become out of sync with the rest of the industry. All of those factors made our plant noncompetitive."

PROFITS AND PRICE FREEZES – Obsolescence of the Austin plant and the incentive system were two key issues for the company. Another challenge was a government-imposed price freeze that dampened the company's net earnings in 1972 and 1973.

In 1970, net sales increased from $626 million to $695.7 million and net earnings reached a new high of $9.9 million. Joint earnings shared with employees reached $2.7 million and the company spent just under $12 million on additions to property, plants and equipment.

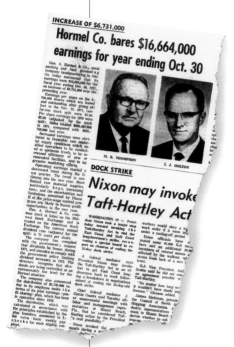

In the company's 80th year, net earnings reached $16.5 million, or $3.50 per share. Eligible employees shared $3.7 million in joint earnings — thanks to efficient operations and aggressive marketing.

*Marketing of Dinty
Moore beef stew featured a
thumbprint of the fictional
character, "Dinty Moore,"
who appeared in product
advertising and promotion.*

*In this heart-warming
advertising campaign,
Hormel directed attention
to the popularity of hot dogs
among children of all ages.*

During the company's 80th anniversary in 1971, sales dropped to $686.5 million due to government and competitive pressures that lowered prices. Despite the downturn in sales, net earnings soared to $16.5 million, thanks to plentiful livestock, increased efficiency of the company's new or renovated facilities and aggressive marketing efforts. For the 33rd consecutive year, eligible employees shared joint earnings totaling $3.7 million. Each share of common stock earned $3.50 and stockholders approved a two-for-one stock split, increasing the total number of outstanding common shares to more than 4.7 million.

Between 1972-75, sales continued their upward thrust, leaping from $719.7 million in 1972 to $943.2 million in 1974 and nearly reaching the one billion mark at $995.6 million in 1975. But, during the period, net earnings tumbled from a high of $16.5 in 1971 to $7.6 million in 1972 and then dropped even lower to $7.2 million in 1973.

As James A. "Jim" Silbaugh, then vice president of the Grocery Products Division, explains, "Net earnings were down because the government, in an attempt to curb inflation, imposed price controls on a variety of products. Once Hormel set its ceiling price for an item, we couldn't raise the price except in specialized cases. The farmers, however, didn't have price controls. They could sell livestock at whatever price the market could bear. It hurt our margins and net earnings dropped accordingly."

When the government lifted its price regulations, net earnings for Hormel bounced back to an all-time high of $16.9 million in 1974, then rounded off at $12.9 million the following year.

PRODUCTS AND PROMOTIONS MULTIPLY – What accounted for the company's hefty sales in an era marked by war, Watergate and an oil embargo? An array of Hormel products bolstered by advertising, promotional campaigns and an ambitious salesforce. During the 1970s, an assortment of new products, many of them line extensions geared for specific market segments, was introduced. For example, in 1970, L. D. Housewright, Jr., group vice president, and his Meat Products Group, introduced the **Curemaster** ham which weighed 1½-2¼ pounds, ideal for four to six servings and aimed at "making ham an everyday family meal." The Group also introduced seven exact-weight, vacuum-packed dry sausages in new, smaller, more convenient packages. Also during 1970, Hormel upgraded its wiener production capabilities and promoted its hot dogs with a "Not Too Spicy For Kids" theme. Once again, Hormel teamed up with the National Football League in a new nationwide promotion called "Kitchen Quarterbacks," including advertisements in *Life, McCall's, Ebony* and *Better Homes and Gardens*, in-store displays and local advertising.

CANNED FOODS AND A BRIGHT SALESMAN – Like the Meat Products Group, the Prepared Foods Group, led by Raymond J. Asp, group vice president, was busy testing, introducing and marketing new products. The Grocery Products Division test marketed smoke flavored **SPAM** luncheon meat and **SPAM** luncheon meat with cheese chunks, both offshoots of the famous best-seller, **SPAM** luncheon meat. A new canned ham also debuted – the **EXL** ham, extra lean and boneless, topped with a sugar and spice glaze and baked in its own juices. To the canned chili line, Hormel added an "extra hot" version in 7½- and 15-ounce cans. And to increase sales of the **Dinty Moore** line of canned foods, Hormel created a new salesman named "Dinty Moore," a lumberjack with a red watch cap, blond hair, red suspenders and a robust look. The new character appeared on day- and nighttime network television and in national magazines and trade publications.

ENDEAVORS NATIONAL AND INTERNATIONAL – In 1970, the Industrial Products and Foodservice Divisions also introduced new products, including four new hot food vending items – **Dinty Moore** Brunswick stew, **Dinty Moore** 3-meat mulligan stew, **Hormel** chili mac and **Hormel** extra hot chili. Hormel created a casserole vending line and also added three new taste treats to its frozen entree family – lasagna, fillet of haddock in butter sauce and a Mexican-style lasagna.

Internationally, Geo. A. Hormel *&* Company was breaking new ground. In 1970, the company signed an agreement creating a new joint venture pairing a subsidiary of Hormel with J. M. Schneider Limited of Kitchener, Ontario, Canada. Schneider-Hormel produced and marketed a complete line of canned meat products and dry sausages for distribution only in Canada.

In Australia, Hormel-Cerebos exceeded its year's projections while the company's Okinawa joint venture, First Enterprise Corporation, began producing **Mary Kitchen** corned beef hash. Hormel also established the Okinawa Premier Food Sales Company to market food products on the island.

Curemaster ham was introduced in 1970 for the convenience of consumers preferring smaller portions.

In 1972, product code dating identified peak freshness periods of selected wieners, bacon, luncheon meat and cooked ham products.

Hormel was the first meat-packer to introduce nutritional and ingredient labeling of products.

*FULL FLAVOR
7 DAYS BEYON*

MEETING TOMORROW'S NEEDS – These were the product introductions – 21 altogether – in the opening year of the decade. Throughout the 1970s, new products would arrive at a similarly rapid pace. Bringing them into the world was the job of various Hormel groups working together.

Richard E. Goldstrand was manager of applied research and process development in the company's Research and Development Division. "R&D always worked hand-in-hand with marketing and production," explained Goldstrand. "Among marketing, advertising and production, you could hardly tell where an idea came from. Together, we worked out the product basics, then devised the production process and did initial tests to measure shelf life and product stability. It would take three or four years, sometimes more, to bring a product to market.

"R&D also helped develop products for the vending business in the single-serving can," noted Goldstrand. "If it caught on in vending, we would sell it in the retail market. I remember years spent developing what is called the retort pouch, a packaging innovation for foods like pork chops and hamburgers. We had several U.S. Army contracts for the pouch but couldn't get the packaging to fly further than that. Later, when microwaveable foods came along, we hauled it off the shelf again and it became the precursor to the **Top Shelf** main dish entrees packaging technique."

"We weren't looking for a new **SPAM** luncheon meat," says Jim Holton, concerning the company's R&D strategy in the '70s. "That is, we didn't expect to find 'the' product for the era. Instead, we worked hard to develop new line extensions, like **SPAM** Spread, and we moved regional foods into national distribution wherever it was feasible."

In addition to extending product lines and helping to create new products, the Research and Development Division, which grew from 25 to about 70 people by 1979, attacked a variety of other issues. "Food safety was always paramount," Goldstrand said. "We were continually working to improve shelf life and maintain freshness. We endorsed the Food Council of America's campaign to increase nutritional awareness among American families and to encourage consumers to choose well-balanced, nutritious meals. In 1972, we began code dating our products for freshness and, in 1973, Hormel became the first company in the meatpacking industry to introduce nutritional and ingredient labeling on its products."

DEC 21

THE CONSTANT QUEST – The company's concern for nutritional labeling, code dating and product improvement did not start in 1970, however. The quest for quality began nearly 80 years earlier with George A. Hormel, always a stickler for cleanliness and quality. "What you will get out of this business," he wrote to one of his employees in 1923, "depends wholly on how much you put into it. . . . Don't expect big results unless you are personally analyzing your work to see how you can bring it up to a higher standard."

The Hormel quality quest, an ideal bred into the culture of the company, was highlighted numerous times over the years. The September 1970 issue of *Hormel NEWS*, for example, congratulated employees for their dedication, craftsmanship and enthusiasm which exemplified the Hormel quality process. Among many singled out for quality service were Bonita J. Allen, Arlene F. Hemphill and Garret L. Loverink in the Sliced Bacon Department; Harold P. Mandler and Maynard G. Weis in the Gelatin Department, and Harold L. Gomer and Ronald D. Sunkin in the Pork Processing Department.

Quality also meant cleanliness at Hormel. George A. Hormel's great-uncle Jay was fond of telling his nephew that clean meat stayed fresh for days while dirty meat spoiled before your eyes. In the 1970s, the crew in the Hormel Sanitation Department kept the plant spotless.

"Cleanliness is a way of life," the Rules of Sanitation brochure stated. The generals in the war who ensured optimum company cleanliness were members of the Corporate Sanitation Committee, including John W. Trollen, director of sanitation; Dr. Tracy E. Barber, medical director; Jim Holton, president; Frank M. Brown, director of engineering; Richard E. Goldstrand, manager of applied research and process development, and Robert P. Dudley, director of research and development.

"We expect our employees to follow these rules," said Trollen, without equivocation. "Not once in a while, but every day and every hour."

"The white-glove Navy admiral inspection technique," Dudley added, "which I remember from inspections during World War II, is still an effective method of determining the general level of cleanliness in the plants." To keep everyone on their toes, Dudley explained, "any sanitation committee member can take a survey of any facility at any time." Swabs in this case were not Navy personnel or their mops but puffs of cotton used to test bacteria counts. Low counts meant high marks for Hormel cleanliness.

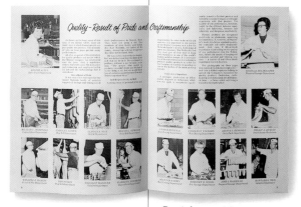

Special recognition was given to employees who maintained the high-quality standards established years earlier by George A. Hormel.

Dorothy K. Stern, in the Austin Dry Sausage Department, was among several Hormel employees recognized for quality efforts in 1970.

Announcing those high marks was the job of the *Hormel NEWS*. In the August 1977 issue, numerous employees were identified for their dedication to the "quality touch," including John W. Dunton, Teresa P. Jennings and Margaret R. Roberts in Atlanta; Gerald C. Vondenkamp in Fremont; Terry G. Gill in Houston, and Lloyd W. Peacock in Mitchell. "A quality touch," the *NEWS* preached, "has been largely responsible for the company's success over the past 85 years. How well Hormel does in the next 85 years will depend on a continuing quality emphasis by all employees."

In its 85th year, employees throughout the organization were reminded that quality was the fundamental reason for continued success.

A PLETHORA OF PRODUCTS – The success of Hormel also depended on its ability to provide a rich and varied assortment of products and to bring them to market and the public's attention. In 1971, the company launched its biggest advertising and sales promotion to date for **Cure 81** ham with commercials on prime time TV shows, large display ads in newspapers, radio spots, consumer and trade magazine ads, point-of-purchase displays and holiday promotions. The result? More **Cure 81** hams moved out of stores and into homes than ever before. Also gaining a national presence that year was the **Curemaster** ham, smoke flavored **SPAM** luncheon meat and **SPAM** luncheon meat with cheese chunks. These products were marketed heavily through the media with special tie-ins and related promotions. In 1971, **EXL** ham was distributed in key regions as an upscale, premium ham developed to complement the company's first canned ham introduced 45 years earlier.

Hormel introduced and test marketed **Brown 'n Serve** sausage, Polish sausage and Italian sausage in 1972. These **Brown 'n Serve** brand name products were variations of old sausage favorites with added cooking convenience. Also debuting in 1972 were **Wranglers** smoked franks, a larger coarse-ground wiener for adults.

Despite the Arab oil embargo and the government's price freeze in 1973, the company added **Lumberjack** beef roll to its expanding line of dry sausages and heavily marketed its **Cure 81** ham, **Range Brand** bacon, **Black Label** bacon, **Hormel** wieners and **Little Sizzlers** pork sausage.

Hormel chili received similar promotional and merchandising attention with extensive print advertising and commercials that emphasized this "fun-for-all-ages" product. To cost-conscious consumers, who now found themselves waiting in line to buy expensive gasoline that jumped in price every time they filled up, Hormel advertisements touted **SPAM** luncheon meat – "A lot of meat, but not a lot of money."

Nineteen seventy-four was a banner year both in net earnings and sales, thanks in part to the company's increased production capacity. Expanded facilities in Austin and Fort Dodge, Iowa, helped Hormel begin national distribution of **EXL** ham. The return of the "deli," a small service section tucked away in supermarkets, also strengthened sales. To help retailers promote this fast-growing phenomenon, born on the East Coast, Hormel provided kits of colorful in-store materials based on four themes – Fiesta Italiano, Old Time Deli Days, Super Sandwich Time and Polish Festival. To these delicatessen sections, Hormel brought many existing products and introduced several new ones, including five new meat loaf items – olive, deluxe, old-fashioned, Dutch and barbecue – plus cervelot, thuringer and beef summer sausage. By the end of 1975, Hormel was selling more than 50 products in America's supermarket delis.

Wranglers smoked franks made its market debut in 1972 using a Western theme.

Self-serve and in-service delicatessen departments gained popularity in American supermarkets in the 1970s. This new shopping phenomenon helped boost sales and new product development at Geo. A. Hormel & Company.

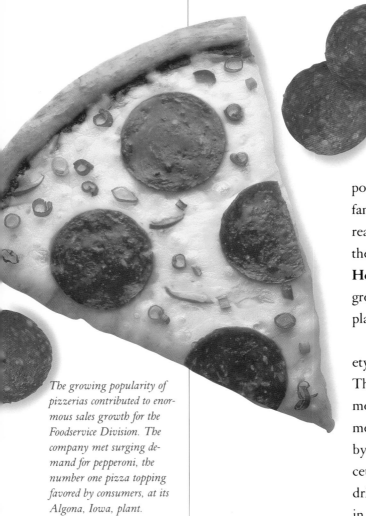

The growing popularity of pizzerias contributed to enormous sales growth for the Foodservice Division. The company met surging demand for pepperoni, the number one pizza topping favored by consumers, at its Algona, Iowa, plant.

Short Orders

*Hormel extended its **Short Orders** individual canned servings line which appealed largely to the growing number of convenience-oriented consumers.*

In the Prepared Foods Group, Hormel increased its line of single-portion entrees called **Short Orders** individual canned servings. This family consisted of chili no beans, sloppy Joes, beef tamales and 21 other ready-to-serve items. Corn dogs, batter-wrapped wieners on a stick, joined the company's repertoire of foods while America's mania for pizza made **Hormel** pepperoni an enormously popular dry sausage topping. Soon, growing pepperoni production would turn the company's Algona, Iowa, plant into "The Pepperoni Capital of the World."

Between 1971-75, the Foodservice Division continued to develop a variety of products for the rapidly growing "eat-away-from-home" market. These included single-purchase vending items and frozen entrees for motels and hotels, restaurants, carry-out services and cafeterias. In the meantime, the Industrial Products Division diverted meat proteins and byproducts for beef stocks, gravies and sauces as well as for the pharmaceutical and cosmetic industries. Gelatin desserts, puddings and instant drink mixes were Hormel-manufactured products that helped swell sales in the early and mid-1970s. Red Owl, Super Valu and other major grocery retailers purchased private label gelatin desserts manufactured by the company. The market potential was so favorable that Hormel began planning for a separate processing facility which eventually became the Davenport, Iowa, gelatin/specialized proteins plant in 1979.

THIS LITTLE PIGGY WENT TO MARKET – While each of the company's operating groups and divisions was producing and marketing new products for an expanding and changing market, Hormel buyers were busy bringing home the bacon. A typical buyer was Donald W. Torgerson, who handled about $1.5 million in livestock purchases every year. "To spend that much money," said Torgerson, "you have to be self-confident – confident you can assess the quality of the livestock you're buying and keep both the seller and your company happy. A buyer is also an agricultural specialist. He answers the farmers' questions on boar selection, feeding and nutrition. The more a buyer can teach the farmer, the better the product and the greater the likelihood he will call Hormel when his hogs are ready for market."

When the livestock arrived at Hormel, the chuck boner, fireman, casing stripper, plate boner, house washer and sawdust man, among others, were ready to swing into action. Orville C. Stoelk, chuck boner, removed meat from the beef chuck. Fireman Carlton E. Thomson didn't put out fires, he made them: "I'm responsible for cooking the product properly while it's in the smokehouse," he explained. "I do that by monitoring the temperature and keeping an eye on the product." Sawdust man Marvin C. Koch assisted Thomson. "My job," he said, "is to feed the proper mixture of sawdust and water into the smokehouse to generate the right amount of smoke." Keeping the smokehouse clean, inside and out, was the job of house washer Leonard Meyers. The house washer uses a cleaning solution and very hot water to maintain smokehouse cleanliness.

At the other end of production, the casing stripper readied wieners for packaging. "It's my job to remove the artificial casing from the wiener," said operator Grace E. Nybo. "I adjust the steam level and make sure the knives of the stripper are properly set."

KEEPING 'EM ROLLING: GOODS AND TRUCKS – As these men and women kept the company's production lines running, another group of employees made sure the products reached the marketplace. In the 1970s, many items manufactured at the Austin plant were delivered by truck. Delivery trips began in the Austin garage which, in 1975, employed 27 people, including 18 drivers, several mechanics and servicemen and a spotter serviceman, night clerk/dispatcher, driver foreman and mechanic foreman.

A team of Hormel specialists is needed to bring products into the marketplace. Among the many who share this vital role are (left to right) livestock buyer, smokehouse operator, packaging line employee and truck driver.

Denver P. Daily, manager of transportation, purchasing and sanitation, explained there were two groups of drivers: "Our 10 territory drivers deliver products directly to the customers' stores and make about 30 stops each day on routes as long as 450 miles round-trip.

"The other eight drivers make regular trips to Fremont, Fort Dodge, St. Cloud, Minneapolis and other destinations within a 300-mile radius of Austin. They haul over-the-road trailers that are often modified for special loads. One trailer has a built-in conveyer for loading and unloading product. It's used primarily for the run between Austin and the Owatonna Canning Company where **Dinty Moore** beef stew is produced. The

DELICATESSEN

*Advertising for selected dry sausage varieties featured this Italian delicatessen proprietor displaying Hormel proscuitto ham, **Di Lusso** genoa and other consumer favorites.*

Well-trained salespeople, dedicated to moving Hormel products into grocery stores nationwide, were vital to the company's success.

W. A. Lampe (right), part of the Hormel distribution salesforce in Los Angeles, calls on his customer, Albert Vera, owner of the Sorrento Market in Culver City, California.

trailer carries approximately 300,000 pounds of product each day and, with the conveyer, can be loaded or unloaded in about a minute and a half."

While Hormel drivers were efficient and safe, they also needed to be courteous. "In some cases," Daily explained, "the driver is the only company representative the retail customer sees on a regular basis. The driver must make a good impression when delivering his products. He's a salesman, too."

A WHOLE LOT OF SELLING GOING ON – Full-time selling, of course, was the domain of the Hormel salesforce which had grown considerably since the late 1890s when John Hormel, George's brother, rode a bicycle across the countryside taking orders for their new sausage product. But whatever the year, 1891 or 1975, the job was the same. Whether the products were canned foods marketed by grocery products, frozen entrees distributed by foodservice, fresh and processed meat products sold by route car and distribution plant salespeople, bulk and vacuum-packed sausages offered by the Dry Sausage Division, or spices and gelatin desserts available through the Industrial Products Division, the mission was clear: "Ultimately the salesman's goal," a *Hormel NEWS* article stated, "is to put every Hormel product in every store in every country in which the company operates."

An ambitious goal. But the Hormel sales staff was ready. "Hormel had 150 to 200 salespeople," says Jim Silbaugh, "devoted to the sale of grocery products. None of the other companies — Wilson, Armour, Morrell — concentrated their people the way we did. We trained our salesforce and paid them well with the best compensation package in the industry."

To sharpen their talents, Hormel salespeople attended seminars and workshops conducted by corporate personnel. They studied company history and sales and management philosophies and goals. In classroom sessions, they learned about markups and the mechanics of pricing which helped them analyze costs on a shelf space basis.

In addition to selling, Hormel salespeople were responsible for service, building supermarket displays and preparing advertisements for local newspapers. The salesforce was the link, sometimes the only link, between Hormel, its customers and consumers.

To keep the salesforce challenged, Hormel introduced numerous contests. One year, for example, meat products district managers, sales representatives and distribution plant sales managers competed for top honors in a campaign dubbed "Brandwagon." To win, salespeople had to meet or exceed established tonnage quotas and sell a variety of products. After two months, the overall winner was John T. Rooney of the Twin Cities who amassed one of the highest personal tonnage quotas and personal sales gains.

N. D. "Bill" Gahagen, then vice president of Distribution Plants and Route Car Sales, said, "Our salespeople experienced nine weeks of tough selling in what appears to be the most competitive situation they've ever faced. Their record-breaking performance proves that the Hormel salesforce ranks among the best in the world."

Demonstrating the wisdom of Gahagen's words, sales surpassed the billion dollar mark for the first time in company history in 1976. They rose to $1.1 billion in 1977, reached $1.2 billion the following year and topped $1.4 billion in 1979. While sales were strong, net earnings in 1975 fell to $12.9 million from a high of $16.9 million the previous year; rose to $14.4 million in the nation's Bicentennial year, and then climbed to a record high of $21.5 million in 1977. Earnings slipped slightly to $19.5 million in 1978 as if to gain momentum for the prodigious leap that occurred in 1979 when, with a boost from inflation, earnings jumped to $30 million.

As Jim Holton recalls, "The fluctuations in net earnings between 1975-79 were due to a number of factors. In 1975, for example, pork supplies decreased and plants were operated at less than optimum levels. Livestock prices and other costs soared because of inflation. That put a crimp in our earnings. In 1977, net earnings rose thanks to newer, more efficient facilities, aggressive marketing and increased pork supplies at lower prices. However, earnings declined in 1978 because livestock supplies were short while accompanying consumer demand pushed wholesale prices upward. We were riding a roller coaster in the '70s but streamlining our plants and building new ones certainly helped smooth out the ride. That's why the company performed so well in 1979."

PROLOGUE TO PROGRESS: NEW PRODUCTS – Salesmanship was one factor that contributed to solid sales and earnings growth in the 1970s. Other key factors included the company's continued efforts in marketing and advertising, its new, people-pleasing products and ongoing construction of new, efficient plants.

Sales seminars educated and challenged the Hormel salesforce to achieve record-breaking performances.

*Hormel chunk ham was
introduced in 1977 with an
advertising theme aimed at
demonstrating its versatility.*

In 1976, **Little Sizzlers** pork sausage improved its popularity with a significant increase in sales and market share. **Wranglers** smoked franks, introduced in 1972, also enjoyed sales increases and Hormel began test marketing smoke flavored chunk ham in a can that was strategically placed next to tuna fish in supermarkets.

"The idea," says Stuart H. "Tate" Lane, former director of marketing, Grocery Products Division, "was to create a ham product that could be used like tuna fish. You could serve it cold in a salad, dice it for sandwiches or put it in casseroles. The merchandising theme for chunk ham emphasized its tuna likeness. We used to say, 'It does everything tuna does except swim.'" Chunk ham went national in 1977, followed by chunk turkey, chunk chicken and chunk salmon.

Another significant product introduction in the late 1970s was Deviled **SPAM** luncheon meat, introduced originally as **SPAM** Spread. Network TV, newspaper and magazine advertisements in *Reader's Digest, McCall's, True Story, Woman's Day* and *Family Circle* explained the name change and provided helpful serving hints.

New also were cocktail smokies and **Pillow Pack** pepperoni. The Perma Fresh luncheon meats line added smoked cooked ham and pepper loaf. Italian sausage, a heavily spiced, smoked product, achieved national

*Dinty Moore beef stew
went head-to-head with a
chunky competitor and won
in this visual comparison.*

distribution in 1978. Smoked sausage made its appearance that year, along
with cocktail wieners and cocktail smokie cheezers. Honey loaf and pepper loaf joined the family of other popular loaf items which could be
found in supermarket deli sections.

Throughout the period, the Grocery Products Division promoted its
products with spot television and radio commercials and advertisements
in national magazines and newspapers. Hormel supported the introduction of chunk chicken and chunk turkey, for example, with four-color,
full-page ads in major women's magazines and newspapers, spot television
commercials and a direct-mail coupon campaign.

"In 1978," Tate Lane says, "**Dinty Moore** beef stew had the biggest
promotional program in its history. We hit the air with a new 30-second
commercial on network television. The theme was 'The meaty meal that
outchunks chunky soups.' We chose to challenge major soup companies
that were introducing chunk-style soups."

An expanded product lineup offered by the Food-service Division competed for a share of a $100 billion market in 1979.

Meanwhile, estimated annual sales in the foodservice market had
reached more than $100 billion. To improve its presence in that growing
market segment, Hormel added new items to its frozen entrees line which,
in 1979, numbered 42. The latest additions — stuffed peppers and stuffed
cabbage rolls — were marketed in a form allowing foodservice operators to
add their own special sauces. At the same time, the Industrial Products
Division began operations in its new multimillion dollar gelatin/specialized
proteins plant in Davenport, Iowa. The plant produced pharmaceutical
and food-grade gelatin used in such diverse products as oral medication
capsules, dessert, pudding and cocoa mixes, protein supplements for diets,
photographic film coatings, carbonless business paper, dishwashing
detergents and shampoos.

FROM SOUTH OF THE BORDER TO DOWN UNDER – "Our company continues
to have a modest but meaningful involvement in international operations," Jim Holton reported to stockholders in 1979. "The activities conducted under the umbrella of the Hormel International Corporation include imports, exports, joint ventures and licensing agreements."

By the end of the decade, Hormel International Corporation also consisted of Vista International Packaging, Inc., with facilities in Kenosha,
Wisconsin, for importing sausage casings from overseas for the U.S.
market.

The company's joint ventures abroad included investments in First
Enterprise, Ltd., in Okinawa and Stefanutti Hormel, S.A., in the
Dominican Republic. Hormel also owned a 20 percent interest in Pure

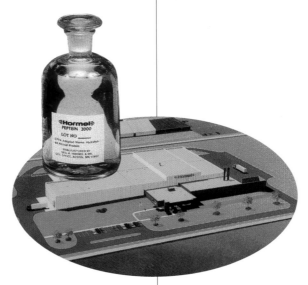

In 1979, operations began in a highly mechanized gelatin/specialized proteins plant in Davenport, Iowa, that manufactured pharmaceutical and food-grade gelatin for a wide variety of food and industrial product applications.

Foods Corporation in the Philippines. Each joint venture involved agreements that provided technical assistance and the use of company trademarks. In addition, Hormel licensed several important trademarks to Blayney Meat Products Pty. Ltd., a member of the Huttons Group in Australia, and the **SPAM** luncheon meat trademark to Lovell & Christmas (Northern) Ltd., in England.

"Our strategy," said Jim Holton, "for opening new international markets was tentative during the 1970s. We didn't have a lot of money to invest in overseas projects because numerous capital investments were being made at home. We were hopeful, however, that one of our joint ventures would take off; if it did, we were ready to devote more time and money to it."

Although business through Hormel International Corporation was modest in the 1970s, aggressive programs introduced by international brokers would accelerate overseas growth for Hormel in the next decade, creating record sales, tonnage volumes and revenues. Licensing and/or joint venture arrangements continued in the Philippines, Great Britain and Australia and new agreements were signed in the Republic of China, the Republic of Korea and Panama.

SPENDING WITH A CAPITAL $ – Throughout the 1970s, Geo. A. Hormel & Company was providing the American consumer with a variety of new products. The company's trend watchers could see traditional family eating patterns changing: women were joining the workforce in increasing numbers and the population of young adults and the elderly was growing rapidly.

To capitalize on these demographic changes, enlarge production capacity, improve the economy and efficiency of its operations and provide products at competitive prices in an inflationary era, Hormel launched a building boom that was unprecedented in company history. Between 1967-82, Hormel spent more than $300 million on new plant construction and capital improvements.

In the West, Hormel built new plants in Seattle, Washington, and Fresno, California. In Stockton, California, Hormel purchased and modernized a food canning plant. In the Southwest, the company built processing and/or distribution facilities in Oklahoma City, Oklahoma; Dallas, Houston and San Antonio, Texas, and acquired a frozen food

plant in Fort Worth. In the Southeast, new plants were constructed in
New Orleans and Shreveport, Louisiana; Atlanta and Albany, Georgia,
and Orlando, Florida. In the Midwest, Hormel built plants in Beloit,
Wisconsin; Algona, Davenport, Knoxville and Ottumwa, Iowa, and
Austin, Minnesota.

To meet burgeoning production demands, Hormel soon found it
necessary to expand many of its older plants and some of its newly constructed ones as well. In 1971, the Fremont plant received a 65,000 square
foot addition to accommodate increased grocery products demands and,
three years later, another 17,500 square feet boosted its smoked meats
manufacturing capacity. In Algona, Hormel enlarged the existing structure by 30,000 square feet and, in Knoxville, added 21,000 square feet to
its dry sausage facility.

Expansion also enhanced the Beloit grocery products plant; the Atlanta
meat products/grocery products plant, and the Stockton grocery products facility. In 1972, Hormel doubled the size of the Austin Corporate
Offices with completion of a 38,000 square foot addition and, the following year, expanded its Research and Development Center by 32,000
square feet.

THE COWS COME HOME – Geo. A. Hormel & Company was investing in
the present. Technology was changing the industry and now it revolutionized business. The meat industry had undergone dramatic changes
since the days when food processing plants were first built. Those huge,
inefficient multistoried plants were replaced by modern, single-story
facilities that used technologies unheard of 10 years earlier.

At Hormel, dramatic changes could not be forestalled. Management
scrutinized the bottom line and that line, especially in beef operations,
ran heavily into red ink. As a result, in 1977, Hormel discontinued beef
operations at the Austin and Fremont plants.

President Jim Holton explained this difficult decision in the *Hormel
NEWS*: "We were unable to operate these plants on a break-even basis.
Our losses were substantial over quite a number of years; this was
especially true in Austin. Not only were the losses large but they were increasing every year. A substantial segment of our competition in the beef
industry [the independent beef packers] has been operating with newer,
more efficient plants with considerably lower base rates and, even more
significant, lower unit labor costs."

*In the period between
1967-82, Hormel invested
more than $300 million in
new plant facilities and
equipment – by far the
largest sum in its history.*

*Fierce competition from low-
cost nonunion independent
operators forced Hormel to
discontinue beef operations
in 1977.*

You're running late on the way to a summer picnic. You hop in the shower, wash and condition your hair, then smooth on some moisturizer and a touch of sunblock before throwing on your clothes. Moving into the kitchen, you put film in your camera, swallow a vitamin capsule and grab a handful of gummi bears to eat on the way. Then you pull the lime-flavored gelatin dessert out of the refrigerator and dash to your car.

An average scenario, right? Of the 10 things accomplished in those few minutes, eight of them were achieved with the aid of a single product—gelatin.

Gelatin, a meat by-product manufactured by the Industrial Products Division, is found in countless products used everyday by millions of people throughout the world. In fact, Hormel gelatin is used in such diverse products as oral medication capsules, sugar and sugar-free desserts, marshmallows, yogurt, gummi-type candies, protein diet supplements, photographic film coatings, carbonless business paper, dish detergents, shampoos, conditioners, moisturizing skin creams and other hair and skin care products.

Hormel began gelatin manufacturing at the Austin, Minnesota, plant in 1947 to make use of

continued on next page

TO BE OR NOT TO BE (IN AUSTIN), THAT IS THE QUESTION – Austin's inefficient plant, in part dating back to the company's earliest days, and the employee incentive system created significantly higher unit labor costs for Hormel. Dick Knowlton, general manager, and his management team sought to operate the plant at a profit. "The sales operation was part of the plant," Knowlton says. "Being a salesperson, I wanted to sell everything we produced. And we did." The great team Knowlton described included Kenneth O. Dahlgren, Denver P. Daily, Elroy F. "Al" Zehner, Samuel House, Joseph A. Carmody and James J. Irwin. "The strategy worked," continued Knowlton. "Between 1969-72, we were profitable. But, in 1973, we broke even and, in 1974, ran into the red. The plant just could not handle the load in a cost-effective way."

"The question was," says Jim Holton, "what should we do with the Austin plant? Close it down? Keep it running? If so, at what level? The plant was a most important factor to the people of Austin. The company's roots were here. In 1975, we asked Dick Knowlton, group vice president of operations and a member of the Hormel Board, to study the plant to see what it would take to bring it up to the productive level desired. We identified all the projects and all the production capabilities needed. To straighten out the inefficiencies, to modernize the plant to industry standards and meet existing federal safety and pollution control requirements would have cost the company $35 million. Dick presented this report to the Board of Directors. Then he recommended that we phase out the plant and build a new one. 'If we pour all that money into the old plant,' he told the Board, 'we'll *still* have an old plant.'"

In 1975, the Hormel Board was composed of I. J. Holton, president; R. L. Knowlton, group vice president, Operations Group; L. D. Housewright, Jr., group vice president, Meat Products Group; Raymond J. Asp, group vice president, Prepared Foods Group; E. C. Alsaker, vice president and treasurer; Bruce Corey, vice president, engineering; Robert M. Gill, vice president, personnel and industrial relations, and Robert F. Potach, vice president and controller. The Board had four nonemployee members, including Elmer L. Andersen, former Minnesota governor and chairman of H. B. Fuller Company; Herrell F. DeGraff, agricultural economist and former president of the American Meat Institute; Donald R. Grangaard, president and chief executive officer of First Bank System, Inc., and Geraldine M. Joseph, contributing editor, *Minneapolis Tribune*.

The decision the Board had to make was a difficult one. Historical considerations argued strongly for a new plant in Austin. But the only way the company could justify the cost of a new plant was to eliminate the time-honored incentive pay system.

"Hormel was paying the highest wages in the industry," Holton recalls. "In addition, we had the incentive system. In theory, the system shouldn't cost the company anything because our workers produced more. But our situation had eroded over time to the point where the wages of our people – those not at machine-controlled operations – averaged 87 percent above the top rates in the industry. Unfortunately, the company was not getting anything like 87 percent more production. The only way to justify the cost of a new plant was to eliminate the incentive system. That was the major hurdle."

A THREE-YEAR TUG-OF-WAR – What management considered a hurdle, union employees considered a birthright. And to many it was. Incentive pay, Jay C. Hormel's farsighted program, had been part of the corporate culture since the late 1930s. To union workers, incentive pay meant extra income for hard, laborious work. To management, incentive pay had the same meaning for many years. But by the mid-1970s, the system had become unrealistic. "Each time management established new work standards," says David A. Larson, vice president of human resources, "the new standard had to provide an opportunity for workers to earn their previous incentive pay. Modernization and labor-saving equipment solved some problems for the short term. But the union had negotiated a machine allowance amounting to a 35 percent bonus on top of base wages for those workers who lost their incentive pay opportunity because of automation. We simply couldn't afford to pay those kinds of bonuses above an already top industry rate and build a new plant."

To work out their differences, labor and management began bargaining in October 1975. For a period of many years, relations between management and labor had been good. Both sides had developed an informal bargaining arrangement that ensured minimized friction. Disputes rarely progressed beyond the grievance stage. Frank W. Schultz, president of Local 9 of the United Packinghouse Workers of America for more than two decades, and Fayette W. Sherman, Hormel vice president of industrial relations, had together negotiated many labor contracts.

By 1975, Schultz's role had been assumed by Richard Arnold and Sherman's by Robert M. Gill. Both knew the history they inherited – virtually every one of Schultz and Sherman's agreements had been ratified by rank and file. Therefore, when Jim Holton announced plans to construct a

GELATIN

continued from previous page

pork skins remaining from bacon and canned ham production. Nearly 50 years later, Hormel ranks among the largest producers in the United States, serving a rapidly expanding world market with specialized sterile gelatin of the highest grade.

In 1979, Hormel replaced the Austin-based facility with a new gelatin/specialized proteins plant in Davenport, Iowa. In operation for 12 years, the 117,000 square foot facility is the largest, most technologically advanced plant of its kind, manufacturing pharmaceutical and food-grade gelatin for companies throughout the United States, Europe and the Far East.

Frank W. Schultz, president of Local 9 of the United Packinghouse Workers of America and a veteran labor negotiator.

*Hormel employees over-
whelmingly rejected a company contract proposal July
27, 1977, in voting held at
Riverside Arena, Austin,
Minnesota.*

$100 million state-of-the-art plant in Austin — if the union and the com-
pany could negotiate new work rules and consent to the elimination of
the incentive system — Austinites and Hormelites alike expected Arnold
and Gill to reach terms quickly.

The union, however, was not prepared to scrap its treasured incentive
system and the company was not willing to replace the Austin plant
without a new labor agreement. Holton recalls meeting with the union's
president, a union economist and the business agent at the start of the
talks. "We were a small group and it was a short meeting. They proposed
a move into the new plant with the existing agreement, believing the
company would have all the advantages of a modern plant. The
economist sought to explain to us why this would be a good decision. I
replied, 'We're people of goodwill but we can't build that plant and move
the incentive system into it.' They could not accept a proposal to
eliminate the system; the meeting ended. Negotiations continued some
weeks later."

A January 1976 agreement deadline came and went. In June 1977, the
union agreed to vote on a contract for the new plant that eliminated incentive pay and the threat of a strike until the replacement Austin plant
had been in operation for three years. Workers overwhelmingly rejected
the offer despite a layoff threat. With negotiations stalemated, Hormel
management decided to look at other plant sites. In a question-and-
answer interview in the January 1978 issue of *Hormel NEWS*, Holton explained the company had taken options on industrial sites in Waverly,
Iowa, and Mankato, Minnesota. "Although we were exploring other
site options," Holton says, "we really did not want to build a new plant
anywhere but in Austin. Dick Knowlton, especially, fought hard for
building the plant here. He was an Austinite, his father had worked in
the plant and he had worked there, too. He realized the devastating impact the decision would mean to Austin if we built the plant somewhere
else. Of course, all of us were well aware of the historical reasons for
locating here but we had to confront the alternatives."

Nevertheless, negotiations collapsed in May 1978 and the company
once again considered building a new plant elsewhere. Subsequently, the
company made its final offer and the union, Local P-9, now under President John E. Hanson, voted by a sizable majority to accept the agreement. Reflecting upon the union's decision, Holton says, "I was convinced

Local P9
SPECIAL RANK & FILE MEETING
Austin High School Auditorium
11:00 a.m., Saturday, June 24

the union voted affirmatively because the people understood the serious-
ness of the situation. The new Davenport plant, replacing former gelatin
facilities in Austin, demonstrated that the company could leave the community."

During this long negotiation period, a committee, headed by
Knowlton, then group vice president of operations, and including William
R. Hunter, general manager, among others, met almost daily with
Hanson, Richard H. Schaefer, business agent, and other P-9 Executive
Board members. It was their function to arrive at a special transition
agreement whereby the move into the new Austin replacement plant
would be smooth and acceptable to both the company and the union.

"Hanson contributed greatly to the union decision to arrive at this
agreement and accept the new contract," added Holton. "He realized we
had to break the stalemate, but it cost him. He lost the presidency which
became an important moment in company and union history, as we eventually found out."

Adopted in June 1978, the new contract dropped the incentive system
and curbed a strike threat for three years after the plant opening. For its
part, Hormel promised to pay industry wage rates and agreed to a complex escrow fund that would make up for the lost incentive pay. The new

*A June 1978 meeting to
discuss the company's final
contract offer was announced
in* The Unionist.

*A new contract was ratified
in 1978 that paved the way
for construction of a
1,089,000 square foot re-
placement plant in Austin.*

plant would employ 1,025 people — a figure reached prior to the actual plant opening four years later because of special employee retirement plans and normal attrition.

It was a welcomed day for everyone in Austin when Hormel and Local P-9 reached agreement; yet, the lengthy, three-year negotiations augured poorly for later rounds of contract talks in the mid-1980s. Another obstacle, unforeseen at the time, was the company and union understanding that its laborers receive industry wage rates. No one imagined those rates would drop.

BUILDING FOR THE YEAR 2000 – Once a settlement was reached, John Hanson exclaimed in *The Unionist*, "This is good news for Local P-9, the city of Austin and the entire community." In the *Austin Daily Herald*, Jim Holton announced, "We will build the best plant we know how to build."

And what a plant it was going to be. It would cover more than one million square feet — roughly the size of 23 football fields — situated on a 33-acre tract of land located directly north of the existing plant. Ironically, this was the same piece of land Jay C. Hormel had considered using years before for a new plant. Capital expenditures would be the largest in company history with approximately one-third of the company's total assets invested in the Austin plant. The new facility was designed to process 1.5 million hogs a year and to produce more than 200 million pounds of product.

Thirty-one-year Hormel veteran Frank M. Brown, corporate manager of construction planning and development, and later company vice president of engineering, told readers of the October 1979 *Hormel NEWS*, "The new plant promises to be a showpiece of modern and innovative meat processing techniques. It will have the latest equipment and the best engineering ideas and newest production methods possible. The plant will be a model of food processing efficiency."

Phase I of the construction began June 25, 1979. "Specifications for the Austin plant," said Brown, "fill a book as thick as the New York City telephone directory. The company's planning specialists did nearly all the design with only a little help from outside consultants."

The planners designed a one-story structure consisting of a basement, a main floor, a mezzanine and a loft area. Facilities for pork processing required work areas on each level. Rendering operations were located in the basement and on the main floor while grocery products, smoked meats, and fresh and prepared sausage departments were situated on the main floor and loft.

Local P-9 President John Hanson (left); Austin Mayor Robert Enright (center), and Hormel President I. J. Holton (right) broke ground for the new plant on June 25, 1979.

Frank M. Brown, corporate manager of construction planning and development, inspected building plans.

Building specifications for the new Austin plant filled a book as thick as the New York City telephone directory.

FROM FRESH MEAT TO FINISHED PRODUCT – In conjunction with the large processing facilities, numerous manufacturing operations were installed for smoked meats and fresh and prepared sausages, including **Cure 81** ham, **Curemaster** ham, **Black Label** bacon, **Old Smokehouse** bacon, **Little Sizzlers** pork sausage, **Wranglers** smoked franks, the Perma Fresh line of products and the family of **Hormel** wieners.

Dry sausage production would take place in the north side of the plant which would also be home to the Grocery Products Division's major product lines – **SPAM** luncheon meat, canned hams and bulk luncheon meats. Grocery products packaging and dry storage areas would be located in the plant's northwest corner where a 13-story automated warehouse system ensured minimal manual handling of products and efficient stock rotation.

The designers placed the canning operations in the west-central portion of the building with the six-story hydrostatic cooker and sterilizer for **SPAM** luncheon meat, capable of processing 435 cans per minute, as the centerpiece.

ENVIRONMENTALLY SOUND – The new building would also house the Market Shipping Department, the company's Quality Control Department and a Medical Department, including a doctor's office, dispensary and reception area. There would be a new facility for changing clothes, a laundry room, three large cafeteria areas and a new general office area, located in the loft, with room for approximately 125 people.

Despite its immense size, the new Austin plant would be efficient, using about one-third less energy than the old plant. In addition, designers equipped the building with a number of environmental control devices

Hormel construction personnel reviewed blueprints and specifications during Phase I construction. Pictured (left to right) are Jean A. Burton, corporate manager of mechanical engineering; Harry W. Willmott, supervising staff engineer; Merlyn R. Gutz, superintendent of construction; Richard T. Bremner, senior staff architect, and Paul D. Langstaff, staff engineer.

that regulated odors, smoke and dust entering the atmosphere. Protecting
the environment extended within the plant as well. In the food-handling
area, plans called for interior walls of reinforced fiberglass panels, rather
than plaster, to minimize maintenance and maximize production line
hygiene.

THE FUTURE IS NOW – With construction of the new plant underway and
with the recent expansion of the Ottumwa and Knoxville, Iowa, plants,
Geo. A. Hormel & Company was ready for the 1980s and beyond. Nineteen seventy-nine had been a profitable year with dollar sales rising to $1.4
billion and net earnings reaching $30 million. But management's outlook
on these figures was sober and reflective. "Earnings and dollar sales were
at record levels," Jim Holton said at year-end. "In viewing these numbers,
however, we need to remember, although earnings and sales dollars are
larger, the forces of inflation erode the dollar's value. Still," he added,
"the year, in many respects, was outstanding."

And the future looked outstanding, too. Austin was still home to
Hormel and a native son had become company president.

*More than 80,000 cubic
yards of existing soil was
replaced with firmly com-
posed fill to ensure a sound
base for the foundation and
floor of the Austin replacement plant.*

In choosing Knowlton, the winner was Geo. A. Hormel & Company. Jim Holton had been the right man to lead the company in the 1970s. Quiet and unassuming but progressive in his thinking, Holton had changed the way the company operated. He carefully monitored financial performance. By nature a delegator, Holton had the courage to instigate the end of a corporate ideal – incentive pay. Holton's decision was a formidable one.

While he was not a marketing man, Holton saw the value of new product development and advocated increasing research and development expenditures. He pursued international ventures with the promise of expanding the company's markets. Holton focused on issues of corporate governance; for example, advocating outside directors long before business stewardship and ethics became a hot topic of the 1980s.

Perhaps most important, Jim Holton championed rebuilding existing facilities or construction of new ones that upgraded the entire Hormel infrastructure in the 1970s. With these facilities in place, the company was uniquely positioned for growth and transformation in the decade ahead.

Finally, Holton groomed and recommended an able successor to the Board.

For his part, 47-year-old Richard L. Knowlton, the new president, was an entrepreneur in the Jay C. Hormel mold. He was willing to take risks with new products, packaging ideas, acquisitions and expansion. He was eager to push his marketing personnel to expand the company's presence in world markets. He saw the wisdom of automation and technology and easy-to-prepare foods for the changing American family. With new products, new plants, a new union contract and the most modern flagship facility in the meatpacking world rising within view of the company's original 1891 site, the future of Geo. A. Hormel & Company looked bright indeed.

In July 1979, I. J. Holton was elected chairman of the board and R. L. Knowlton advanced to president.

Consumers on low-salt diets enjoy Black Label bacon.

All The Taste. Without The Waist.

Introducing Light & Lean® from Hormel; a line of meats as health conscious as you are. Each variety of Light & Lean® Franks, Ham, and Luncheon Meats have less fat than other so-called light meats. And coupled with their great taste, they're the perfect way to satisfy today's healthier appetites. With our coupon, save 35¢ and try the new line of Light & Lean meats from Hormel. No matter how much you buy, they won't go to waist.

THERE'S A NAME FOR FOOD THIS GOOD.

Hormel

Recent advertising for the Light & Lean product line emphasizes quality and healthy eating.

A 1984 advertising campaign introducing Light & Lean ham appealed to calorie-conscious consumers with the theme "Eat right without eating less!"

Light & Lean™ **HAM**
180 CALORIES
6.0 OZ.

Frank Shorter breezed through the finish line of the Olympic marathon in 1972 to bring the gold medal home to the United States. Long-distance running quickly caught the imagination of Americans who began lacing their jogging shoes and racing toward new health goals. They assumed better control of their lives by exercising, quitting smoking and eating properly.

As health consciousness swept the nation, people became concerned about calories, fat and salt in their diets. New words entered the American vocabulary in the 1970s — yogurt, alfalfa sprouts, tofu, kelp and miso, to name a few.

While some of these foods never moved out of specialty health food stores, others competed for the food-buying dollar.

By offering familiar foods high in protein but low in calories, fat and salt, Geo. A. Hormel & Company helped homemakers and their families improve their eating habits. In 1981, Hormel introduced many of its luncheon meats under a new **Light & Lean** brand. Diet and nutrition concerns were addressed with a line of calorie-controlled products — smoked cooked ham, red peppered ham, black peppered ham, glazed ham, cooked ham and Canadian-style bacon — that were 90 percent lean and only 25 calories per slice. The hard-hitting **Light & Lean** luncheon meat advertising slogan,

"Great taste doesn't come any leaner," was a welcome signal to health-conscious people that it wasn't necessary to compromise taste for nutrition.

When **Light & Lean** franks were introduced in 1989, consumers responded enthusiastically. Gary E. Esbeck, director of marketing for the Meat Products Group, remembers: "Parents seeking wholesome food products were pleased with the introduction of low-fat **Light & Lean** franks. They appreciated being able to serve a quick and economical meal their children loved that also offered important health benefits."

Following the 1980s introduction of multiple varieties of **Light & Lean** luncheon meats, **Light & Lean** ham and **Light & Lean** franks, consumers who had "exited these categories" returned, according to Esbeck. "In addition," he says, "other consumers switched their meat preferences and turned to the diversified families of **Light & Lean** products."

Low-fat and high-protein content also contributed to the rise in

popularity of poultry and fish products in the 1980s. In 1983, Hormel acquired Farm Fresh Catfish Company, Inc., now headquartered in Hollandale, Mississippi. Catfish is synonymous with Cajun cooking and when spicy southern food caught on nationally, so did this regional fish favorite.

Until the mid-1980s, ham was the traditional number one seller in the deli case but, waiting in

Hormel proves that wholesome eating doesn't mean giving up meat.

With the purchase of Chicken By George, Inc., in 1988, Hormel introduced a new product line offering flavor, nutrition and convenience.

the wings, was poultry. Capitalizing on this growing trend, Hormel introduced turkey-based luncheon meats such as smoked breast of turkey. More significant, however, was the late 1986 acquisition of Jennie-O Foods, Inc., Willmar, Minnesota, the largest privately held

turkey processing company in the United States.

Then, in 1988, Hormel added to its poultry lineup by purchasing Chicken By George, Inc., a cottage industry started by former Miss America,

sportscaster and first lady of Kentucky, Phyllis George. She created a tantalizing line of marinated chicken breasts in several popular flavors, including lemon pepper, Cajun and teriyaki. In 1990, Hormel supplemented the line with a four-item family of fresh, marinated turkey varieties which are to be joined by an expanded selection of marinated beef and pork items.

Among the family of chunk products, **Hormel** chunk breast of chicken, **Hormel** chunk white and dark chicken and **Hormel**

chunk turkey provide consumers with a high-protein source relatively low in calories and cholesterol.

Hormel has also adapted products for people on low-salt diets — **SPAM** luncheon meat, with 25 percent less salt/sodium; reduced salt **Hormel** chili with beans; the lower salt variety of **Hormel** microwave bacon, and no-salt-added **Hormel** chunk breast of chicken — to gain popularity among health-conscious Americans.

By lowering fat and salt in its meat and food products, Geo. A. Hormel & Company continues to offer nutritious selections made especially for the American palate. "The accelerated consumer interest in nutrition, weight control and leisure foods is a fitting complement to many of our product groupings," says Esbeck. "We remain committed to introducing additional health-oriented products to satisfy the increased demand for top-of-the-line nutritious meals."

*Low calories and high nutrition of **Light & Lean** franks are emphasized in a lighthearted 1989 advertising campaign that claims "Anything with Fewer Calories . . . Just Wouldn't Be a Hot Dog."*

FARM FRESH

Hormel acquired Farm Fresh Catfish Company in 1983 to meet the growing demand for fish as a low-fat, high-protein meal alternative.

Hormel chili and SPAM luncheon meat, American favorites for more than 50 years, are now available in low-salt varieties.

CHAPTER SEVEN

An Era

of Teamwork

and Product

Innovation

1979-1991

*"At Hormel, an environment exists that encourages people to take risks
and be entrepreneurial."*

R. L. Knowlton

1979

R. L. Knowlton in 1987.

H ormel was fortunate that young R. L. "Dick" Knowlton chose to invest his competitive spirit, tactical thinking and commitment in his hometown company. Hormel and Knowlton were in for a whirlwind ride through the 1980s — a decade characterized by intense competition, an industry shakeout, dazzling new product introductions, trouble in Austin and what some observers called the "reinvention" of Hormel.

Light & Lean luncheon meats combine good taste and low calories.

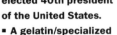

- Ronald Reagan is elected 40th president of the United States.
- A gelatin/specialized proteins plant in Davenport, Iowa, is fully operational.

1981 I. J. Holton relinquishes his responsibilities as the company's chief executive officer.
- The company opens a plant in Hayward, California, and expands its Ottumwa, Iowa, plant.
- Hormel introduces **Light & Lean** luncheon meats.
- **Hormel** bacon bits completes its second full year of national distribution.

Torrential rains did not dampen the enthusiasm of Austin residents when they gathered for the opening of the Austin flagship plant.

1979-1981

1980 The company introduces **Fast'N Easy** precooked bacon.
- Hormel invests $55.6 million in property, plants and equipment.
- The company adds three new items to its **Perma Fresh** luncheon meat line.

1982-1984

1982 Hormel begins full operation of its new $100 million, 1,089,000 square foot Austin flagship plant.
- Hormel closes plants in Fort Dodge, Iowa, and Albany, Georgia.

Two-term President Ronald W. Reagan.

- The company expands plant operations in Beloit, Wisconsin, and Stockton, California.

1983 The company acquires Farm Fresh Catfish Company, Greensboro, Alabama.
- Hormel introduces **Homeland** hard salami.
- The company starts its first major venture into the mail-order industry with the development of the *Austin Street Market* catalogue.

1984 *The Wall Street Transcript (TWST)* names R. L. Knowlton best chief executive officer in the meat and poultry industry.
- Hormel debuts **Light & Lean** ham.

• The company acquires Dold Foods, Inc., Wichita, Kansas.

1985-1987

1985   The company moves its annual stockholders' meeting from Austin for the first time in history, selecting Atlanta, Georgia, as the alternate site.
• Near midnight, August 16, Local P-9 President James V. Guyette delivers notice of a strike at the Austin plant. The plant operates on a limited basis while the strike continues.
• An agreement with FDL Foods, Inc., Dubuque, Iowa, leads to the formation of FDL Marketing, Inc., a wholly owned subsidiary.
• Sales reach $1.5 billion.

1986   Despite the ongoing strike, Hormel hires nearly 600 new employees and 500 former strikers in an effort to bring the plant back to full operation.
• Hormel and Local P-9 announce a new four-year contract on August 27, ending the 13-month strike.
• Hormel implements a companywide Quality Improvement Process (QIP).
• The company acquires Jennie-O Foods, Inc., Willmar, Minnesota.

1987   Hormel introduces **Top Shelf** main dish entrees.

New Traditions breakfast sandwiches helped distinguish Hormel as "New Products Company of the Year."

A company divided: Hormel struggled with a bitter, 13-month strike in 1985-86.

• The company's Frozen Foods Division introduces **New Traditions** breakfast sandwiches.
• The company acquires Sunshine Shippers, Inc., San Jose, California.

• *Prepared Foods* magazine names Hormel "New Products Company of the Year."
• Sales break the $2 billion mark.
• **SPAM** luncheon meat celebrates its 50th birthday.

1988-1991

1988   The company acquires Chicken By George, Inc., a two-year-old company founded by former Miss America Phyllis George.
• The company introduces **Hormel** microwave bacon.
• **Cure 81** ham celebrates its 25th anniversary.

1989   Hormel introduces **Light & Lean** franks.

• Hormel introduces Special Recipe pork sausage links and patties.

1990   Geo. A. Hormel & Company begins trading its common stock on the New York Stock Exchange.
• Hormel acquires Parkin Food Products, Ltd., South Kirkby, England.
• The company purchases the mail-order operation of S. E. Rykoff & Co.
• Hormel acquires Gourmet America, Inc.
• A two-for-one split of the company's common stock represents the seventh split in a 30-year period.

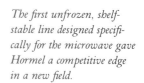

The first unfrozen, shelf-stable line designed specifically for the microwave gave Hormel a competitive edge in a new field.

The fall of the Berlin Wall in November 1989 united East and West Germany after more than 25 years of separation.

Making the commitment real, Hormel employees in Atlanta, Georgia, signed pledges to strive for quality during Zero Defects Day activities.

1991

SPECIAL REPORT

**Wall Street Examines
The Meat Industry**

The 1980s became the shakeout decade for the American meatpacking industry, but Hormel had a survival strategy.

As the 1980s dawned, America — and the world — had good reason to view the new decade with trepidation. In November 1979, the Shah of Iran was deposed by the Ayatollah Khomeini, a religious extremist who kept 49 Americans hostage. Russian soldiers invaded Afghanistan and, to send a clear message to the Kremlin, President Jimmy Carter ordered a U.S. boycott of the 1980 Olympic Games in Moscow. But that was only the start. More international upheaval lay ahead — the assassination of Egyptian President Anwar Sadat; the controversial British invasion of the Falkland Islands, and explosive, continuous fighting in Beirut, Lebanon.

Americans, struggling with skyrocketing interest rates and rising unemployment, rejected Democratic party leadership and elected a former screen star to the White House. In January 1981, Republican Ronald Reagan embarked on what would become a two-term administration, gaining widespread popularity and renewing the nation's confidence.

At the same time, the American family was in flux. Divorce and single parents became almost as common as nuclear families. A growing number of children were "latch-key kids" who, upon returning from school, found their homes empty because both parents worked. Instead of "high touch," the decade was "high tech" as Americans nationwide became computer oriented and computer literate. More than 315,000 personal computers were sold by early 1980, causing *TIME* magazine to take the unprecedented step of naming the machine its "Man of the Year."

SHAPE UP OR SHAKEOUT – In 1980, Geo. A. Hormel & Company entered a shakeout decade. For the meatpacking industry, 20 years of evolution culminated in unprecedented upheaval for America's leading companies. Unlike the steel industry, however, media coverage and public understanding of meatpacking turmoil were limited.

The shakeout started in 1962 when the upstart Iowa Beef Processors (IBP) revolutionized the industry with a plan to be the low-cost producer largely through substantially reduced labor costs. In the 1970s, stalwarts in the business had been confronted with the dual burdens of inefficient, outdated plants and historically high labor rates. Efforts to remain competitive were slow and costly. A few companies anticipated the changes and adapted; most, however, could not cope and floundered. Still others, particularly the large, old-line firms, survived through sometimes questionable acquisitions. Swift & Company, a once preeminent player in the industry, was now one of a number of companies held by Esmark, Inc., a company later known more for panty hose than meat. Wilson & Co., Inc., was acquired by LTV Corporation, then, as one trade journal observed, "bled dry and thrown back onto the market." Greyhound acquired Armour & Company, sold a majority of its pork and beef processing facilities, and offered the remainder to a new buyer, Con-Agra, Inc.

Despite the downward pressure that regional, nonunion packers such as IBP were putting on wage rates, union leaders clung steadfastly to outdated "master contracts" that preserved wages at higher levels and made their companies noncompetitive. Strike after strike over wage negotiations, frequently in tandem with plant closings, characterized the industry in the late 1970s and early 1980s. At the same time, efforts to become more efficient by retrofitting old plants and building new ones saddled meatpackers with heavy debt.

There were added blows. In the early 1980s, pork supplies were short, raising prices to an all-time high of $67 per hundredweight. American eating habits were changing, forcing companies in the red meat industry to listen. Health food was gaining broad popularity with fitness-conscious consumers. Countless choices ranging from frozen yogurt and tofu to alfalfa sprouts, whole grains and pasta competed successfully for the food-buying dollar. Furthermore, Americans who chose to eat meat tended to select poultry and fish while others followed vegetarian diet patterns.

SEEKING THE COMPETITIVE EDGE – This was the business environment R. L. Knowlton faced as president of Geo. A. Hormel & Company in 1979. He believed the company had two choices: Hormel could change to compete effectively in the new marketplace or it could risk extinction as had other once-strong companies such as Rath Packing Co. and Cudahy, Inc.

Knowlton had a competitive streak that made him uniquely suited for this challenge. His willingness to compete probably had its start at Austin High School where Knowlton lettered in four sports – tennis, track, basketball and football – and it was enhanced when he played offensive and defensive guard on the varsity football team at the University of Colorado.

When Richard Knowlton graduated from Austin High School in 1950, the chairmanship of Hormel was beyond his ken.

Sports took a backseat to business when Dick Knowlton graduated in 1954 with a degree in geography and economics. He joined Hormel at a starting salary of $5,400. But if sports taught Knowlton anything, it was the importance of teamwork – drawing on the talents of many to achieve a common goal. This emphasis on creative teamwork would produce more new products in the 1980s than during any other era in company history and prompt *Forbes* magazine to call Hormel one of the most innovative companies in the food processing industry.

Knowlton's advocacy of teamwork would also guide the company through the 1980s – a turbulent, devasting and sometimes violent decade in which almost all of the industry leaders disappeared, were acquired or dropped substantially from their once-proud positions.

The decision to build a flagship processing plant in Austin, Minnesota, underscored the strong and historic ties that Hormel had with its hometown. While construction continued on the Austin plant, executives of Hormel convened in strategic planning retreats that yielded a new mission for the 1980s and beyond.

The decade began with the company reporting one of its best all-around years in history. Geo. A. Hormel & Company performed admirably following a two-for-one stock split early in the 1980 fiscal year. Net earnings reached a record high of $32.8 million on sales of $1.3 billion, an increase of 9.3 percent. Stockholders' equity increased by 13 percent to $208.3 million and the company raised its dividend level for the 12th consecutive year. In addition, capital investments were the highest ever, totaling $55.7 million, a 103 percent increase over record expenditures the year before.

Threatened government wage and price controls had not materialized and the company was on schedule with construction of its replacement Austin plant. A new Davenport, Iowa, gelatin/specialized proteins plant, coupled with expansion of the Ottumwa, Iowa, processing plant, signaled greater manufacturing efficiencies. At the same time, Hormel continued to phase out unprofitable operations.

Equally important, the company was introducing new products, debuting 12-ounce, exact-weight packages of **Burgermeister** thuringer, **Old Smokehouse** thuringer and **Lumberjack** beef summer sausage.

FIRST, YOU PLAN – Hormel 1980-81 annual reports devoted only a sentence to it, but brevity was no indication of the importance Dick Knowlton and his management team placed on strategic planning. One such planning session was held at a retreat where the management team discussed the company's future. Amid all the industry upheaval, this process gave Hormel a chance to capitalize on change rather than be a victim of it.

"We went into our company retreat knowing we had to surrender some traditional ways and adopt new strategies and tactics," Knowlton says. "While those traditional ways had been effective for us — and for others — for many years, we could not assume they would continue to

  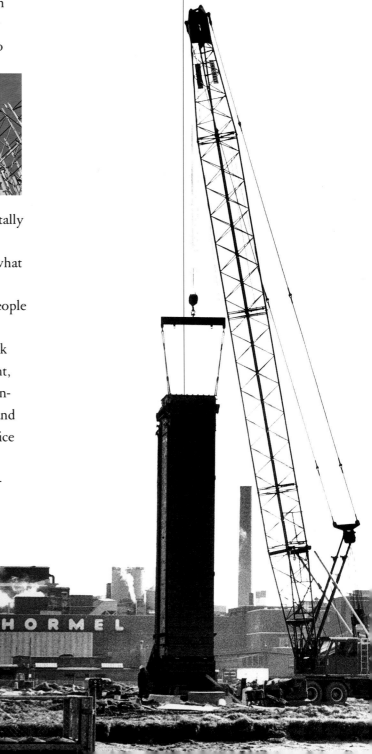

be. The environment was changing all around us. That called for a totally fresh look at our role and future in the marketplace. We surrendered some time-honored ideas and, in several product areas, we practiced what might be identified as 'creative destruction.'"

Participating in this first of many retreats were such key Hormel people as Raymond J. Asp and Lee D. Housewright, Jr., executive vice presidents; William R. Hunter, group vice president, operations; Frank M. Brown, vice president, engineering; John R. Furman, vice president, Dry Sausage Division; Robert M. Gill, vice president, personnel and industrial relations; Stanley E. Kerber, vice president, Route Car Sales and Distribution Plant and Foodservice Divisions; Clayton T. Kingston, vice president, pork operations; Robert F. Potach, vice president and controller; James N. Rieth, vice president, strategic planning and development; James A. Silbaugh, vice president, Grocery Products Division; Donald S. Sorenson, vice president, beef operations, and Charles D. Nyberg, general counsel and secretary.

*A six-story hydrostatic cooker and sterilizer for **SPAM** luncheon meat allowed Hormel to process 435 cans per minute in the new Austin plant.*

Austin, Minnesota, was a farming town of 4,000 when George A. Hormel arrived on a hide and wool buying trip from Des Moines, Iowa, in the 1880s. In frequent visits over the next seven years, George became increasingly involved in the community. His contacts and circle of friends grew and, in 1891, when Hormel decided to open a meatpacking business, he chose Austin.

The city of Austin and Hormel grew together in the century that followed. Today, Austin is a prosperous community of 23,000 and Hormel is a $2.6 billion *Fortune* 200 corporation employing 8,300 people, including subsidiaries. More than one in five employees, about 1,700, are Austin residents with an annual payroll exceeding $66.9 million, providing an economic boost to the Austin area of more than $400 million.

The close alliance between Hormel and the community is found in various settings. Social service agencies, cultural organizations and recreational facilities such as the United Way, YMCA, Mower County Senior Citizens Center, Austin Symphony Orchestra, St. Olaf Hospital, the Salvation Army, the multisport Riverside Arena and the Austin municipal pool are all beneficiaries of the Hormel corporate giving program.

continued on next page

The YMCA is one of several community organizations supported by Hormel.

"Focus" and "specialization" were words spoken often in those meetings and they inspired the company's new mission statement. Not since George A. Hormel used three words to sum up his strategic vision — "Originate, don't imitate" — had the company fine-tuned its strategic focus to such a degree.

"We felt obliged to think our statement through carefully in order to successfully commit meaningful words to daily practice. This statement was meant to be powerful — something that would guide us in our every action . . . in our every decision," said Knowlton. "This was no exercise in trite phrase making."

A MISSION WITH MEANING – Four years of thoughtful integration and practice passed before the company's mission "went public" on the cover of the 1984 Annual Report. Geo. A. Hormel & Company resolved . . . "To be a leader in the food field with highly differentiated quality products that attain optimum share of market while meeting established profit objectives."

Like the company's products, its mission was a mouthful because it packed several critical concepts into a single sentence.

"There are three key terms in our mission statement," Knowlton told analysts at a Piper, Jaffray & Hopwood gathering, "and they are 'highly differentiated,' 'quality' and 'optimum.' *Highly differentiated* means we examine every product, every process, every package for a point of difference. There is no point in producing a wiener or a sausage that is similar to our competition. Without that point of difference, we don't go to market. In addition, all of our marketing efforts will focus on establishing that 'point of difference' for the products to be introduced.

"*Quality* is the heritage that George A. Hormel gave us and it's up to this generation to keep that standard intact. Quality has been the single most important reason for our success. Quality products, a quality image and quality performance.

"Finally, *optimum* does not necessarily mean maximum or number one. It means developing niches in major food categories and capitalizing on them. For example, **Cure 81** ham is the leader in the nonwater-added, boneless ham category but it is part of a much broader boneless ham market."

What will it take, the Piper analysts asked, to make this mission statement worth more than the paper it's printed on? Plenty, replied Knowlton, known for his tenacity in business. It meant Hormel would invest heavily in research and development to ensure its technological leadership in manufacturing, packaging and new product development. It meant taking more risks and living with failures that are part of the equation. "In today's marketplace, 90 percent of all new products fail in their first five years," Knowlton explained. "Today, the race is on to create products that satisfy our customers' lifestyle changes. The proliferation is staggering — new or improved entries arrive daily. We must create an environment at Hormel that encourages people to take risks and be entrepreneurial. And, if an idea fails, we move on. I approve every new project. As a result, we're all involved, committed and at risk. No one individual is ever identified with failure."

MATCHING WITS WITH THE GIANTS — There was a big risk in the Hormel decision to become a leader in the food field. It meant the company would match wits and products with the giants, including General Foods Corporation, Libby, Swanson, The Pillsbury Company and General Mills, Inc. Then again, in Knowlton's office, a small, framed quotation summed up his view of risk and reward: "On the edge of the ravine, you will always find the most beautiful flowers."

Closing inefficient operations, investing heavily in new facilities and creating a more centralized organization were key — some would call them risky — decisions designed to bring the Hormel mission to life. In 1981-82, the company closed several facilities — the Fort Dodge, Iowa, processing plant, the last multistory facility; a custom beef operation in Scottsbluff, Nebraska, and a distribution plant in Albany, Georgia. In turn, Hormel invested in a new distribution plant in Hayward, California; made additions to processing or distribution plants in Beloit, Ottumwa, Dallas, Los Angeles, Algona and Knoxville, and celebrated the much-anticipated start-up of the flagship Austin plant that easily commanded the largest capital commitment in Hormel history — more than $100 million.

The plant that required the largest capital investment in Hormel history also generated front page coverage on Sept. 13, 1982.

continued from previous page

Austin is also supported through The Hormel Foundation, a philanthropic organization founded in 1941 for the support of local educational and charitable activities. The Foundation funds a variety of community organizations, including The Hormel Institute, an internationally renowned biochemical research center, and the Jay C. Hormel Nature Center, a preserve and environmental education facility located on the former estate of the founder's only son and successor. In a similar vein, George Hormel's turn-of-the-century manor now houses the Austin YWCA.

Over the years, Hormel has fielded many attractive relocation offers from other larger communities. Interestingly, one such offer came from Austin, Texas, the city with which many mistakenly identify Hormel. But the Austin, Minnesota-bred company was not willing to tear up 100-year-old roots and there was no price tag high enough to replace its partnership with this bedrock Minnesota community. That loyalty was reaffirmed in 1982 with the opening of a new $100 million state-of-the-art replacement plant in Austin. For Geo. A. Hormel & Company, there's no place like home.

Hormel plant functions were also becoming more focused. Rather than manufacture franks, sausage and stew in one location, many plants specialized in one or two items and reaped greater economies of scale. In addition, the "plant as profit center" philosophy, an industry tradition, was replaced with a more centralized approach to operations. While autonomy had worked well for Hormel in earlier decades when distribution and communications were less sophisticated, the decentralized approach also meant generally poor economies of scale for company manufacturing capabilities as well as inconsistency — intolerable traits in the unforgiving market environment of the 1980s.

PRESSURE ON THE BOTTOM LINE – Along with most of its competitors, Geo. A. Hormel & Company keenly felt economic pressures of the new decade. After setting a record in 1981, dollar sales of $1.4 billion declined slightly in 1982 and, again, in 1983 as the critical and difficult transition from the old plant to the newly constructed facility was made. During this time, the company had more than $100 million invested without any returns; yet, the costly expenses associated with the transition and start-up from the old to new plant continued. In 1983, net earnings decreased $.02 per share. The company reduced its capital expenditures to $20 million — less than one-third the previous year's allotment — and announced cost-cutting measures to weather what Knowlton called "challenging and frustrating" times.

Nevertheless, there were signs of hope. "Our net income wasn't record-breaking," he told shareholders at the 1983 annual meeting, "but it was highly satisfactory when compared to others in the industry." During 1983, Hormel implemented a successful cost-control program designed to reduce operating expenses by 10 percent and embarked upon aggressive marketing efforts aimed at emphasizing that "point of difference" between Hormel products and the competition. In addition, the company completed a reorganization that created a more centralized and streamlined operation.

Under the new plan, manufacturing — once part of Meat Products and Prepared Foods Groups — was transferred to the Operations Group. Responsibility for the company's major plants in Austin, Fremont and Ottumwa was also vested in operations. In addition, Hormel adopted a new management plan for the Meat Products Group encompassing seven geographic regions and designed to improve group communications, gain efficiencies in operations and focus sales efforts on the most promising opportunities in local markets.

Hot dog! Hormelites celebrated the opening of the new Austin plant with a 1,200 foot frank.

ADDED VALUE SET HORMEL APART – When it came to products and promotion, Geo. A. Hormel & Company, circa 1983, began to reflect the priorities set forth in its developing mission statement. To offer highly differentiated products and attain optimum share of market, Hormel would convert its remaining commodity-type products to consumer-branded, value-added lines. For example, the Meat Products Group developed an atmosphere-controlled package designed to extend product shelf life. The new package, introduced under the **Super Select** brand, included boneless whole loins, shoulder butt roasts, tenderloins and ham roasts, each packed in its own natural juices inside a clear, vacuum-sealed container. These large, hand-picked, knife-ready pork cuts offered retailers a convenient alternative – they could price and sell the packages whole or cut and package the meats as boneless roasts, butterfly chops, country-style ribs, ham, cubed steaks, tenderloin chops or pork kabobs. In this manner, Hormel positioned its basic pork products a cut above the commodity-style competition.

Super Select brand meats from Hormel made life easier for retailers with value-added cuts and packaging.

Other new products qualified as "highly differentiated" because they dominated a special niche or supplied innovative answers to consumers' demands for new tastes and greater convenience. In 1983, for example, Hormel introduced **Homeland** hard salami, a product with a hearty flavor of spice and garlic reminiscent of Old Country recipes rarely found in supermarket cases. And, with **Great Beginnings** entrees, consumers could have a "simple or elegant meal in a hurry" – chunky beef, pork, turkey or chicken, combined with a variety of gravy combinations. Heated before serving, the entree was served over biscuits, pasta, rice or noodles, or in a pastry crust.

Hormel introduced Homeland hard salami in 1983 with a distinctive flavor reminiscent of the Old Country.

Although the new product seemed to have a future consistent with its name, **Great Beginnings** entrees failed to catch on. The product's rise and fall, however, offers a good example of how risk and failure are viewed at Hormel. "Failure is something we all share," Knowlton told a business reporter. "**Great Beginnings** entrees seemed to be a successful concept and, as chief executive officer, I supported the idea, along with the project manager. We seek to create a safe environment for risk. When people work hard, there's no such thing as failure."

IN THE SWIM – Hormel also chose to enter new fields, such as aquaculture, to capitalize on changes in consumer diets. Early in 1983, Hormel acquired Farm Fresh Catfish Company, now headquartered in Hollandale, Mississippi. Fish – like pork – could be easily processed into value-added, convenient foods. By renovating the company's existing plants and building a new one, Hormel quickly established Farm Fresh Catfish Company as a leading low-cost producer in the business. This timely acquisition was tied to the success of aquaculture, a fish farming technique barely 20 years old, that had enjoyed surprising growth. Between 1981-83, production of farm-raised catfish jumped from 60 to 160 million pounds because consumers were often opting for fish – a low-cholesterol, high-protein food source.

As American consumers increasingly chose fish as a protein alternative, Hormel capitalized on the trend by acquiring Farm Fresh Catfish Company.

Capitalizing on America's health consciousness, Hormel decided to expand its **Light & Lean** luncheon meats concept to other products. Introduced in 1981 and distributed nationally one year later, the smoked cooked ham, red peppered ham, black peppered ham, glazed ham, cooked ham and Canadian-style bacon all had a unique quality – each slice was 90 percent lean and contained no more than 25 calories. Demonstrating that a healthful choice was also a flavorful choice, Hormel promoted its **Light & Lean** line with this hard-hitting slogan: "Great taste doesn't come any leaner." Before long, consumers had additional **Light & Lean** branded alternatives, including bologna, franks and ham.

KUDOS TO A 'COOL COMPETITOR' – Trouble in 1984 bubbled around Hormel like a kettle of simmering chili. Consumption of meat continued its downward trend for the third straight year and intense competition among struggling meatpackers led to narrower profit margins. Companies clinging to the old style of doing business suffered the most.

Hormel, on the other hand, was realizing the positive impact of its shift from commodity-based to value-added, consumer-oriented products bolstered by aggressive promotion and new-found economies in manufacturing. In 1984, Hormel reported record net sales of $1.5 billion and net earnings of $29.5 million. Remarkably, the company achieved these results while paying wages well above the industry average.

No wonder *The Wall Street Transcript* (*TWST*) chose to name Dick Knowlton the best chief executive officer in the meat and poultry industry for 1984. Hormel was buoyant in a year when other companies could barely keep their heads above water.

TWST cited as key strengths the company's willingness to embrace technological improvements and its ambitious new product development linked to shifts in consumer demographics.

"Hormel has been a cool competitor," one analyst commented. "They have consistently remained profitable throughout this chaotic time. They saw the need to reduce exposure to high labor costs and pursued the high technology route very early. Their capital expenditures have been aimed at that goal and they have achieved it in their flagship Austin plant."

Industry observers interviewed by *TWST* were impressed with the $250 million Hormel spent between 1978-82 on new and modernized facilities, including the $100 million Austin plant with its automatic ham deboners and huge automated warehouse. Well before other manufacturers had taken their first look at robotics and mechanized labor, Hormel engineers had developed robots to lift bulk luncheon meat cans into retort crates, put picnic hams into automatic deboning machines, thread bacon slabs into molding machines and haul packaging materials from one corner of the one million square foot plant to another. Before long, company engineers envisioned robots tackling precise cutting tasks once reserved for humans.

"While Hormel has traditionally been plagued by the vagaries of hog supply and pricing trends, the chief executive officer made real progress in mitigating the adverse effects of those trends," *TWST* noted. "Management embarked upon an ambitious capital improvement program targeted at achieving superior operating efficiencies. The technological advancements incorporated in Austin, Beloit and Stockton have significantly cut processing time and product shrinkage, yielding excellent cost benefits."

The Wall Street Transcript *credited Hormel and Dick Knowlton with weathering a series of tough years in the meat and poultry industries.*

Hormel proved in 1984 that ham lovers could still watch their weight and enjoy this traditional entree.

TUNNEL VISION – Hormel also turned its expertise for technological innovation to products. After three years, R&D researchers discovered how to combine the proven taste of **Hormel** franks with the number one selling chili. The result was **Frank 'N Stuff** franks with a unique tunnel of **Hormel** chili inside. American hot dog lovers embraced the new combination following its 1984 introduction.

In Knowlton's mind, product convenience was paramount in 1984. "We know close to 60 percent of America's homemakers work outside the home," he said. "In addition, the population of people over 60 is growing rapidly. They insist on convenience as well as healthy, nutritious foods. A recent Gallup Poll showed 88 percent of consumers surveyed are concerned about nutrition; 80 percent believe avoiding too much salt is important, and a growing number are on low-fat diets.

"For too long," Knowlton said, "the food industry has been selling to a consumer who no longer exists." Knowlton meant the "traditional" American family – a houseful of kids, a single breadwinner and a full-time homemaker preparing a robust evening meal. Knowlton and his colleagues could see that the real American family of the 1980s often had as many careers as children.

Light & Lean luncheon meats, **Light & Lean** ham, **Broiled & Browned** pork sausage and **Farm Fresh** catfish fillets, along with stalwarts **Hormel** chili, **Mary Kitchen** corned beef hash and **Black Label** ham – all proved their timeliness and viability in 1984.

Significant sales increases in these and other products compensated for sales lost when Hormel terminated its beef contract in Huron, South Dakota; eliminated a pork processing shift in Austin, and closed its Ottumwa pork processing plant for six weeks. Value-added Hormel

*The "drip test" in 1985 – there was only one graphic way to show the thick and rich texture of **Not-So-Sloppy-Joe** Sloppy Joe Sauce.*

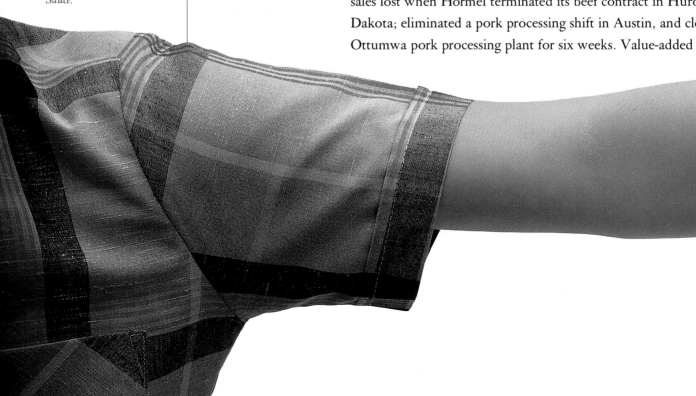

products offset the loss because typical profit margins on these products were higher than traditional narrow margins on fresh meat.

What some had called the "reinvention" of Geo. A. Hormel & Company was well underway. Before decade's end, commodity-type products would diminish to a minority of the total product line and Hormel would shut down most of its pork processing operations to change its focus from meatpacker to "total food company."

NO RETREAT, NO SURRENDER – When 1985 began, Geo. A. Hormel & Company faced a year of recordbreaking performance – and heartbreaking conflict. At this time, also with an eye to the future, the company invested $29.4 million on building or modernization projects – a sum 36.8 percent higher than the preceding year.

New products, including additional **Light & Lean** luncheon meat selections, dry sausage snacks, **Old Smokehouse** pork spare ribs, **Old Smokehouse** bar-b-q sauce, **Hormel** chunk salmon, frozen Mexican-style entrees, catfish snacks, prepared salads and a turn-of-phrase rival to a favorite sandwich, **Not-So-Sloppy-Joe** Sloppy Joe Sauce, would appear on grocery shelves throughout the year.

Furthermore, Hormel would capitalize on another megatrend by introducing its first product adapted for the microwave oven – **Broiled & Browned** sausage. "With this introduction, Hormel became the first food processor in the nation to offer retail and foodservice outlets a pork

Frank 'N Stuff franks revolutionized the hot dog in 1984 and these Hormel researchers and marketers helped. Shown (left to right) are Noel H. Goss, Gary A. Jones, Katherine F. Benkler, Kenneth E. Tribbett and Paul W. Stegemann.

Business publications confirmed what Hormel and other U.S. meatpackers already knew. The industry would never be the same.

sausage developed specifically for microwave use," noted Stanley E. Kerber, senior vice president of marketing for the Meat Products Group. "We recognized that 50 percent of American households in 1985 owned microwave ovens and the percentage was likely to grow beyond 70 percent by decade's end." In fact, by 1989, there were more microwave ovens in American homes than televisions.

But, in this year of shrewd product innovation, unprecedented advertising efforts and outstanding financial performance, there were painful business decisions to confront.

Hormel had to reduce its labor costs to continue to compete successfully. The stakes were higher than they had ever been because the competition was fast becoming leaner and tougher. By this time, meatpackers who failed to increase efficiency and sales and decrease labor costs had gone out of business. The remaining players in the industry were savvy, sophisticated and tenacious.

In 1981, union leaders settled on three-year agreements with Hormel, Oscar Mayer & Company, Armour & Company, Wilson & Co., Inc., and Swift & Company. These agreements froze wages at $10.69 an hour and suspended cost-of-living increases in exchange for protection from plant closings. Labor and management hailed the agreement as a win-win proposition — union workers had a decent pay scale and job security and the companies had additional capital to spend on plant modernization. But, when Wilson lost $26 million in the first nine months of fiscal 1983 and declared bankruptcy, the future and those jobs did not seem secure after all. In Austin, Minnesota, the Wilson failure was chilling — just 25 miles away in Albert Lea, Minnesota, 1,350 people who worked at a Wilson packinghouse waited for pink slips.

Although it was stronger than Wilson and others in the industry, Hormel could not overlook the high labor costs associated with pork processing. In many cases, nonunion competitors enjoyed labor costs as much as 50 percent less. When Hormel sold surplus pork supplies not needed in its own operations, it did so at a loss.

A NEED FOR ADJUSTMENT – Knowlton and Hormel management braced themselves for a reaction by other company unions to proposed wage adjustments. The industry had already reacted. Bankrupt, Wilson and its labor leaders settled on a 25 percent reduction in its master agreement, pegging base pay at $8 an hour. Before long, Morrell cut its rates to

$8; Swift Independent Packing reduced wages to $8.25; Armour, now owned by Con-Agra, Inc., was largely a nonunion shop and paid $6, and Oscar Mayer & Company had initiated wage reduction talks.

In late 1983, Hormel told workers to expect a wage reduction. A labor arbitrator ruled the company could invoke the "me-too" provision in its Austin contract which allowed for adjustments in wages, upward and downward, if industry trends warranted it.

Labor leaders at Hormel plants representing workers at local unions in North Carolina, Georgia, Texas, Wisconsin, Nebraska, Iowa and Minnesota met long and often in the ensuing weeks and months to decide what strategies to use in negotiating with Hormel management. In light of industry wage cuts, union representatives debated what wage rate they would accept and what would trigger a strike. Knowlton knew it would be difficult for Hormel employees to accept the $8 package negotiated throughout most of the industry. Therefore, he offered what became known as the $9-10 package. It was an improvement over others in the industry and the company believed its technological advantages would help offset this industry-high wage proposal.

While most union leadership was willing to accept a wage compromise, one leader would not – James V. Guyette, president of Austin Local P-9. A native of Austin and son of a Hormel meatpacker, Guyette would hang tough – no wage cuts, no compromise. "His agenda," wrote reporters Dave Hage and Paul Klauda in their book, *No Retreat, No Surrender,* "often seemed detached from the reality of events around him. The rank and file did not send him to meetings to bring back concessions. And, as long as Hormel was making money, he wasn't about to accept any wage reductions. What his boyhood friends remember as an unusually wide stubborn streak in such a quiet kid had become the passion of a labor leader who would let nothing diminish his principles."

Guyette's passion ultimately led to a bitter break between the leadership of Local P-9 in Austin and other unions representing workers in seven company plants. After tough negotiating, six locals settled on a wage agreement with Hormel that paid $9 an hour Sept. 1, 1984, with a raise to $10 a year later. According to one union leader, this was the best settlement in the industry, but Guyette and the membership of Local P-9 didn't agree.

James V. Guyette – Austin native, son of a Hormel meatpacker and uncompromising union leader.

P-9 STANDS ALONE – "P-9 leaders made it clear to David A. Larson, vice president of human resources and chief labor negotiator for Hormel, that they wouldn't consider taking a wage cut while the company was making money," Hage and Klauda said.

Perplexed by P-9's intransigence, Hormel had no alternative but to implement wage reductions according to the contract in Austin. The company preferred not to reduce wages but, on Oct. 8, 1984, the hourly base pay was lowered to $8.25 when the contract allowed for a 23 percent cut from the $10.69 rate which had survived in Austin longer than at any other meatpacking plant in the country.

Business observers were surprised by this outcome. Had P-9 chosen to vote with its sister unions to ratify the new wage agreement, Austin workers could have been working for $9 per hour instead of $8.25 with the assurance their base pay would increase 12 months later.

Three men represented Hormel on the "front line" during the company's 13-month labor dispute. Pictured (left to right) are David A. Larson, vice president of human resources and chief labor negotiator; Charles D. Nyberg, senior vice president, general counsel and corporate secretary, and Deryl D. Arnold, Austin plant manager.

Within a year of the Austin showdown, five members of the six-member P-9 governing board were replaced and Guyette was fully in charge of the organization. Ray Rogers, labor strategist and controversial cofounder of Corporate Campaign, Inc., was retained by Local P-9 and, according to news accounts, assured his new clients that "we're going to kick the living hell out of this company."

Breaking a longstanding tradition, Hormel held its 1985 Annual Meeting in Atlanta, Georgia. Anti-Hormel leaflets appeared on Austin doorsteps and handmade signs endorsing one side or the other surfaced in Austin shop windows and homes. Where once the company's union and management workers shared favorite restaurants and after-work hangouts, now purposeful segregation occurred.

Negotiating attempts continued throughout the first half of 1985 but, when P-9 offered its proposal in July, a strike seemed inevitable. The P-9 proposal called for a wage rate of $12.50 an hour, reinstatement of the incentive pay system discontinued in 1979 and a "well-pay" bonus of 10 percent per week for every employee who showed up for work everyday. One observer called the P-9 proposal "an attempt to rewrite 45 years of bargaining history in one stroke." The company's final offer to the union included a two-tier wage program — $10 an hour beginning September 1, $9 for new employees — and changes in the seniority system that gave management more control over job assignments. The offer elicited boos from the rank and file. On Wednesday, Aug. 14, 1985, Local P-9 rejected this offer by a vote of 1,261-96 and the executive board began preparing a 48-hour strike notice for Hormel.

"Cheers and hooting rose from the back of the hall," union members said. "The showdown was on."

On Friday, August 16, just 30 minutes before midnight, Guyette walked into the Austin plant and handed Plant Manager Deryl D. Arnold a letter officially informing him that Local P-9 was going on strike. "A few minutes later, Guyette emerged from the plant leading a procession of night shift workers," reporters Hage and Klauda said. "They marched to the gate, chanting and cheering under the glare of television cameras."

The strike lasted 13 months and everyone in Austin and Hormel was affected. Incidents of name-calling, vandalism and violence occurred frequently. Knowlton and other key Hormel managers were shadowed by bodyguards. There was concern for the safety of their families. Childhood friends who had grown up together and attended the same schools in Austin found themselves at odds — often bitterly — because they didn't share the same allegiance. The strike soon generated headlines in national newspapers and commanded almost daily broadcast coverage in Minnesota. Families of the rank and file wondered how long they could stretch their limited resources to cover mortgages, car payments and groceries. Militant union supporters were attracted to Austin and joined the fight against Hormel.

An Aug. 14, 1985, union vote defeated the final Hormel contract offer by an overwhelming margin.

On Aug. 15, 1985, Local P-9 union members drew battle lines.

While the community hoped for reconciliation, both Hormel management and P-9 found little common ground for negotiations. As management had promised, the Austin plant operated on a limited basis, using 200 Hormel supervisors to run processing lines. This was one-tenth the size of the normal workforce but the benefits of this sophisticated new plant were now evident. About 20 workers could produce thousands of cans of **SPAM** luncheon meat in a day. Arnold's skeleton crew worked in highly automated sections of the plant where they could be most productive. Because this small crew couldn't handle live hogs, Hormel purchased pork from other meat processing companies happy to find another customer in a market depressed by excess capacity.

Outside Austin headquarters, Local P-9 picketers rallied daily.

HARD WORK PAYS OFF – During 1985, even though the pain of the strike was evident in Austin and felt keenly among those who once earned Hormel paychecks, the company prospered. At year-end, Knowlton reported sales for 1985 had increased 3.3 percent to $1.5 billion while profits climbed to $38.6 million, up 30.9 percent from the year before. Although the Austin plant had been shut down from August 16 through October 26, company sales increased by nearly 7 percent during that quarter and profits rose 83 percent compared to the same quarter in 1984. As Knowlton had predicted when the strike began, Hormel could grow even without its "star plant" in Austin.

"By all measurements," Knowlton told stockholders at the off-site annual meeting, "fiscal 1985 has been the company's finest. Record earnings and dollar sales were the result of an extraordinary performance throughout the organization. Creative and innovative marketing programs, coupled with highly successful sales programs and professional management, were key ingredients in the year's success."

In a year circumscribed by the strike, Hormel spent more than $70 million on promotion and advertising – 50 percent more than the 1984 expenditure – to increase market share for existing products and to introduce new branded foods. Many new items served the rapidly expanding delicatessen industry. By mid-decade, close to two-thirds of all American supermarkets included a service deli counter, an increase of 20 percent since 1979. Within two years, deli sales were projected to reach $6.5 billion in America and Hormel was ready to capitalize on that growth.

As the Local P-9 strike wore on, friends, coworkers and neighbors became soldiers in a heartbreaking battle.

Another important development in 1985 had a direct bearing on the Austin strike and the company's demand for fresh pork. In 1985, the company signed a marketing agreement with FDL Foods, Inc., Dubuque, Iowa, which led to the formation of FDL Marketing, Inc., a wholly owned subsidiary of Hormel. Under terms of the agreement, FDL Marketing would supply Hormel with fresh and processed meat products under Hormel and Dubuque brand names. When the Austin plant was crippled, FDL became a major supplier of pork raw materials and branded products and helped the company meet consumer demand.

AN AGONIZING DECISION – After five months of virtual shutdown at the Austin plant and recognizing labor leadership was not interested in settling, Hormel announced it would reopen the plant with a full workforce Jan. 13, 1986. The company further stated it would give Local P-9 union members the first opportunity for available jobs, then hire new, permanent employees at $8 an hour, the industry average wage, to fill the plant's employment needs if it could not be adequately staffed by Local P-9 members.

Hormel needed 1,050 people to run one eight-hour shift at the plant. The continuous flow of applications during the strike had assured the company it could find top-quality workers. Hormel hoped hundreds of experienced and hardworking Local P-9 members would return to the plant, but the chasm between the company and the union had grown wider every week.

"Scab!" was the word hurled at union members who crossed the picket line. Within a few days, taunts and accusations escalated to broken windshields, slashed tires, assaults and gunshots.

Until Governor Rudy Perpich called in the Minnesota National Guard, law and order was no longer guaranteed in this once-placid Minnesota town. The ironies were abundant. "Bright white banks of lights shone down from utility towers, making the Austin plant glow in the morning

In a graphic demonstration of the new replacing the old, the former Austin plant was razed in February 1985.

By February 1986, the Local P-9 strike attracted more than 2,000 union supporters from across the U.S.

darkness and illuminating an eerie standoff," authors Hage and Klauda observed. "Civilian Minnesotans who stepped out of ordinary lives into military garb were standing in mute ranks against fellow Minnesotans who stepped out of equally ordinary lives into a big-time labor war."

That was January 1986. Within four months, union supporters by the thousands would march through the streets of Austin; some would block plant gates and refuse to leave. For the first time in Austin history, the smell of tear gas soured the morning air.

Convinced Local P-9 was not operating in the best interests of its membership and respecting the policies of the United Food and Commercial Workers (UFCW) union, international union leadership ordered an end to the strike and boycott of Hormel. When Local P-9 resisted, the UFCW international president appointed a trustee for the local union — an action supported by a district court ruling. In an environment that was no less emotionally charged than it had been for months, the new union trustee, Joe Hansen, began contract negotiations with Hormel.

On Aug. 27, 1986, Hormel and the union announced a new four-year contract for the Austin plant. Called "the best contract in the meatpacking industry," it was comparable to agreements reached at seven other company plants where the old contracts would expire September 1. With the new contract, wages would reach $10.70 an hour by the end of the third year (1988) and wages would be tied to a "me-too" clause with the company's Fremont plant in the fourth year. The two-tier wage system, in which workers hired in January 1986 were paid less than senior employees, was eliminated.

Five hundred P-9 members who had returned to work at the Austin plant joined nearly 600 newly hired employees in accepting the new contract.

One of the fundamental questions that helped fuel the strike was answered by authors Hage and Klauda: "Why does a profitable company need wage cuts? It's well to remember," the pair wrote, "that Hormel had been operating under an income freeze of its own. Its profits had been flat or declining for three years when it first asked for wage cuts in 1983. In 1984, its profit of $29.5 million was actually lower than in 1979. For a company that routinely plowed profits back into plants and equipment, it was not a healthy situation or an attractive one for investors.

"By our calculations, if Hormel labor costs had remained where they were in 1984, the last fiscal year before the wage and benefit reductions, the company would have gone into the red by 1987. Had Local P-9 triumphed in 1985 or 1986, it almost certainly would have been a Pyrrhic victory, one that would have forced Hormel into the same financial pinch that led Wilson to slash wages in 1983. Either solution would have been unpalatable to the union: financial distress, resulting in plant closings and layoffs, or subcontracting work — and eventually jobs — to low-wage or nonunion packers."

This outcome was one I. J. Holton warned against in the 1970s and Knowlton was forced to act upon in the 1980s. Thirty years earlier, Jay Hormel had foreseen such problems when he reviewed his company's salaried workers and incentive pay system, programs he originally created to make Hormel one of the best places to work in the nation.

DOING THE RIGHT THING – When Knowlton addressed the Minnesota Agri-Growth Council at its annual meeting just three months after the strike ended, he could say his company had acted honorably during those 13 heartbreaking months of strike.

"First, we agreed to always state our position firmly and positively, to stand by that position and live by it," Knowlton said. "After all, for nearly 100 years, our company has been proud of its employee programs which include the best wages and fringes in the industry, profit sharing and free shares of stock.

When the strike ended Aug. 27, 1986, Hormel and the union announced a four-year contract that was called the best in the meatpacking industry.

"Second, we agreed to be open with the press. We would not be reactionary.

"Third, we agreed to operate our business as professionally as possible and minimize the effects of the strike on our plans for Hormel progress.

"Fourth, we decided to have one spokesman for the company so the rest of us could continue to run the business with minimum interruption.

"Last, but most important, we were committed to reexamining every action necessary to assure everyone we were doing the most responsible thing for our employees."

Throughout the strike, the determination in Knowlton was apparent and the solid values born of George A. Hormel were evident. If there was any winner, it was the corporation which came out of the labor crisis stronger than ever. A testimonial to Knowlton's leadership was his selection by Carnegie Mellon University in 1987 as outstanding crisis manager.

Appropriately, the 1986 Annual Report carried a theme that underscored the flip side of discord and distrust. On the simple white cover were just three words – "We're Better Together" – and the Hormel logo.

A TRIBUTE TO GEORGE – During 1986, Hormel implemented a companywide Quality Improvement Process (QIP), a concept the founder embraced 95 years earlier. QIP was created to complement and refine the company's already solid quality systems and to extend quality improvement efforts throughout the organization. The QIP commitment meant thousands of hours of educational programs involving nearly 7,000

Hormel employees around the country earned special recognition for their individual contributions to quality. Pictured are Houston coworkers who each received "Employee of the Month" awards.

Hormel employees and the creation of employee-run Quality Improvement Teams (QITs) in 24 Hormel locations. They had a major assignment — to plan local quality programs, educate fellow employees and devise ways to monitor quality and measure the outcome.

"Our commitment," Knowlton told an audience of investment analysts, "is to do it right the first time. That means zero defects. We agree to supply defect-free products and services that conform to clearly defined requirements. When a company's culture is ingrained from top to bottom with such a philosophy, it's worth millions. We can eliminate errors others tend to take for granted as an everyday cost of doing business. We'll be a better company and have more satisfied customers and employees."

TALKING TURKEY – Another way Hormel could satisfy customers was to further diversify its line of meat protein products. This was accomplished with the acquisition of Jennie-O Foods, Inc., the largest privately owned processor of turkeys in the country, in December 1986. Founded 46 years earlier in Willmar, Minnesota, by the highly entrepreneurial Earl B. Olson, Jennie-O Foods had grown in stature because of its high-quality turkey products and reputation for consistently fair treatment of turkey suppliers.

When Hormel acquired Jennie-O Foods in 1986, the Minnesota-grown company had achieved preeminent status as the nation's largest, privately owned processor of turkeys.

For Hormel, acquiring this neighboring enterprise with shared values meant the company could capitalize on the country's fast-growing poultry business and heightened consumer demand for turkey year-round, not just for holiday feasts.

Two new product lines, refined several years earlier, test marketed in 1986 and introduced in 1987, set the tone for several years to come and gave *Prepared Foods* magazine good cause to name Hormel "New Products Company of the Year." Those products were **New Traditions** breakfast sandwiches and **Top Shelf** main dish entrees. Created to serve consumers who were beginning to rely on microwave ovens as staple appliances in their kitchens, both products emerged from the company's ability to innovate, take risks and bring leading-edge technology to market.

The **New Traditions** sandwiches was not only a new product line but also the cornerstone for a new Frozen Foods Division created in 1987 to handle a growing number of products formerly marketed through the Meat Products Group. This new initiative and the increased focus given to frozen foods was meant to expand the company's industry presence and national stature as a supplier of value-added consumer products. To accomplish this goal, all eyes were on **New Traditions** sandwiches — the

Product innovation that produced Top Shelf main dish entrees and New Traditions sandwiches made Hormel an acknowledged leader in 1987.

New Traditions sandwiches successfully combined frozen food and microwave technologies into a popular, portable product.

line that began in 1985 with a single product, skinless pork sausage links, and later included a full family of breakfast sandwiches. Now consumers on the run could cook up, in two to three minutes, hot, nutritious, portable breakfasts with hearty ingredients – Canadian bacon, eggs, cheese, ham, sausage and biscuits.

Before long, Hormel introduced **New Traditions** hamburgers, cheeseburgers and bacon cheeseburgers aimed at the legion of Americans who consume no less than 34 billion hamburgers a year.

"A quality product at a great price," a trade press reporter commented, "it's a simple idea that excites me." Subsequently added to this distinctive product line were **New Traditions** chicken and fish fillet sandwiches.

But even more than whetting the collective appetites of sandwich lovers, Hormel took steady aim at the microwave market. By this time, the appliance could be found in 60 percent of America's homes, not to mention offices, plant cafeterias, convenience stores, even tractors driven by farmers who chose not to waste time leaving the fields for meals.

CAN YOU TOP THIS? – With **New Traditions** sandwiches, Hormel successfully combined frozen and microwave technologies. But, with the introduction of **Top Shelf** main dish entrees in 1987, the company proved its willingness to innovate by creating an entirely new category of prepared foods. Call it hedging bets, Hormel now offered consumers multiple microwave preparation options – off the shelf or straight from the freezer.

Top Shelf main dish entrees was both a packaging and food innovation. Industry historians agreed it ranked with the introduction of America's first canned ham in 1926. Four years of extensive research, testing and capital investment in the millions preceded the introduction of **Top Shelf** main dish entrees – the first unfrozen, shelf-stable line designed specifically for the microwave.

In addition, the R&D effort involved a joint development project with a major packaging supplier that yielded the first shelf-stable, microwaveable plastic container. **Top Shelf** main dish entrees consisted of 10 specially prepared entrees of beef, fish and chicken that stayed fresh without preservatives or refrigeration for 18 months or more and could be prepared in the microwave in two minutes or less. Each entree was vacuum-packed in a multilayered plastic serving dish that provided a barrier to moisture and oxygen. Each tray was sealed with a semirigid, airtight plastic lid. The product was then precooked and sterilized with a unique heating technique to ensure retention of the food's natural flavors and complete freshness.

No one underrated the significance of **Top Shelf** main dish entrees. "This is one of the most important products ever produced by Hormel," Knowlton reiterated. "It represents a revolutionary breakthrough in packaging technology and offers consumers a new level of convenience."

"It's the number one priority development project for Hormel," James E. Hall, group vice president of the Prepared Foods Group, added with unabashed enthusiasm. "Without question, it is the most heavily researched product development line in company history. It's also one of the great packaging innovations of this century."

Forrest D. Dryden, vice president of research and development, explained that development of **Top Shelf** main dish entrees really had two equally important focal points — package and product. "The package had to be shelf stable, fully microwaveable and easy to open," Dryden said, "and it had to be adaptable to retort package cooking while looking and tasting good."

With Top Shelf *main dish entrees, the innovation of new packaging was just as important as the meals themselves.*

Hormel began experimenting with more than 100 product ideas and finally narrowed them to 10. The entrees were even more complicated because they had three or four individual components needing precise processing without overcooking.

When **Top Shelf** main dish entrees reached the market, they were supported with the largest advertising and promotional campaign ever launched by Hormel — TV and print advertising, coupons, special trial offers, in-store displays, sampling programs and local and national publicity. Hormel had learned years earlier the huge costs associated with being a leader.

Skeptical consumers had to be convinced that a product with no preservatives could last more than one year without refrigeration — and taste so good.

"One of the prices we must pay as pioneers is the cost involved in educating the consumer about a new product line," Robert F. Patterson, then vice president of the Grocery Products Division, explained. Hormel enlisted the respected, nationally known entertainer, Dick Cavett, to present **Top Shelf** main dish entrees to skeptical consumers who could hardly imagine a product that required no refrigeration, had no preservatives, lasted more than a year, was ready for the table in only minutes — and tasted good, too. Along with Cavett, Hormel launched a "Send **Top Shelf** to a Friend" campaign, to prove the product's stability and uniqueness. In

Introduced in 1988,
Hormel *microwave bacon took the muss and fuss out of traditional bacon frying.*

To celebrate the 50th anniversary of **SPAM** *luncheon meat in 1987,* **Hormel** *employees at the Houston plant cooked up a special birthday cake.*

addition, the company reached into history for a promotion used to introduce **Hormel** chili five decades earlier. Consumers were guaranteed "Double your money back, if you don't like it."

Patterson believed the offer sent a strong message about Hormel. "It shows we have confidence in our products," he said.

Years of research and development and promotional support began to pay off immediately when **Top Shelf** main dish entrees appeared on supermarket shelves. "It's flying off the shelves in Denver and Indianapolis," one jaded food industry reporter observed with uncharacteristic support. "Most important, the **Top Shelf** main dish entrees technology opens doors for Hormel to introduce line extensions."

THE $2 BILLION THRESHOLD – **Top Shelf** main dish entrees and **New Traditions** sandwiches were major contributors to a record year for Hormel in 1987. The company exceeded $2 billion in dollar sales for the first time while net earnings and tonnage volumes also reached record levels. In addition, Hormel declared a two-for-one stock split effective June 1, the second in less than two years and the sixth in 27 years. Performance of this magnitude was particularly noteworthy because pork prices had climbed dramatically in 1987 and the people of Hormel were recovering from the pain and upheaval of the 13-month strike.

Longtime Hormel shareholders who purchased stock in 1960 were happy to hear in 1987 that every share they owned now equaled 64 shares.

With an eye on growth and specialization, key people were advanced to leading roles at Hormel. Among them, Ronald E. Plath was named president of Hormel International Corporation; Forrest D. Dryden was elected a vice president responsible for the company's linchpin Research and Development Division; Scott A. Wallace joined Hormel as senior vice president of strategic planning and corporate development, and Marvin F. Moes, a vice president of the corporation, was named to oversee the newly formed Frozen Foods Division.

LIVING THE MISSION – Propelled by the success of **Top Shelf** main dish entrees and committed to taking the lead in new product development, Hormel, in 1988, saw new opportunities to introduce other unique products.

The sit-down family meal, for example, once an American norm, was now the exception. Fast foods, eating out, take-home foods and direct-home delivery had become staples as two-career couples began to dominate the social landscape and leisure time grew scarce. When Americans did eat at home, meals were smaller and they were cooked in the microwave. A growing number were take-out meals brought home to enjoy. Hormel researchers predicted take-out, take-home meals would account for 21 percent of food dollar expenditures by 1992.

In the second year of the **Top Shelf** main dish entrees national rollout, not a single food retailer turned the product down. In a major food and beverage marketing survey, it was dubbed "the most influential product of 1988." The shelf-stable food category was considered by experts the equivalent of the frozen food phenomenon 25 years earlier. Shelf stable, one seer announced, "is going to explode."

As more retailers committed shelf space to microwave sections, Hormel created handy, single-serving microwaveable cups of **Hormel** chili, **Dinty Moore** beef stew, **Mary Kitchen** hash and other well-known favorites.

A PAYOFF IN POULTRY – While Hormel grew through new product development, it also expanded with a timely acquisition in 1988. Watching poultry consumption continue to rise, the management of Hormel chose to expand even further into poultry products after the successful acquisition of Jennie-O Foods, Inc., two years earlier.

Opportunity knocked when former Miss America, Phyllis George, agreed to sell her two-year-old company, Chicken By George, Inc., to Hormel in 1988. Founded in her Kentucky kitchen, the line included light, fresh, marinated chicken breast entrees, all specially formulated by the former beauty queen and NFL sports co-anchor. All of those activities aside, George found relaxation in her kitchen, whipping up lemon herb, mesquite barbecue, teriyaki, Italian bleu cheese, Cajun, tomato herb and country mustard and dill marinades and sauces for her special food line.

Not only were the items wholesome, tasty and nutritious, but they fit the highly differentiated criteria for new products established by Hormel because they contained no preservatives, were low in calories, versatile in preparation and eminently convenient.

It was a perfect match. George would remain involved in new product development and promotion while Hormel gained a solid, distinctive entry in the value-added chicken category.

Phyllis George

As American consumers sought tasty alternatives to red meat entrees, Hormel made the strategic acquisition of a company whose specialty was fresh chicken.

INTERNATIONAL

George A. Hormel was not a man of limited vision. "We must hold our head up in the world," he wrote in a letter to his mother in 1887 when expressing dreams and ambitions for his fledgling partnership with Albrecht Friedrich.

When he went into business on his own, his ambitions fueled growth and expansion in regional, national and, as early as 1905, international markets. Within 15 years, for example, Hormel was shipping 100 carloads of Wiltshire sides, Cumberland middles, English bellies and Irish backs to the British Isles each week.

But international exports declined after World War I when Geo. A. Hormel & Company turned its attention to domestic growth and development. By 1955, Hormel, a $350 million company, revived its international presence through a licensing arrangement with a company in Cork, Ireland, for the production of SPAM luncheon meat. Similar arrangements followed throughout the 1950s and 1960s with companies in Canada, England and Venezuela. SPAM luncheon meat even went "down under" to Australia in 1969. Other product exports followed as did joint ventures in the Philippines and Okinawa.

Today, Hormel International Corporation serves

continued on next page

INNOVATION ON A GLOBAL SCALE – Hormel entered its final year of the 1980s committed to unprecedented advertising support of multiple new products and to full-scale research and development that would yield new entries in the increasingly competitive food field.

During 1989, the company took its **Top Shelf** main dish entrees and **Micro Cup** shelf-stable entrees nationwide and announced seven hearty soups would be added to this expanding microwave line. In addition, after solid consumer acceptance in Minneapolis, Denver and Los Angeles, Chicken **By George** prepared packaged chicken was made available to 65 percent of the United States with a four-item line of Turkey **By George** prepared packaged turkey varieties introduced at the start of fiscal 1990.

In a nod to America's dual love of hot dogs and the desire for fewer calories, less fat and lower cholesterol, the company's Meat Products Division introduced **Light & Lean** franks in six test markets. The product offered a surprisingly healthy frank alternative with 20 percent more protein, 50 percent fewer calories, 67 percent less fat and 20 percent less cholesterol. Similarly, the division's **Light & Lean** luncheon meats and **Hormel** microwave bacon with 35 percent less salt performed well in supermarkets as sophisticated consumers made buying choices based on good health.

The industry also recognized Hormel for its packaging innovations. Hormel and joint venture partners received the *Food Processing* magazine award for a new approach to microwave bacon packaging that included a "MicroInsorb" pad designed to soak up bacon drippings and eliminate the cleanup required with traditional pan frying. One year earlier, Du Pont and the National Food Processors Association (NFPA) had singled out **Hormel** microwave bacon packaging as an example of consumer-inspired innovation. "Among the winning entries, nearly 60 percent were developed in response to consumer demands for more convenience," *Meat Processing* magazine reported. "**Hormel** microwave bacon is a prime example of how combined efforts solved the problem consumers had in getting a uniformly cooked breakfast meat safely, easily and neatly from refrigerator to table."

The four-year-old Frozen Foods Division expanded its **New Traditions** sandwich line to include two new microwaveable items — **Hormel** chili dog with cheese and **Hormel** hot chili dog with cheese.

Hormel subsidiaries also brought new products to market, including a new **Jennie-O** turkey meat loaf and Mexican-style loaf; a fresh pork loin

FOR TOMORROW'S HIGH FLYERS

Reach for SPAM® and surprise yourself. Because this world-famous food is tasty, nutritious and is made with the best British pork. For families growing high flyers, this versatile meal-maker is the perfect answer.

THE ORIGINAL SPAM® MADE WITH PRIME CUTS OF BRITISH PORK

In the spirit of Prime Minister Margaret Thatcher who served SPAM luncheon meat as a young home-maker, the British leap for the perennial canned meat favorite today.

roast debuted by FDL Marketing, Inc., for the foodservice industry, and eight new seasoned entrees introduced by Farm Fresh Catfish Company.

On the Pacific Rim, Hormel International Corporation distributed **SPAM** luncheon meat and **Hormel** Vienna sausage to test markets in mainland Japan; inaugurated production of **Hormel** franks and **Black Label** bacon in the Republic of China; exported many Hormel products to Singapore and Malaysia, and introduced Australians to smoke flavored **SPAM** luncheon meat. To the company's delight, Koreans considered **SPAM** luncheon meat a delicacy — in fact, one of the "classiest" of all imported American products, according to *The Wall Street Journal*. Re-markably, the product that had been the focal point of World War II jokes had acquired an upscale image overseas.

In Central America, Hormel began production of several traditional products at a new 35,000 square foot processing plant in Panama City, Panama, and Hormel-branded products even began appearing on grocery shelves in Mexico.

The year 1989 was strong — one that would ultimately end Oct. 28, 1989, with net sales of $2.3 billion and net income of $70.1 million, up 16.5 percent over 1988. In recognition of this financial performance, the Board of Directors authorized a two-for-one stock split on November 22 — the seventh in 30 years — and approved the 24th consecutive annual increase in the company's dividend rate.

continued from previous page

markets in 36 countries throughout the world and offers multiple families of food products in Japan, the Philippines, Republic of China, Republic of Korea, United Kingdom, Australia and Panama. Acquisition of Parkin Food Products, Ltd., of South Kirkby, England, was completed in 1990, signaling the company's plans for continued global expansion.

"Dramatic political change in Eastern Europe presents Hormel with enormous opportunities for growth in the 1990s," says Ronald E. Plath, president of Hormel International Corporation. "Eastern Bloc countries, such as Poland, Hungary and Czechoslovakia, offer the potential for joint ventures or licensing arrangements for our basic canned foods while Western Europe is more receptive to new concepts like shelf-stable microwave products. Hormel is also growing in the Pacific Rim and with our neighbors—Canada and Mexico."

As global trade and in-stantaneous communica-tion bind continents and cultures together, high-quality brand names are not limited by geographic boundaries. Hormel Inter-national Corporation has much to look forward to in the future.

Hormel celebrated a "rite of passage" in business when the company joined the New York Stock Exchange in 1990.

By 1991, Hormel had processing plants in 10 cities outside of Minnesota, including (left to right) Algona, Iowa; Atlanta, Georgia; Beloit, Wisconsin; Davenport, Iowa; Fremont, Nebraska; Houston, Texas; Knoxville, Iowa; Oklahoma City, Oklahoma; Springfield, Missouri, and Stockton, California.

On the eve of a new decade, Geo. A. Hormel & Company celebrated still another milestone — the company applied to have its common stock listed on the "granddaddy" of American exchanges, the New York Stock Exchange (NYSE). For many companies, this listing is a rite of passage, acknowledging premier status in American business. For Hormel, it also represented a chance to broaden its shareholder base to fuel future growth.

1990 AND COUNTING – The new decade began with a homecoming. Since 1985, when labor issues loomed large, Hormel had moved its annual meeting outside of Minnesota — a wrenching, but necessary decision. Now the meeting returned to the familiar Austin High School auditorium and a record 1,600 shareholders attended. The homecoming drew unabashed applause when the evening began.

Two weeks earlier, Knowlton and members of his management team stood on the historic trading floor of the New York Stock Exchange and witnessed the symbol for their company, "HRL," flash across the NYSE electronic ticker tape for the first time. It was a dramatic event, indeed.

Back home in Austin, earth movers and construction crews provided visible affirmation of the company's commitment to its hometown. Work on a 42,000 square foot addition to the Corporate Offices was clearly visible, along with interior renovation of the entire existing building.

Other expansion in 1990 was global. Hormel announced its purchase of Parkin Food Products, Ltd., of South Kirkby, England, a company that manufactures, sells and distributes shelf-stable, microwaveable pasta, fish and meat entrees. It was an ideal fit and a timely acquisition to capitalize on opportunities in Eastern and Western Europe. With elimination of the Berlin Wall, the prospect of a unified Germany and removal of trade barriers in the Eastern Bloc, Hormel could envision promising new markets, especially for products not requiring refrigeration such as **SPAM** luncheon meat, **Dinty Moore** beef stew and **Top Shelf** main dish entrees.

Two additional acquisitions, although small, represented the company's willingness to match growth with internal expansion. In August, Hormel announced the purchase of the S. E. Rykoff & Co. mail-order

catalog operation based in Los Angeles, specializing in fine restaurant-quality foods, distinctive cookware and accessories. This acquisition was designed to supplement the company's existing mail-order business and to strengthen its market position in the highly competitive gift catalog industry. Catalogue Marketing, Inc., a wholly owned subsidiary in San Jose, California, employs approximately 145 people during its peak months; they handle orders from three catalogs that feature an array of food products, fresh and dried fruits, desserts and fresh meats, including many traditional Hormel products.

Expanding the fare even further, Hormel added such delicacies as escargots, wild mushrooms, caviar and smoked salmon to the menu when it acquired Gourmet America, Inc., in September 1990. The three-year-old company based in Hingham, Massachusetts, had made a name for itself by importing tasty specialty items from such diverse locations as Canada, Denmark, Italy, Tahiti and Belgium. The entrepreneurial Gourmet Foods had already built a broad customer base, including department stores, hotels, airlines, restaurants and supermarkets. For Hormel, Gourmet America represented an opportunity to expand into the rapidly growing specialty foods business by offering distinctive products through the company's existing retail, foodservice and mail-order catalog channels.

As the year progressed, strategic growth inspired corporate restructuring. Two new groups created at Hormel gave heightened attention to three important areas — foodservice, frozen foods and international development.

James W. Cole, a 30-year sales and marketing veteran and former director of the Foodservice Division, was named group vice president of the newly created Foodservice Group. Cole had proven his leadership while serving as president and chief operating officer of Farm Fresh Catfish Company and as chairman, president and chief executive officer of another Hormel subsidiary, FDL Marketing, Inc.

What more can be said about a state-of-the-art plant that covers 23 football fields? The Austin replacement plant from the air in 1990.

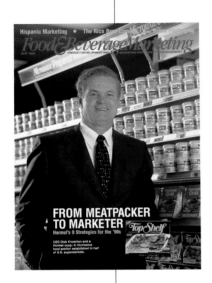

R. L. Knowlton described his nine strategies for the '90s in a leading trade journal.

David N. Dickson, senior vice president of strategic planning and corporate development, was elected group vice president of the new International, Frozen Foods and Planning and Development Group. Dickson joined Hormel in August 1989 after 19 years with the Carnation Company where he was an officer and board member.

Emphasizing the importance of manufacturing to improve sales growth and service, the Board of Directors also named Gary J. Ray, senior vice president of the Operations Group, to a new position as group vice president. In his new assignment, Ray's responsibilities expanded to include transportation and distribution.

Late in the year, five new members were elected to the Board of Directors and named to the Executive Committee. In addition to Cole, Dickson and Ray, also added to the Board and Executive Committee were Stanley E. Kerber, group vice president, Meat Products Group, and Robert F. Patterson, group vice president, Prepared Foods Group. Coupled with these executive advancements at fiscal year-end, the company reported its best year in history with earnings of $77.1 million and sales exceeding $2.6 billion.

A RECIPE FOR THE '90S – On the eve of 1991, George A. Hormel's admonition seemed as appropriate as it had been when he opened for business on the banks of the Red Cedar River in 19th-century Minnesota – "Originate, don't imitate," the pragmatic entrepreneur said.

One analyst with a national brokerage firm summed up the company's willingness to honor the axiom: "This is," he said, "a changed company since 1980."

In a single decade, Hormel had moved steadily out of the commodity business that had characterized the company and the industry for decades. While other major meat processors had withered, Hormel consistently posted new records in sales, earnings and earnings per share. Furthermore, Hormel focused R&D money on consumer trends that called for healthy, highly portable, convenient, single-serve, microwaveable products. Hormel was willing to innovate with ambitious new product introductions and experiment with leading-edge packaging technologies such as a microwave entree that children could prepare themselves. "Willing" to Hormel meant accepting the risk, cost and frustration of failure in order to realize product success. By late 1990, **Kid's Kitchen** shelf-stable entrees was one of those products considered both risky and costly because Hormel was dealing with a consumer group known for its finicky tastes.

Now the company that had taken George A. Hormel's words to heart – and put them into practice – was ready to begin its second century in 1991. Knowlton identified nine strategies designed to carry the corporation to the next billion dollars in sales and what ultimately could be unqualified leadership in the food industry.

▪ First, Hormel will continue to capitalize on its shelf-stable technology and create an entire line of products offering convenience and wholesome choices to consumers;

▪ Second, fresh prepared foods represented by the Chicken **By George** and Turkey **By George** lines will become even more important as consumers insist on attractive, easy-to-prepare meals with no preservatives or additives;

▪ Third, poultry will not be secondary to the company's basic red meat or pork focus. Through its **Jennie-O** and **By George** product offerings, Hormel will give consumers more choices;

▪ Fourth, Hormel will capitalize on its lower fat, lower calorie **Light & Lean** line with new additions offering nutritional benefits;

▪ Fifth, what's in a name? Plenty. In consumer surveys, the company found a strong association between the Hormel brand name and quality. The company will make greater use of its well-known identity and the 100-year reputation behind it. In an era when nine out of 10 new brands fail, Hormel has a distinct edge in this realm;

▪ Sixth, Hormel will become a growing force in the freezer case, expanding upon its **New Traditions** sandwiches with compatible frozen food companies;

▪ Seventh, another area of opportunity is the deli business — one of the fastest growing sectors in America's supermarkets. Because of the long-standing Hormel presence in service and self-service delicatessens, the company plans to develop additional freshly prepared foods;

▪ Eighth, while prepared foods cooked at home have been a long-standing Hormel focus, equally important is the away-from-home category. Hormel intends to become an even stronger entity in the foodservice industry with additional products that cater to restaurants, hotels and other high-volume establishments, and

▪ Ninth, if Koreans love **SPAM** luncheon meat, the Taiwanese prefer **Black Label** bacon and Mexicans have discovered the good taste and convenience of **Top Shelf** main dish entrees, can the Eastern Bloc be far behind? Hormel will aggressively pursue export of its popular American products all over the world.

Nine key business strategies — designed to propel Geo. A. Hormel & Company into its second century — will ensure *The Hormel Legacy* is as real and vibrant as it was intended 100 years ago.

On the eve of its Centennial year, Geo. A. Hormel & Company reported the best financial performance in history. Evidence of the company's success and growth captured the attention of numerous trade and financial publications.

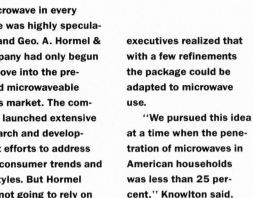

Top Shelf is:

a) An unfrozen entree.

b) Stored anywhere.

c) Faster than frozen.

d) Without preservatives.

e) All of the above.

The answer: e) All of the above.
You see, new Top Shelf unfrozen entrees don't need a freezer, a refrigerator or any preservatives to stay fresh. So you can keep them in your cupboard, briefcase or backpack and not worry about them spoiling or melting.
The Breast of Chicken Acapulco, the Boneless Beef Ribs, the Lasagna and all the other varieties are ready to eat in just two microwave minutes. And without any coldspots.
And there's one more thing Top Shelf is a great way to get fresh-from-the-kitchen taste. Find them on your grocer's shelf in the new microwave entree section.

It leaves frozen entrees cold.

When a product is a pioneer, it requires more than a little explanation.

Top Shelf main dish entrees became combat rations for Operation Desert Shield when Hormel signed a contract Nov. 17, 1990, to supply front-line soldiers in the Persian Gulf with 12 varieties of the shelf-stable meals. A two-part contract, valued at $44.4 million, was the company's first defense rations business in a decade.

Microwave cooking. It all started with a chocolate bar. In 1947, at the Raytheon Company in Waltham, Massachusetts, Percy LeBaron Spencer noticed that microwaves used for signal transmission melted the chocolate bar in his pocket. This accidental discovery led to the invention of the microwave oven which became a standard household appliance during the 1980s.

By 1991, nearly 85 percent of American homes had one microwave oven and many had two. In addition, 70 percent of offices, plants and other worksites were equipped with them. College dorms, cabins and even cabs of high-tech tractors included microwave ovens. Although still in its infancy, the microwaveable food business is expected to reach $800 million in sales by the end of 1991.

In 1981, the notion of a microwave in every home was highly speculative and Geo. A. Hormel & Company had only begun its move into the prepared microwaveable foods market. The company launched extensive research and development efforts to address new consumer trends and lifestyles. But Hormel was not going to rely on accidents — like the invention of the microwave — for new product development. Some good fortune did come into play, however, when cutting-edge packaging technology landed on the company's doorstep on New Year's Eve, Dec. 31, 1982. The package was a semirigid, multilayered plastic tray with an airtight lid. This container kept vacuum-packed foods fresh for more than a year without refrigeration or freezing. Company

executives realized that with a few refinements the package could be adapted to microwave use.

"We pursued this idea at a time when the penetration of microwaves in American households was less than 25 percent," Knowlton said.

He was gambling that Hormel could assume a leadership role by introducing the industry's first shelf-stable microwaveable foods. Three chefs with extensive restaurant experience were hired to create dinner entrees that would appeal to modern consumers. These chefs, together with Hormel food scientists, food technologists, home economists and outside consultants, developed varieties adaptable to the company's specially developed retort cooking process.

After experimenting with more than 100 recipes, the 10 best were introduced in 1987 under the **Top Shelf** main dish entrees label. The varieties included breast of chicken Acapulco, Italian-style lasagna, tender beef roast and boneless beef ribs.

Critics applauded the flavor but consumers were skeptical that a product which sat on the shelf for 18 months could be packed without preservatives. Hormel called on the credibility of Dick Cavett, nationally known celebrity, to assure consumers that **Top Shelf** main dish entrees were, indeed, top-quality and preservative-free. If that wasn't enough, the company backed the product

Another Hormel microwave market entry featured established favorites.

with a double-your-money-back satisfaction guarantee.

After launching **Top Shelf** main dish entrees, Hormel took advantage of its new packaging technology to revitalize traditional favorites such as **Dinty Moore** beef stew, **Hormel** chili and **Mary Kitchen** corned beef hash by introducing these longtime favorites in microwave bowls and cups. The company also developed two new

lines—**Kid's Kitchen** shelf-stable entrees and **Micro Cup** shelf-stable soups and entrees.

Similarly, two other Hormel microwaveable product lines were introduced—**New Traditions** breakfast and dinner sandwiches and **Hormel** microwave bacon. The **New Traditions** hamburgers, cheeseburgers and bacon cheeseburgers were aimed at the legions of Americans who eat more than 34 billion ham-

burgers a year—three every week for every man, woman and child in the United States. Joining this family were **New Traditions** fish fillet sandwiches and **New Traditions** chicken sandwiches. Microwave-ready breakfast items—Canadian bacon, egg and cheese biscuit; ham and egg biscuit; sausage biscuit; bacon, egg and cheese biscuit, among others—offer consumers popular alternatives to fast-food restaurant menus as well as other selections found in grocery store frozen food sections.

By the late 1980s, nearly 40 varieties of shelf-stable Hormel products enhanced the selection of microwaveable foods available, giving Americans convenient, portable meals for home, school, work or on the road.

Through packaging technology, Hormel also improved the microwaveability of bacon. **Hormel** microwave bacon, first test marketed in 1988, is sold in a unique package that simulates broiling in the microwave. It produces crisp, tasty bacon in a disposable cooking package. "Microwave bacon is so quick and convenient consumers will use it in salads, sandwiches and a variety of foods, in addition to serving it for breakfast," says Stanley E. Kerber, group vice president, Meat Products Group.

By 1991, the microwave oven was about as common as the toaster and an entire meal could be microwaved as fast as Percy Spencer's chocolate bar melted. Through innovation and product leadership, Hormel survived a critical time in its history and, today, competes shoulder-to-shoulder with major food conglomerates.

New Traditions bacon cheeseburgers offer consumers flavorful alternatives to fast-food restaurant menus.

Hormel microwave bacon has a unique packaging system that simulates broiling in the microwave.

For the next generation of consumers, Hormel created Kid's Kitchen shelf-stable entrees.

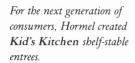

Our first one hundred years provide a valuable perspective for the direction and development of Geo. A. Hormel & Company during its second century of growth. Unquestioned is the fact that we will continue to encounter changing consumer lifestyles and sweeping food trends such as have unfolded in the past decade. Ongoing industry challenges will require increasing attention and adherence to production, marketing and distribution services that form the "lifeline" of the organization. Historically, because Hormel is a food company choosing to lead — rather than follow — clear vision and understanding of emerging new marketing opportunities will be essential.

The company will undergo widespread internal transformation in the years leading to 2091. At the same time, new outside competition, highly innovative and aggressive, will be ever present to challenge us. Our focus will need to be steadfast to the principles and values which have led us to where we are today — a preeminent food company with a longstanding reputation for quality products with distinct points of difference distinguishing us from others in the industry.

Tomorrow's foods will be targeted to specific market segments, resulting in "niche" products meeting the selective, specialized needs of consumers young and old. Continued market fragmentation will result not only in expanded product offerings but also in even greater competition for the food dollar.

In the century ahead, truly successful food companies must be innovative as they create products responsive to new lifestyles and changing family eating patterns. Development of technological advantages through state-of-the-art production methods will provide economies of scale essential to continued leadership.

For Hormel, the consumer foods marketplace is quickly evolving with new global dimensions. The economic collapse of the Eastern Bloc, the advancement of Third World nations and exploding communications capabilities offer new avenues of opportunity.

Hormel will succeed in meeting these industry challenges because our employees, at all levels, continue to live *The Hormel Legacy* — a legacy deeply rooted in innovation, teamwork and, above all, an intense commitment to quality.

The company moves into its second century solidly positioned for the journey of new opportunities before us. Ours, I believe, is one of endless opportunity. We dedicate this wonderful book to those very special people who have been a part of this magnificent company's history as well as to those who will shape its future.

R. L. KNOWLTON
Chairman of the Board
President and Chief Executive Officer

This history of Geo. A. Hormel & Company would not have been possible without the efforts of hundreds of people who contributed information, photographs, time and skills.

We regret that we cannot name every person who had a part in this book, because their contributions are valuable and greatly appreciated.

The following people deserve a special note of appreciation for their direct contribution to this history:

Antonio E. Alonso
Sharon M. Barnes
William M. Bernardo
Virginia M. Bissen
Thomas M. Blumhardt
Renee L. Braun
Robert R. Braun, Jr.
Richard A. Bross
Eric A. Brown
Harold B. Butler
Gayle L. Carey
Kenneth F. Carlson
Joseph A. Carmody
John J. Chihak
Howard Cohrt
Alan B. Condra
Richard L. Crane
Julie H. Craven
Victor Croes
Paulette M. Cummings
John M. Dick
Knowles Dougherty
Mrs. Richard Dougherty
Forrest D. Dryden
Gary E. Esbeck
Jean E. Fitzlaff
Ferris F. Furtney
David N. Gardner
R. F. Gray
Mrs. R. F. Gray
Jeffrey A. Grev
Vern Grove
Milton O. Gustafson
Merlin R. Gutz
Kay Gutzmann
Michael Haeuser
Adeline Hanson
John E. Hanson
Meri G. Harris
Clifford R. Hess

I. J. Holton
Benjamin F. Hormel, Jr.
William R. Hunter
Karen K. Jacobs
Kevin C. Jones
Stanley E. Kerber
Richard J. King
R. L. Knowlton
V. Allan Krejci
Mahlon S. Krueger
S. H. Lane
David A. Larson
Thomas J. Leake
Gene A. Lifka
Lowell J. Linderman
Dr. Doniver A. Lund
Bert P. Maus
David E. McConnell
Earl J. McEnaney
Marvin F. Moes
Daniel Mollner
Ray Neilsen
Steve Neilsen
Ralph C. Nelson
Charles D. Nyberg
Bruce Olson
Earl B. Olson
Rebecca J. Otterness
Robert F. Patterson
Helen Paulson
Neil A. Perry
Ronald E. Plath
Don L. Pohlman
Thomas J. Purcell
Richard Qualer
Gary J. Ray
Mark N. Reed
Kenneth P. Regner

Stephen E. Rowe
Edward Ryder
Harald H. O. Schmid
Leonard L. Schulke
Victoria A. Schulte
James A. Silbaugh
Scott Sprang
Richard D. Stanley
Joe C. Swedberg
P. H. Swift
Robert J. Thatcher
M. B. Thompson
Lance Wallin
Tom White
Richard Woita
Kenneth E. Young
Julius A. Zillgitt

Others
Austin Public Library
Gustavus Adolphus College Library
In Quest of Quality (author: Richard C. Dougherty)
James J. Hill Reference Library
Mankato State University Library
MINITEX
Mower County Historical Society
National Archives and Records Administration
National Archives – Chicago Branch
The Oral History Collections of the Minnesota
   Historical Society
The Procter *&* Gamble Library
The State Historical Society of Wisconsin
University of Nebraska Archives

Local 9
John Anker
John Morrison

BBDO
Thomas Keating
Vivian Martinson

Austin Daily Herald
Richard Barrett
James Negen

Austin Chamber of Commerce
Larry Haugen

Diversified Graphics, Inc.
Mike Alexander
Cherie Baker
John Bonstrom
Brian Crombie
Craig Jeska
Bob Powell
Don Smith

Mower House Color Graphics
Shirley Jenkins

Minnesota Historical Society
Bonnie Wilson

Peregrine Publications
Judith M. Gilats
Paul J. Hintz

Nancekivell Design Office
Catherine Johnson
Darlene Ludlow
James S. Nancekivell
Lisa Pettit
Robert Shauer

Yeager Pine & Mundale
Bonnie Anderson
Miriam Butwin
Craig Caligiuri
Nancy R. Chakrin
Elizabeth Child
Alvin Handelman
Lisa Jordahl
Nancy Mueller
Mame Osteen
Carol L. Pine
Mary Tickle
Diana Witt

AP/Wide World Photos

p. 55, World War II

p. 86, President Harry S Truman

p. 86, Korean War

p. 110, President John F. Kennedy

p. 111, Dr. Martin Luther King, Jr., and others

p. 134, President Richard M. Nixon

p. 134, Apollo moon landing

p. 170, President Ronald W. Reagan

p. 171, Berlin Wall

Austin Daily Herald

p. 47, newspaper headline

p. 54, front page

p. 67, front page

p. 87, newspaper headline

p. 135, front page

p. 135, Hormel plant construction

p. 141, newspaper headline

p. 160, Hormel employees going to vote

p. 161, front page

p. 162, Hormel plant ground breaking

p. 171, strikers

p. 175, **SPAM** luncheon meat cooker

p. 177, front page

p. 185, James V. Guyette

p. 187, front page

p. 187, newspaper headline

p. 188, Hormel 1985 strike

Austin YMCA

p. 176, children in pool

BBDO

p. 50, ladle with beef and vegetables

p. 51, Hormel microwave advertisement

p. 54, **Dinty Moore** beef stew can

p. 55, **SPAM** luncheon meat advertisement

p. 55, Hormel Girls

p. 55, **Hormel** chili con carne can

p. 68, **Hormel** onion soup advertisement

p. 68, **SPAM** luncheon meat can

p. 69, Hormel Chili Beaners

p. 78, World War II rationing advertisement

p. 79, Hormel Girls advertisement

p. 80, Hormel Girls business card

p. 82, bowl of **Hormel** chili

p. 82, Hormel Chili Beaners

p. 83, **Hormel** chili advertisement

p. 83, "It's Chili Time" advertising theme

p. 99, **Mary Kitchen** roast beef hash advertisement

p. 102, **Hormel** bacon advertisement

p. 106, **SPAM** luncheon meat can

p. 106, **SPAM** luncheon meat advertisement

p. 106, Burns and Allen advertisement

p. 107, "Slice it . . ."

p. 111, National Football League symbol

p. 122, **Little Sizzlers** pork sausage

p. 123, **SPAM** luncheon meat sandwich

p. 125, Re-Seal luncheon meat

p. 129, Hormel advertisement

p. 130, **Cure 81** ham advertisement

p. 131, **Cure 81** ham advertisement

p. 134, nutrition information panel

p. 142, boy with hot dog

p. 144, **Hormel** meat wieners

p. 147, **Wranglers** smoked franks advertisement

p. 154, **Hormel** chunk ham

p. 166, **Light & Lean** ham advertisement

p. 166, **Light & Lean** ham

p. 167, carrot

p. 170, **Light & Lean** ham advertisement

p. 179, **Homeland** hard salami advertisement

p. 181, **Light & Lean** ham advertisement

p. 182, **Not-So-Sloppy-Joe** Sloppy Joe Sauce
advertisement

p. 197, **Top Shelf** main dish entrees advertisement

p. 206, **Top Shelf** main dish entrees advertisement

p. 206, **Dinty Moore** beef stew

Chicago Historical Society

p. 8, meat packers (from *Views of the Chicago
Stockyards*, publ. 1892 by A. Wittemann, New York)

Chuck Ruhr Advertising

p. 154, **Dinty Moore** beef stew advertisement

Ferris Furtney

p. 112, illustration from Hormel cookbook

Food & Beverage Marketing *[magazine]*

p. 204, 1990 cover

Fremont Tribune, *Fremont, Nebraska*
p. 157, newspaper headline

Ray Gillson
p. 76, employee badge

Green Bay Gazette, *Green Bay, Wisconsin*
p. 90, newspaper headline

I. J. Holton
p. 137, I. J. Holton in Boy Scout uniform

Hormel family photos, *courtesy of Stephen Rowe*
p. 6, birth record
p. 7, Hormel family
p. 48, Hormel home in Bel Air, California

Kansas City Public Library, Missouri Valley Special Collections
p. 10, Kansas City, Missouri

R. L. Knowlton
p. 173, R. L. Knowlton, high school graduation

Local 9, United Food and Commercial Workers
p. 161, meeting announcement
p. 161, *The Unionist* front page

Meat Industry *[magazine]*
p. 184, article, "Hog Industry 'Shake-Out'"

Meat Processing *[magazine]*
p. 172, article, "Wall Street Examines the Meat Industry"

Minnesota Historical Society
p. 2, Civil War (photo: F.C.& I.)
p. 3, President Abraham Lincoln
p. 18, immigrants (credit: Library of Congress)
p. 23, World War I
p. 23, President Theodore Roosevelt
p. 24, map of Upper Midwest
p. 30, Panic of 1893
p. 54, President Franklin D. Roosevelt
p. 64, farmers
p. 65, Frank Ellis

p. 66, Hormel 1933 strike
p. 67, Hormel 1933 strike
p. 67, Minnesota Governor Floyd B. Olson and others
p. 78, meat ration line

Minneapolis Public Library
p. 101, map of West Coast

Mower County Historical Society
p. 13, Austin, Minnesota

Prepared Foods *[magazine]*
p. 196, cover and spread

St. Paul Pioneer Press, *St. Paul, Minnesota*
p. 44, front page

Star Tribune, *Minneapolis-St. Paul, Minnesota*
p. 44, front page
p. 62, front page
p. 190, march in Austin
p. 191, front page
p. 202, stock listing

Toledo-Lucas County Public Library, *Toledo, Ohio*
p. 7, front page, *Toledo Daily Democrat*

University of Nebraska, Lincoln
p. 90, 1917 *Cornhusker* yearbook

The Wall Street Transcript *[magazine]*
p. 181, 1984 article, "TWST Names Knowlton . . ."

Net sales and net earnings of Geo. A. Hormel & Company for an 89-year (1902-90) period of its 100 years are summarized below. Figures were obtained from company annual reports and from a listing provided by the treasurer's office.

(Dollars in thousands)

Year	Net Sales	Net Earnings
1990	$ 2,681,180	$ 77,124
1989	$ 2,340,513	$ 70,114
1988	2,292,847	60,192
1987	2,314,082	45,944
1986	1,960,237	39,079
1985	1,502,235	38,618
1984	1,454,527	29,492
1983	1,417,705	27,897
1982	1,426,596	28,051
1981	1,433,966	27,283
1980	1,321,966	32,758
1979	$1,414,016	$29,970
1978	1,244,865	19,471
1977	1,106,274	21,499
1976	1,094,832	14,352
1975	995,593	12,863
1974	943,163	16,916
1973	825,671	7,191
1972	719,755	7,605
1971	686,487	16,477
1970	695,768	9,933
1969	$ 626,017	$ 9,236
1968	585,879	9,134
1967	548,819	8,658
1966	491,733	3,511
1965	441,600	4,351
1964	411,827	5,725
1963	393,740	2,965
1962	384,742	3,062
1961	384,145	3,147
1960	372,276	4,533

Year	Net Sales	Net Earnings
	(Dollars in thousands)	
1959	$ 401,723	$ 5,839
1958	373,181	3,000
1957	347,989	3,315
1956	333,035	5,126
1955	350,245	3,821
1954	344,035	1,833
1953	325,309	3,020
1952	317,162	2,142
1951	313,081	2,411
1950	258,764	2,330
1949	$ 250,301	$ 1,737
1948	272,223	3,779
1947	231,979	3,229
1946	129,312	2,541
1945	116,983	1,274
1944	138,774	1,543
1943	128,410	1,312
1942	119,431	1,348
1941	74,599	1,193
1940	62,253	1,601
1939	$ 60,344	$ 1,601
1938	56,922	1,032
1937	60,760	767
1936	55,807	1,103
1935	47,641	655
1934	33,380	776
1933	25,202	636
1932	24,180	464
1931	32,466	(609)
1930	41,141	1,255

Year	Net Sales	Net Earnings
	(Dollars in thousands)	
1929	$ 40,047	$ 2,224
1928	36,599	1,263
1927	36,310	478
1926	38,408	1,182
1925	34,784	966
1924	26,163	1,065
1923	22,649	888
1922	19,778	749
1921	19,754	(437)*
1920	27,703	186
1919	$ 29,739	$ 292
1918	23,911	400
1917	14,202	672
1916	8,730	325
1915	8,720	220
1914	8,249	247
1913	6,943	178
1912	5,324	200
1911	3,965	(19)
1910	4,734	73
1909	$ 3,968	$ 86
1908	3,100	101
1907	3,190	113
1906	2,617	146
1905	1,770	18
1904	1,185	16
1903	859	23
1902	711	17

Embezzlement not included.

A

Adamy, Clarence G. (1977-
Allen, John W. (1989-
Alsaker, E. C. (1969-84)
Andersen, Elmer L. (1972-75)
Ankeny, Jr., DeWalt H. (1983-89)
Arney, R. D. (1957-69)
Asp, Raymond J. (1969-87)

B

Banfield, R. S. (1947-58)
Berg, Sherwood O. (1969-73, 1976-
Butler, Harold B. (1965-71)

C

Catherwood, S. D. (1906-52)
Cole, James W. (1990-
Corey, Bruce (1960-79)
Corey, H. H. (1928-65)
Crane, R. P. (1946-47)

D

Dacey, A. A. (1934-39)
Daigneau, R. H. (1928-55)
DeGraff, Herrell F. (1973-77)
Dickson, David N. (1990-
Doane, E. M. (1914-23)
Dougherty, Park (1936-57)
Dugan, M. F. (1923-56)

E

Eberhart, A. L. (1901-22)
Eberhart, Lena L. (1907-14)

F

Foster, Thomas D. (1903-07)
Foster, William T. (1903-07)

G

Gill, Robert M. (1970-84)
Gower, R. D. (1941-60)
Grangaard, Donald R. (1974-83)
Gray, R. F. (1945-70)

H

Hall, James E. (1984-88)
Higgins, John P. (1939-47)
Hocker, T. H. (1938-61)
Hodapp, Don J. (1986-
Holton, I. J. (1961-84)
Hormel, Benjamin F. (1901-41)
  (George A.'s brother)
Hormel, Elizabeth (1907-11)
  (George A.'s sister)
Hormel, George A. (1901-46)
Hormel, Herman G. (1901-34)
  (George A.'s brother)
Hormel, James C. (1960-69, 1970-75)
  (George A.'s grandson)

GEO. A. HORMEL & COMPANY BOARD OF DIRECTORS (AS OF JAN. 1, 1991)

R. L. Knowlton

James W. Cole

David N. Dickson

Don J. Hodapp

Stanley E. Kerber

Robert F. Patterson

Gary J. Ray

Hormel, Jay C. (1914-54)
  (George A.'s son)
Hormel, John G. (1901-36)
  (George A.'s brother)
Hormel, Lillian B. (1907-14)
  (George A.'s wife)
Housewright, Jr., L. D. (1969-83)
Hunter, William R. (1979-89)

J

Joseph, Geraldine M. (1974-78, 1981-

K

Kerber, Stanley E. (1990-
Knowlton, R. L. (1974-

L

Larkin, A. E. (1953-58)

M

Marquesen, O. L. (1958-69)
Mayberry, W. Eugene , M.D. (1986-
Morrell, John H. (1903-07)
Murray, Gordon (1958-72)

N

Nockleby, C. A. (1947-60)
Nolan, J. H. (1921-22)
Nyberg, Charles D. (1986-90)

O

O'Berg, O. W. (1922-46)
Olson, Earl B. (1987-
Olson, J. L. (1946-64)

P

Patterson, Robert F. (1990-
Potach, R. F. (1970-86)

R

Ray, Gary J. (1990-
Rose, Ray V. (1981-
Ryan, George W. (1954-70)

S

Selby, E. S. (1911-21)
Shepherd, R. E. (1903-06)
Sherman, Fayette W. (1955-68)
Silbaugh, James A. (1983-87)
Sturman, E. N. (1928-37)

T

Thompson, M. B. (1956-74)

W

Wakefield, L. E. (1922-45)
Wallace, Scott A. (1988-90)

Clarence G. Adamy

John W. Allen

Sherwood O. Berg

Geraldine M. Joseph

W. Eugene Mayberry, M.D.

Earl B. Olson

Ray V. Rose